D1765631

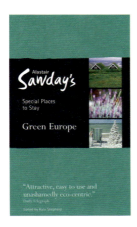

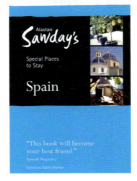

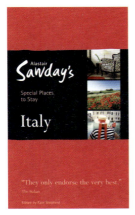

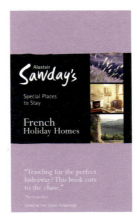

Alastair
Sawday's

Special Places to Stay

Third edition
Copyright © 2009 Alastair Sawday
Publishing Co. Ltd
Published in October 2009
ISBN-13: 978-1-906136-25-3

Alastair Sawday Publishing Co. Ltd,
The Old Farmyard, Yanley Lane,
Long Ashton, Bristol BS41 9LR, UK
Tel: +44 (0)1275 395430
Email: info@sawdays.co.uk
Web: www.sawdays.co.uk

The Globe Pequot Press,
P. O. Box 480, Guilford,
Connecticut 06437, USA
Tel: +1 203 458 4500
Email: info@globepequot.com
Web: www.globepequot.com

Series Editor Alastair Sawday
Editor Kristina Locke
Assistants to Editor Lucy Roberts,
Lianka Varga
Editorial Director Annie Shillito
Writing Alex Baker, Georgina Black,
Jo Boissevain, Matthew Hilton Dennis,
Monica Guy, Honor Peters,
Helen Pickles
Inspections Alex Baker, Vanessa Betts,
Georgina Black, Miranda Davis,
Simon Hayward, Sarah Kostoris,
Kristina Locke, Sophie Muskett
Florence Oldfield, Angie Reid,
Lucy Roberts, Hannah Wilde
*And thanks to those people who did an
inspection or two!*
Accounts Bridget Bishop,
Sally Ranahan
Production Jules Richardson,
Rachel Coe, Tom Germain
Sales & Marketing & PR Rob Richardson,
Sarah Bolton, Bethan Riach, Lisa Walklin
Web & IT Chris Banks, Phil Clarke,
Mike Peake, Russell Wilkinson

*We have made every effort to ensure the accuracy
of the information in this book at the time of
going to press. However, we cannot accept any
responsibility for any loss, injury or
inconvenience resulting from the use of
information contained therein.*

Printing: Butler, Tanner & Dennis, Frome
UK distribution: Penguin UK, London
Maps: Maidenhead Cartographic Services

Alastair Sawday's

Special Places
to Stay

India &
Sri Lanka

4 Contents

The buildings

Beautiful as they were, our old offices leaked heat, used electricity to heat water and rooms, flooded spaces with light to illuminate one person, and were not ours to alter.

So in 2005 we created our own eco-offices by converting some old barns to create a low-emissions building. We made the building energy-efficient through a variety of innovative and energy-saving building techniques, described below.

Insulation   We went to great lengths to ensure that very little heat can escape, by laying thick insulating board under the roof and floor and adding further insulation underneath the roof and between the rafters. We then lined the whole of the inside of the building with plastic sheeting to ensure air-tightness.

Heating   We installed a wood-pellet boiler from Austria, in order to be largely fossil-fuel free. The pellets are made from compressed sawdust, a waste product from timber mills that work only with sustainably managed forests. The heat is conveyed by water, throughout the building, via an under-floor system.

Water   We installed a 6000-litre tank to collect rainwater from the roofs. This is pumped back, via an ultra-violet filter, to the lavatories, showers and basins. There are two solar thermal panels on the roof providing heat to the one (massively insulated) hot-water cylinder.

Photo: Tom Germain

Lighting   We have a carefully planned mix of low-energy lighting: task lighting and up-lighting. We also installed sun-pipes to reflect the outside light into the building.

Electricity   All our electricity has long come from the Good Energy company and is 100% renewable.

Materials   Virtually all materials are non-toxic or natural. Our carpets are made from (80%) Herdwick sheep-wool from National Trust farms in the Lake District.

Doors and windows   Outside doors and new windows are wooden, double-glazed and beautifully constructed in Norway. Old windows have been double-glazed.

We have a building we are proud of, and architects and designers are fascinated by. But best of all, we are now in a better position to encourage our owners and readers to take sustainability more seriously.

What we do

Besides having moved the business to a low-carbon building, the company works in a number of ways to reduce its overall environmental footprint.

Our footprint   We measure our footprint annually and use it to find ways of reducing our environmental impact. To help address unavoidable carbon emissions we try to put something back: since 2006 we have supported SCAD, an organisation that works with villagers in India to create sustainable development.

Travel Staff are encouraged to car-share or cycle to work and we provide showers (rainwater-fed) and bike sheds. Our company cars run on LPG (liquid petroleum gas) or recycled cooking oil. We avoid flying and take the train for business trips wherever possible. All office travel is logged as part of our footprint and we count our freelance editors' and inspectors' miles too.

Our office Nearly all of our office waste is recycled; kitchen waste is composted and used in the office vegetable garden. Organic and fairtrade basic provisions are used in the staff kitchen and at in-house events, and green cleaning products are used throughout the office.

Working with owners We are proud that many of our Special Places help support their local economy and, through our Ethical Collection, we recognise owners who go the extra mile to serve locally sourced and organic food or those who have a positive impact on their environment or community.

Engaging readers We hope to raise awareness of the need for individuals to play their part; our Go Slow series places an emphasis on ethical travel and the Fragile Earth imprint consists of hard-hitting environmental titles. Our Ethical Collection informs readers about owners' ethical endeavours.

Ethical printing We print our books locally to support the British printing industry and to reduce our carbon footprint. We print our books on either FSC-certified or recycled paper, using vegetable- or soy-based inks.

Our supply chain Our electricity is 100% renewable (supplied by Good Energy), and we put our savings with Triodos, a bank whose motives we trust. Most supplies are bought in bulk from a local ethical-trading co-operative.

For many years Alastair Sawday Publishing has been 'greening' the business in different ways. Our aim is to reduce our environmental footprint as far as possible, and almost every decision we make takes into account the environmental implications. In recognition of our efforts we won a Business Commitment to the Environment Award in 2005, and in 2006 a Queen's Award for Enterprise in the Sustainable Development category. In that year Alastair was voted ITN's 'Eco Hero'. In 2009 we were given the South West C+ Carbon Positive Consumer Choices Award for our Ethical Collection.

In 2008 and again in 2009 we won the Independent Publishers Guild Environmental Award. In 2009 we were also the IPG overall Independent Publisher and Trade Publisher of the Year. The judging panel were effusive in their praise, stating: "With green issues currently at the forefront of publishers' minds, Alastair Sawday Publishing was singled out in this category as a model for all independents to follow. Its efforts to reduce waste in its

Photo: Tom Germain

office and supply chain have reduced the company's environmental impact, and it works closely with staff to identify more areas of improvement. Here is a publisher who lives and breathes green. Alastair Sawday has all the right principles and is clearly committed to improving its practice further."

Becoming 'green' is a journey and, although we began long before most companies, we still have a long way to go. We don't plan to pursue growth for growth's sake. The Sawday's name — and thus our future — depends on maintaining our integrity. We promote special places — those that add beauty, authenticity and a touch of humanity to our lives. This is a niche, albeit a growing one, so we will spend time pursuing truly special places rather than chasing the mass market.

That said, we do plan to produce more titles as well as to diversify. We are expanding our Go Slow series to other European countries, and have launched *Green Europe*, both bold new publishing projects designed to raise the profile of low-impact tourism. Our Fragile Earth series is a growing collection of campaigning books about the environment: highlighting the perilous state of the world yet offering imaginative and radical solutions and some intriguing facts, these books will keep you up to date and well-armed for the battle with apathy.

My younger son Rowan, arriving in India for the first time, texted the memorable message "India is mental". He had arrived in Chennai and, assailed on all sides by sights, sounds and experiences that were entirely new to him, one on top of another in a relentless and exhaustingly kaleidoscopic mess, was searching for a word to describe it all. 'Mental', as used nowadays by young people, was the perfect word. I hardly have to say that, week by week, the confusion of things unravelled and Rowan was left marvelling at the startling, colourful complexity of India.

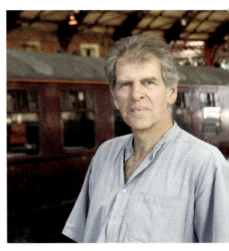

The most helpful aspect of this wonderful little book is the way it introduces you to Indians in their homes and hotels, people who genuinely want to enlighten you. When I was last there, staying in a B&B in Puducherry (Pondicherry), we were invited to join our host, before going out to dinner, for... a drink? No, a 'conversation'. We were invited to join him in his Conversation Hut at 6pm for an hour. It turned out that he wanted only to tell us about India's history, and how the Raj had been but a short-lived and largely insignificant blip in the long history of this great country. We emerged at 7pm, chastened and enlightened – though short of a conversation.

Any attempt to understand India seems to be rendered obsolete within weeks of its beginning. This is not helped by the rapid changes in India, and the counter influences. The middle-class revolution is happening, but the vastness of India's rural population grows apace too. The speed of modern enterprise is exhausting, but so is the sloth of bureaucracy. Democracy flourishes, but hardly functions. There is a new meritocracy but a very ancient hierarchy. The country is modernizing, but the very process generates its own resistance in a place steeped in traditions that mean as much now as they ever did.

Our Special Places are as special here as in any country we cover. Some would say that they are even more special, such is the astonishing exoticism of many of the buildings and people, not to say their ideas. You will meet kindness, generosity and novelty in equal measure. Through these pages you will meet India – and now Sri Lanka too – in some of their many manifestations.

Alastair Sawday

Photo: Tom Germain

My first trip to India, several years ago, was to Goa, with its fascinating fusion of Portuguese influences and Indian exoticism. Cows wandered on the beach, Rajasthani women clutched baskets of trinkets to sell and you could get a Kingfisher beer and a prawn curry for Rs20. A drive away from the crowds rewarded you with lush green paddy fields, quaint villages with crumbling Portuguese houses, the architectural joys of Panaji (Panjim) and endless palm-swayed beaches – not to mention delectable home-cooked food and a warm hospitality shining through it all. I was smitten.

Since then I have been back numerous times and have had, over the years, a particular love affair with Indian food. I remember the taste of my first butter, pepper and garlic crab at one of Mumbai's renowned lunch houses, when a succulent crab the size of a football was placed in front of me, along with a huge pile of paper napkins. And, straight off the overnight train from Delhi, a freshly cooked plate of onion pakoras, served at dawn on a hillside cafe on the way to Almora in the Himalayas. I remember the crispest masala dosa with an eye-wateringly fierce lentil stew presented at a local cafe in Chennai, and juicy Alphonso mangoes fresh off the trees that you peel open and devour, their rich nectar trickling down your chin. And the specialities of the diverse regions: the fabulous fish curries and masala-grilled seafood of the southern coast, the marinated kebabs of Delhi, the sumptuous vegetarian thalis of Rajasthan, the Bhelpuris on the streets of Mumbai and the stuffed velvety momo dumplings of Dharamsala. Above all, I have enjoyed the meals cooked in Indian homes with local produce and spices, brought to the table with love and care.

The dramatic beauty of India never fails to astound me: the vast panoramas of the Himalayas, the lush coconut groves of Goa, the dreamy backwaters of Kerala, the dazzling temples of Tamil Nadu, the majestic palaces and forts of Rajasthan, and the unspoilt wildernesses of the forests and national parks.

India is changing, and changing fast. IT hubs, modern cities and skyscrapers merge with chai wallas, rickshaw drivers and barefoot beggars. And yet, 100 miles out of the city, you go back 200 years, where carts and bullocks are treasured possessions and people walk five miles for fresh water.

Photo: Chhatra Sagar, entry 75
Photo: Amritara - Shalimar Spice Garden, entry 160

Tourism in India and Sri Lanka has changed enormously in the past few years too, and the quality and quantity of hotels has soared. New hotels are emerging daily, but standards vary immensely. Everyone is jumping on the health and tiger travel bandwagon, ayurvedic spas open every week, and jungle lodges spring up without warning. This explosion of niche travel has lead to a massive escalation in guest houses and hotels, with many showing no respect for the land and the locals. Our research has been thorough and we offer you the genuine article: inspiring places that understand the ancient science of ayurveda and the importance of nurturing the land.

Our visits have taken us to exquisite palaces and havelis, crumbling forts, comfy homestays, remote mountain retreats, chic beach shacks and eco-friendly jungle lodges: there's something for everyone here. We have also included Sri Lanka for the first time. This stunning tropical island has beaches and Buddhist temples, tea plantations and hill stations, and very hospitable people. Not only does Sri Lanka have something for everyone, but you can cover many of the treats in two weeks.

It has been a joy for me to visit parts of India that I didn't know before and to share the culture so proudly shown to me. Memories linger — of watching tribal dancers over a camp fire while drinking mugs of homemade soup, of waking in the Himalayas to carpets of vibrant daisies after the monsoon rains, of jubilant breakfast picnics in Kanha National Park to celebrate seeing my first tigers in the wild.

When you visit, do find 'conversation time' with your hosts over a cup — or several — of chai, which, as the hours pass, may become something stronger; you'll leave with new friendships forged. As sure as night becomes day, India will stir up strong emotions and play with your senses, and you'll go home wanting more. We hope you enjoy exploring these wonderful places.

Kristina Locke

Photo: Green Lagoon Resort, entry 136

It's simple. There are no rules, no boxes to tick. We choose places that we like and are fiercely subjective in our choices. We also recognise that one person's idea of special is not necessarily someone else's so there is a huge variety of places, and prices, in the book. Those who are familiar with our Special Places series know that we look for comfort, originality, authenticity, and reject the insincere, the anonymous and the banal. The way guests are treated comes as high on our list as the setting, the architecture, the atmosphere and the food.

Inspections

We visit every place in the guide to get a feel for how both house and owner tick. We don't take a clipboard and we don't have a list of what is acceptable and what is not. Instead, we chat for an hour or so with the owner or manager and look round. It's all very informal, but it gives us an excellent idea of who would enjoy staying there. If the visit happens to be the last of the day, we sometimes stay the night. Once in the book, properties are re-inspected every few years so that we can keep things fresh and accurate.

Feedback

In between inspections we rely on feedback from our army of readers, as well as from staff members who are encouraged to visit properties across the series. This feedback is invaluable to us and we always follow up on comments.

Photo: Ellerton, entry 198

So do tell us whether your stay has been a joy or not, if the atmosphere was great or stuffy, the owners and staff cheery or bored. The accuracy of the book depends on what you, and our inspectors, tell us. A lot of the new entries in each edition are recommended by our readers, so keep telling us about new places you've

discovered too. Please use the forms on our website at www.sawdays.co.uk, or later in this book (page 268).

However, please do not tell us if your starter was cold or the bedside light broken – tell the owner, immediately, and get them to do something about it. Most owners, and staff, are more than happy to correct problems and will bend over backwards to help. Far better than bottling it up and then writing to us a week later!

Subscriptions

Owners pay to appear in this guide. Their fee goes towards the high costs of inspecting, of producing an all-colour book and of maintaining our website. We only include places that we like and find special for one reason or another, so it is not possible for anyone to buy their way onto these pages. Nor is it possible for the owner to write their own description. We will say if the bedrooms are small, or if a main road is near. We do our best to avoid misleading people.

Disclaimer

We make no claims to pure objectivity in choosing these places. They are here simply because we like them. Our opinions and tastes are ours alone and this book is a statement of them; we hope you will share them. We have done our utmost to get our facts right but apologise unreservedly for any mistakes that may have crept in.

You should know that we don't check such things as fire regulations, swimming pool security or any other laws with which owners of properties receiving paying guests should comply. This is the responsibility of the owners.

Photo: Neeleshwar Hermitage, entry 127

Finding the right place for you

All these places are special in one way or another. All have been visited and then written about honestly so that you can decide for yourselves which will suit you. Those of you who swear by Sawday's books trust our write-ups precisely because we don't have a blanket standard; we include places simply because we like them. But we all have different priorities, so do read the descriptions carefully and pick out the places where you will be comfortable. If something is particularly important to you then check when you book: a simple question or two can avoid misunderstandings.

Maps

Each property is flagged with its entry number on the maps at the front. These maps are a great starting point for planning your trip, but please don't use them as anything other than a general guide. Most places will send you detailed instructions once you have booked your stay.

Ethical Collection

We're always keen to draw attention to owners who are striving to have a positive impact on the world, so you'll notice that some entries are flagged as being part of our 'Ethical Collection'. These places are working hard to reduce their environmental footprint, making significant contributions to their local community, or are passionate about serving local or organic food. Owners have had to fill in a very detailed

questionnaire before becoming part of this Collection – read more on page 264. This doesn't mean that other places in the guide are not taking similar initiatives – many are – but we may not yet know all about them.

Symbols

Below each entry you will see some symbols, which are explained at the very back of the book. They are based on the information given to us by the owners. However, things do change: bikes may be under repair or the owners have a new pet. Please use the symbols as a guide rather than an absolute statement of fact and double-check anything that is

Photo: Friday's Place, entry 165

important to you — owners occasionally bend their own rules, so it's worth asking if you may take your child, for example, even if they don't have the symbol.

Wheelchair access — Some places are keen to accept wheelchair users and have made provision for them. However, this does not mean that wheelchair users will always be met with a perfect landscape. You may encounter ramps, a shallow step, gravelled paths, alternative routes into some rooms, a bathroom (not a wet room), perhaps even a lift. In short, there may be the odd hindrance and we urge you to call and make sure you will get what you need.

Children — The ✶ symbol shows places which are happy to accept children of all ages. This does not mean that they will necessarily have cots, high chairs, etc. If an owner welcomes children but only those above a certain age, we have put these details at the end of their write-up. These houses do not have the child symbol, but even these folk may accept your younger child if you ask.

Photo: The Kandy House, entry 199

Types of places

This book covers all types of places to stay in India and Sri Lanka, as long as they are special. Each entry is simply labelled (B&B, hotel, self-catering) to guide you, but it is not always easy to place properties into fixed categories – a palace is not always a palace and some guest houses call themselves resorts. You may even find a tent called a 'hotel'. The write-ups and place names reveal several descriptive terms, and this list serves as a rough guide to what you might expect to find.

Hotels can vary from 'heritage' to 'boutique' – some are lavishly decorated palaces teeming with dusty antiques, others may be surprisingly contemporary.

Homestays are the equivalent of B&B and make up a rapidly growing sector; they tend to be family homes where you get a taste of (mostly middle-class) home life. Although many of the host families have moved away from a strictly traditional lifestyle, it is important to respect the customs of the family; homestay owners adore having guests to stay and friendships are easily formed over sociable dinners.

Havelis are heritage mansions generally found in the older cities and towns in India, particularly in Rajasthan; they can be hotels or homestays.

Guest houses tend to be smaller and less anonymous than hotels, but less intimate than homestays; they are often private houses that have been partially converted and may or may not have a restaurant, room service or telephones in the rooms.

Resorts – and eco resorts – are places of varying size that cater for individuals and small groups; they generally consist of huts, tree houses and cottages throughout the grounds, may put on evening entertainments, have an ayurvedic or a beauty spa, and arrange activities and trips.

Camps may offer rooms, tents or both; meals and safaris are often included in the price. The standard of luxury can vary greatly for tents – some have four-poster beds and en suite showers, others are very simple; be warmed by camp fires and dine by candlelight.

Rooms

Bedrooms – We tell you the range of accommodation in single, twin/double and

Photo: The Brunton Boatyard, entry 142

family rooms, cottage suites, villa suites. tree houses, cabanas and tents. Extra beds can often be added for children; check when booking. In self-catering entries we mention the number of people who can sleep comfortably in the apartment, cottage or house. Where an entry reads eg '3 + 1' this means 3 B&B rooms plus 1 self-catering apartment/cottage. Rooms vary enormously; in one you may find thin mattresses on top of each other, while some of the pricier rooms will have luxurious orthopaedic bedding. Pillows tend to be hard or foam-filled.

Bathrooms – Most bedrooms in this book have an en suite bath or shower room; only those with 'separate' or 'shared' bathrooms do not. The vast majority of places now have western loos. Occasionally you may find the term 'bucket' shower – so expect a bucket and

Photo: Tree House Hideaway, entry 100

a jug in your bathroom. You may also find open-air showers – a joy during the day, less appealing at night when insects are attracted by lights. In rustic places there may be no hot water. Good bathroom toiletries are a bit of a treat and only to be expected in the swishest places. If these things are important to you, please check when booking.

Meals

Except at self-catering properties, breakfast is usually included in the room price. It can be as simple as coffee and toast, but might also include fresh tropical fruits, homemade jams, cheese, eggs and cold meats, as well as traditional Indian breakfasts of parathas (flat breads) and dosas (rice pancakes).

Where meals are available, prices are given per person. Taxes on meals can add a further 8-10%.

Food is generally wholesome, delicious and cheap, with vegetarians well catered for. Dishes change as you pass from state to state reflecting the dizzying array of regional produce. Coconut and fish dominate the dishes of the southern coastal areas and Sri Lanka, while the influences in the Himalayan areas are Pakistani, Tibetan and Chinese. Northern Indian food will feature kebabs and curries cooked with cream and yoghurt. South India has some of the best vegetarian food with dosas, salads and chutneys. The deserts of Rajasthan may deliver some pretty fiery curries, but not all Indian food is spicy.

Note that it is culturally acceptable to use only your right hand for eating.

Some places have a set Western-style menu, which they believe their guests will prefer, but the quality and the ingredients available will often lead to disappointment. The local dishes are usually made from fresher ingredients and are far tastier, but do make sure to ask for them in advance.

Alcohol

Alcohol is not readily consumed in public in India and the number of bars is small, but times are changing and most major towns have an off-license or two. Gujarat and Tamil Nadu are officially dry states though you will find beer/wine in most hotels. Note that in some rural areas you may be offered the local firewater/toddy!

Prices and minimum stays

The prices we quote are generally per night per room with breakfast included. For self-catering we say whether the price is per night or week; for half-board and full-board it is usually per room but it may be per person (p.p.); if in any doubt, do check. Note that tax at 7-10%, or more, may be added to room prices.

Price ranges cover seasonal differences and different types of rooms. We often mention the high season period in the price section, so if you are going out of season, prices may be lower. Always check Christmas and New Year prices, which may be higher, and don't be afraid to ask

for special deals for longer stays. Prices quoted are those given to us for 2009–2011 but are not guaranteed, so do double-check when booking.

Owners have given us their prices in sterling, US dollars, euros, Indian rupees (Rs) or Sri Lankan rupees (SLRs), but we've given an approximate price band, based on exchange rates at the time of printing, for comparison.

Booking and cancellation

Requests for deposits vary, but most hotels now require a payment by credit card or bank transfer on booking to secure the room, and some owners may charge you for the whole of the booked stay in advance.

Some cancellation policies are more stringent than others. It is also worth noting that some owners will take the money directly from your credit/debit card without contacting you to discuss it. So ask them to explain their cancellation policy clearly before booking so you understand exactly where you stand; it may well avoid a nasty surprise.

Remember that both India and Sri Lanka are five and a half hours ahead of GMT.

Payment

The majority of places take credit or debit cards, but do check in advance that your particular card is acceptable. Those places that do not take cards don't have the  symbol, so make sure you have the right currency if you're going to somewhere remote.

Tipping

Tipping is not unusual, but do not feel obliged; you will rarely be made to feel embarrassed if you don't tip. Tips for staff in hotels and guesthouses are always greatly appreciated and you will be making a real difference with your contribution; in a standard hotel Rs50 (65p) per day is about right, or 10% of the bill to spread between various people. A small tip in family-run establishments is also welcome, so do leave one if you wish. In restaurants it is usual to leave 5-10%. A 2km rickshaw ride will be about Rs50-Rs75, so a tip to a rail porter of Rs50 for carrying your luggage would be more than enough. For short drives taxi drivers don't expect a tip, but welcome the gesture of leaving the change with them. When using a driver for long distances or full days it is customary to pay tips of Rs100-Rs200 per day or Rs1,000-Rs2,000 for a week.

Arrivals and departures

In hotels rooms are usually available by mid-afternoon; in B&Bs and self-catering places it may be a bit later, but do agree an arrival time with the owners in advance or you may find nobody there. Several insist on full payment on booking, particularly during the peak season. It remains law that you should register on arrival, but hotels have no right to keep your passport, however much they insist. Check out is generally at 11am.

Closed

When given in months this means the whole of the month(s) stated. So, 'Closed: November–March' means closed from 1 November to 31 March.

Electricity

The current in India and Sri Lanka is 220-240 volts, 50 Hz. Virtually all hotel rooms will have at least one socket that takes a two-pin plug. For UK travellers, a European adaptor plug (available in airports) is ideal.

Photo left: Kurumba Village Resort, entry 191
Photo right: The Kandy House, entry 199

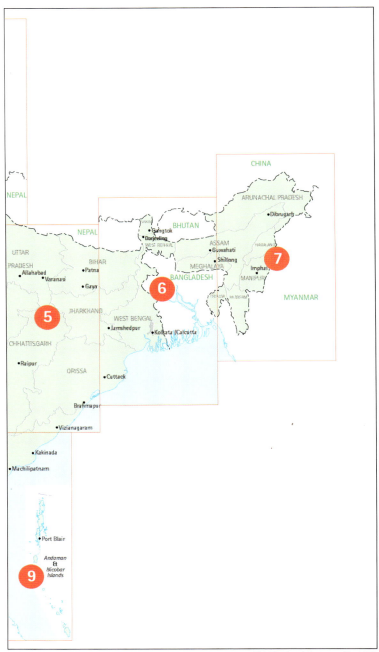

©Maidenhead Cartographic, 2009

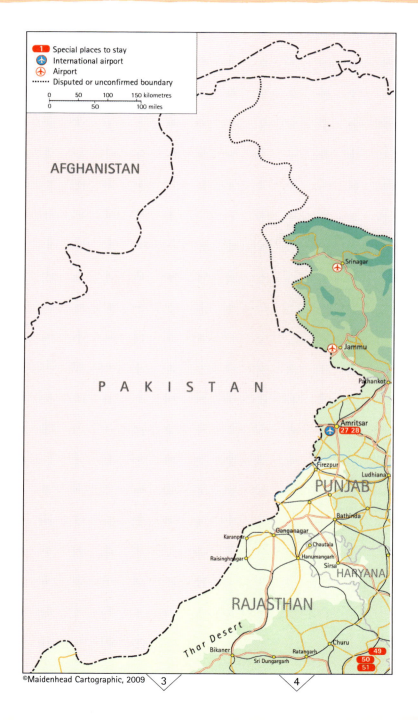

Special places to stay
International airport
Airport
Disputed or unconfirmed boundary

0   50   100   150 kilometres
0   50   100 miles

AFGHANISTAN

Srinagar

Jammu

P A K I S T A N

Pathankot

Amritsar
27 28

Firezpur

Ludhiana

PUNJAB

Bathinda

Karanpur   Ganganagar

Chautala

Raisinghnagar   Hanumangarh

Sirsa

HARYANA

RAJASTHAN

Churu

49

Thar Desert   Bikaner   Ratangarh   50

Sri Dungargarh   51

Map 2   25

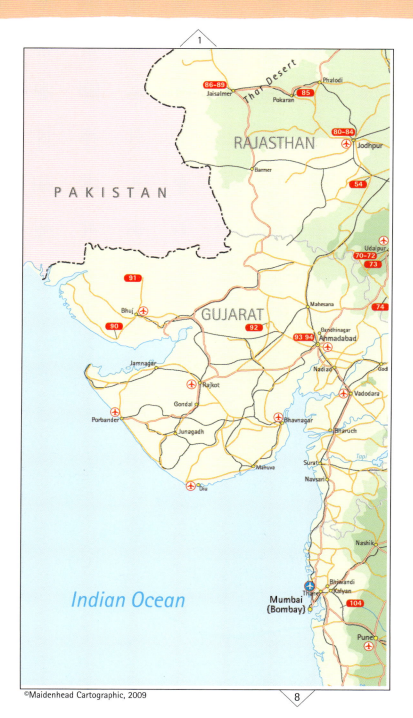

Map 4

27

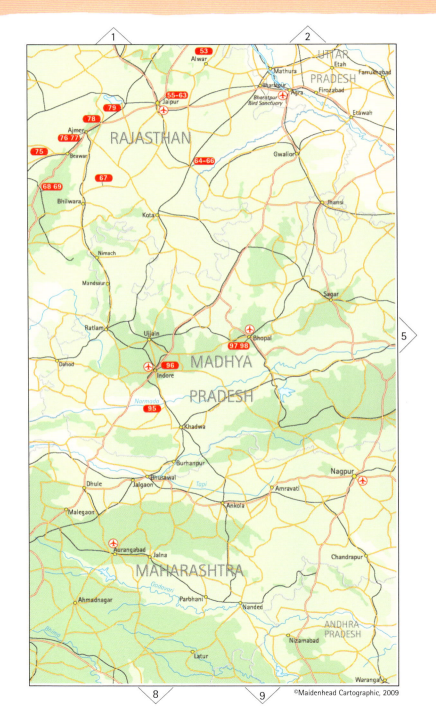

©Maidenhead Cartographic, 2009

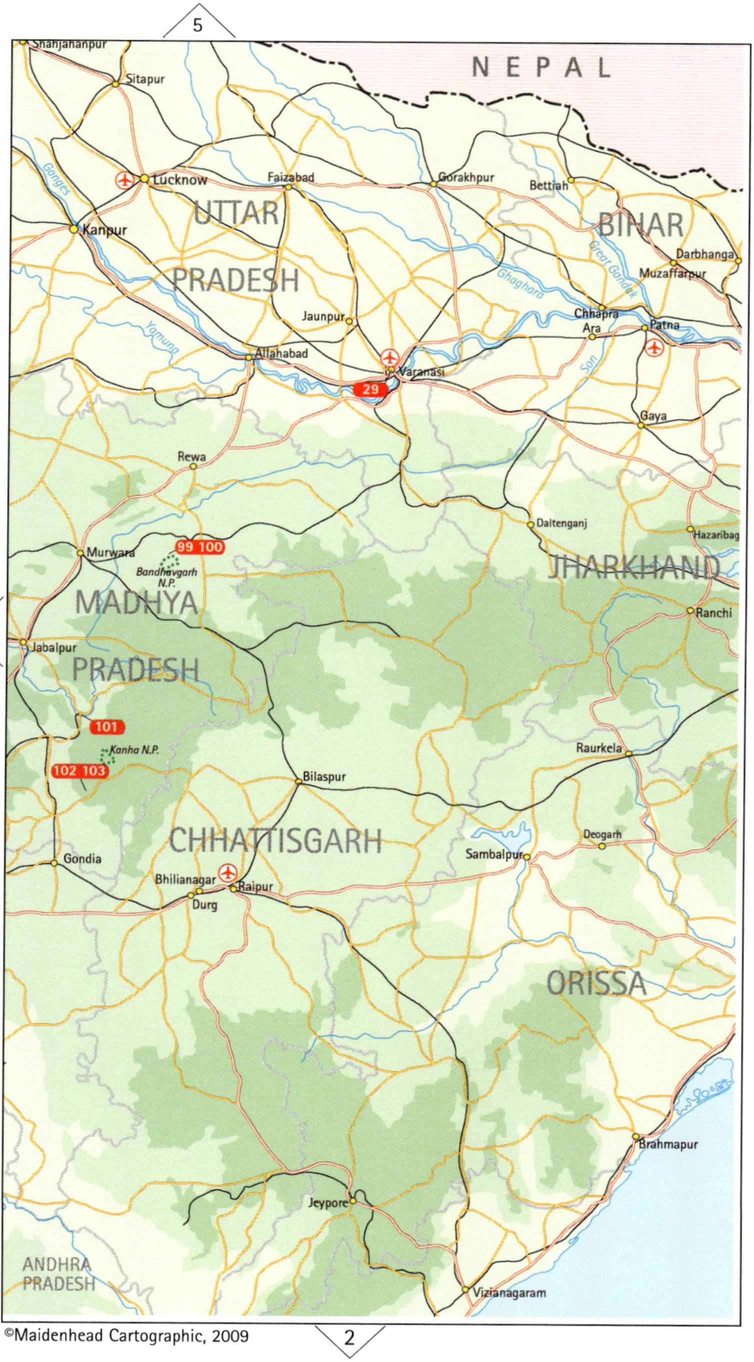

NEPAL

Shahjahanpur

Sitapur

Faizabad   Gorakhpur   Bettiah

Lucknow

UTTAR   BIHAR

Kanpur   Darbhanga

PRADESH   Muzaffarpur

Jaunpur   Chhapra

Allahabad   Ara   Patna

Varanasi

29

Gaya

Rewa

Daltenganj   Hazaribag

JHARKHAND

Murwara   **99 100**

Bandhavgarh
N.P.   Ranchi

MADHYA

Jabalpur

PRADESH

101

Kanha N.P.

102 103   Raurkela

Bilaspur

Gondia   CHHATTISGARH

Sambalpur   Deogarh

Bhilianagar   Raipur

Durg   ORISSA

Brahmapur

Jeypore

ANDHRA
PRADESH   Vizianagaram

Map 6 29

©Maidenhead Cartographic, 2009

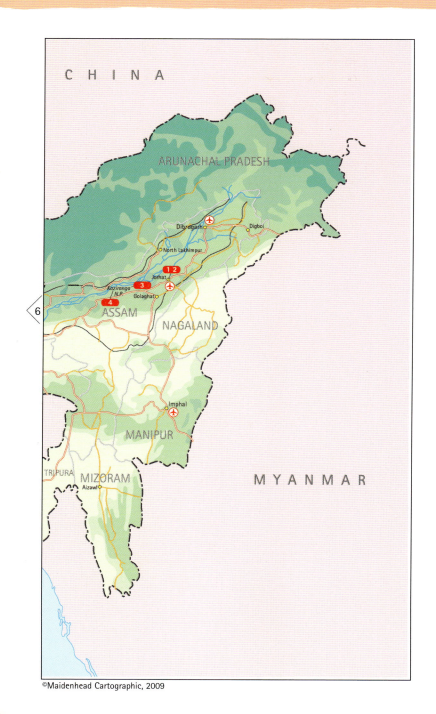

©Maidenhead Cartographic, 2009

Map 8

31

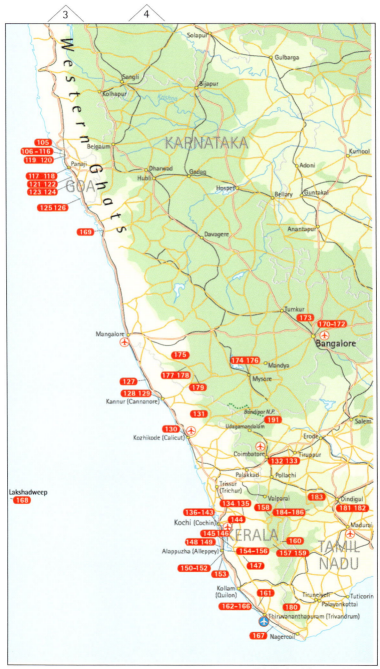

©Maidenhead Cartographic, 2009

Map 10   33

9

0   50   100   150 kilometres
0   50   100 miles

INDIA

SRI LANKA

Kankesanturai
Pandattarippu   Velvettiturai
Chankanai   Point Pedro
Nelliadi
Jaffna   Chavakachcheri

Kilinochchi

Mannar

Vavuniya

Trincomalee
Kinniya   Mutur

Anuradhapura

Kalpitiya
197
Puttalam
196
Anamaduwa

Sigiriya
Polonnaruwa
Dambulla
Eravur
Batticaloa
Kattankudi

Matale
Kalmunai
Kurunegala
Samanturai
Kandy
198 199   Amparai
Negombo   Mawanella
Kotugoda   200   Gampola
Dalugama   Gampaha   Nawalapitiya   Nuwara
Eliya   Badulla
COLOMBO
Sri Jayawardanapura   Kotikawatta
Kotte   Hatton-
Moratuwa   Dikoya
Panadura   Horana
Wadduwa
Kalutara
Beruwala   Madampe
Bentota
Balapitiya   Elpitiya
Ambalangoda   Watugedara
202-205   201   206   Hambantota
Galle   Weligama   Ambalantota
Ahangama   Tangalle
Matara

©Maidenhead Cartographic, 2009

India

Assam, Sikkim & West Bengal

Thengal Manor

A slice of another life – and, although the architecture is colonial, the family that owns it is Assamese, and distinguished. It is on a grand scale, almost opulent, though there is little hint of 'hotel'. The furniture is a busy mix of antique and reproduction with furnishings from all over the world: solidly upholstered and deeply comfortable – perhaps a mahogany drum table or a Louis IV-style sideboard – heavy floral curtains, giant-chequered floor, white walls and old family photos. The main bedrooms are magnificent – maybe a four-poster bed, dark elegant antiques, red polished floors – and big enough to have their own sitting areas and dressing rooms; the single is small and windowless. Somehow it is very European, despite the space and the ceiling fans. The colonial style re-emerges in a splendidly colonnaded quadrangular veranda, with polished red floors and white cane chairs. There are luscious gardens, space galore and delightful staff are eager to please. You are on the edge of a small village and they can organise you a trip to Sangsua Tea Plantation – wonderful.

Price	Rs3,600. Singles Rs3,100. Whole house Rs14,000. Plus 15% tax & 10% service charge. Peak season: October–April.
Rooms	5: 2 doubles, 2 twins, 1 single. Extra beds available.
Meals	Breakfast Rs225. Lunch Rs300. Dinner Rs350. Plus 12.5% tax.
Closed	Rarely.
Directions	15km from Jorhat along the Na Ali (new road) towards Titabor. Signed.

Rupa Barbora
Thengal Manor, Na Ali, Jalukanibari, Jorhat, 785001

Tel	+91 (0)3762 304 673
Fax	+91 (0)3762 304 672
Email	rupabarbora@gmail.com
Web	www.heritagetourismindia.com

Price band: B

Burra Sahib's Bungalow

All you hear are the frogs, the crickets and the charmingly nostalgic but occasional train. The big L-shaped bungalow with the corrugated iron roof is surrounded by gently undulating tea plantations and cloaked by huge trees; here, time stands still. Come for remoteness and tranquillity and gorgeously smiley staff who serve you tasty Anglo-Indian dinners and introduce you to their wives; if you're lucky you'll meet wise Mr Barooah, the owner from Kolkata. Chiku and other fruit trees dot the cow-mown lawns, the flower beds and shrubs have a dusty glaze, and there's a fishing lake that brims beautifully after the rains. If the grounds are dreamy, the interiors are cluttered colonial: countless armchairs and sofas, lacy curtains and layers of rugs, knick-knacks on worn tables. But the antique furniture is glorious – dressing tables with elaborate handles, woven wicker recliners, coloured glass chandeliers. Mattresses and pillows are brand new; bathrooms have been retiled, in 80s pastels and florals. There's a historic golf course you can stroll to, and the early morning tea tours are unmissable.

Price	Rs3,000. Singles Rs2,640. Plus 15% tax & 10% service charge.
Rooms	4: 2 doubles, 2 twins. Extra beds available.
Meals	Breakfast Rs225. Lunch Rs300. Dinner Rs350. Plus 12.5% tax.
Closed	Never.
Directions	Airport: Dibrugarh. Train: Dibrugarh (22km). Pick-up is required (request the scenic route).

Rupa Barbora
Burra Sahib's Bungalow, Sangsua Tea Estate, Dibrugarh, Jorhat, 785001

Tel	+91 (0)3762 304 673
Fax	+91 (0)3762 304 672
Email	rupabarbora@gmail.com
Web	www.heritagetourismindia.com

Price band: B

Wild Grass

If you are planning on making the journey to Assam, a path seldom trodden by the European traveller, seek this place out. Nature lovers come for wild elephants and the one-horned rhino, and for the guides, whose knowledge is a wonder: your eyes and ears will be opened wide. Wild Grass is fully committed to the National Park and to ensuring that its eco and social structure is not damaged; there's not a sweet wrapper in sight and the locally employed staff are supremely helpful and happy. Bedrooms in the chalet-style lodge are airy and spacious with views onto lush gardens or rural Assam – a delight to return to after treks on elephant or jeep. There are mighty trees to rest under and lunches to be lingered over in a dining room awash with light. Feast on authentic Assam cuisine, or continental. For your evening's entertainment, enjoy the cultural performances as the bonfire burns, or relax on the veranda and pick out your favourite birdsong: over 200 species dwell here, bathed in the firefly glow that floods the surrounding fields. Wonderfully relaxing. *Cottage peak season only.*

Price	Rs900–Rs1,950. Singles Rs800–Rs1,450. Cottage Rs1,600. Peak season: November–April.
Rooms	19: 18 twins/doubles, 1 cottage for 2.
Meals	Lunch & dinner for two, Rs700.
Closed	Never.
Directions	5km from the entrance to central range Kaziranga National Park, on the right towards Jorhat. Unsigned; ask for directions.

Manju Barua
Wild Grass, Kaziranga, Golaghat, 785109

Tel	+91 (0)3776 262 085
Email	wildgrasskaziranga@gmail.com
Web	www.oldassam.com

Price band: A

Entry 3   Map 7

Diphlu River Lodge

The dawn elephant safari is followed by a slap-up breakfast at 7.30am, then another jeep excursion – it's all go. Many guests come for two days but we say stay longer, to absorb the peace and unwind. Young local staff greet you on arrival, with fresh lycee juice and cordial smiles, and escort you to your quarters. These lovely thatched cottages are set far enough apart to allow the one-horned rhino (elephants, too) to saunter through, en route between the nearby Kaziranga National Park and the hills behind. Reached via raised bamboo walkways, set on stilts to avoid the monsoon's floods, the houses will delight you with their woven, sloping ceilings, smartly colonial furnishings and Assamese touches. Beds have superb mattresses, showers are roomy, breezy doors open onto cane-furnished verandas, hot water bottles appear (post-sundowners) as if by magic. Dinners are lightly spiced and delicious, you can spot birds on guided river walks and watch hog deer grazing in the wetlands. Light levels outside the rooms are thoughtfully kept to a minimum, and the loudest noise you'll hear is from the frogs in the paddies at night.

Price	Full-board Rs5,000–Rs20,000. Singles Rs15,000. Safaris & walks included.
Rooms	12 cottages for 2 (4 semi-detached).
Meals	Full-board except in low season. Peak season October–April.
Closed	Never.
Directions	Airport: Tezpur (1 hour), Jorhat (2.5 hours), Guwahati (4 hours). Airport pick-up on request.

Price band: E

Ashish Phookan
Diphlu River Lodge, c/o Assam Bengal Navigation, A-1 Mandovi Apts, GNB Rd, Ambari, Guwahati, Kamrup, 781001

Tel	+91 (0)3612 602 223
Email	assambengal@rediffmail.com
Web	www.diphluriverlodge.com

Entry 4   Map 7

Assam Bengal Navigation

Making stately progress along the formidable Brahmaputra, her shiny white and green hull and sparkling rails towering above the water, RV Charaidew is a throwback to the days when colonial tea-planters and forest officers went 'up country'; no wonder she turns heads. RV Sukapha is newer, built in 2006, with the addition of a small ayurvedic spa. Each vessel has 12 cabins; each allows the visitor a rare insight into Assam's history and wilderness. Experience tea gardens and temples, rickshaw rides and deserted river islands, and glimpses of Himalayan snows. The highlight is the wildlife: the one-horned rhinos of Kaziranga National Park, the tigers of Orang, the Gangetic dolphin, and amazing birdlife. The style is brisk and comfortable rather than cruise-ship glam and displays a fondness for bamboo, cane chairs, checked cushions. Cabins are snug, shipshape, air-conditioned and on the upper deck; there's space aplenty on the sundeck, or in the saloon with its wraparound windows and wildlife DVDs. The manager often joins guests for dinner and the staff are delightful. Brilliant for explorers with style. *Minimum stay 3 nights.*

Price	Full-board $700 per night. Transfers & excursions included. Peak season: October-April.
Rooms	2 vessels, each with 12 cabins for 2.
Meals	Full-board only.
Closed	May-September.
Directions	Vessels are boarded in Guwahati, Kaziranga or Jorhat. Transport arranged to departure points on booking.

Andrew & Grania Brock
Assam Bengal Navigation,
A-1 Mandovi Apartments, GNB Road,
Ambari, Guwahati, Kamrup, 781001

Tel	+91 (0)3612 602 186
Email	assambengal@aol.com
Web	www.assambengalnavigation.com

Price band: G

Entry 5   Map 6

Yangsum Farm Homestay

Near the small bazaar village of Rinchenpong, a tranquil farm run by Thendup Tashi and his sister – warm and gracious hosts. No mobile reception here, just birdsong, so come to write, draw or help out on the 44-acre heritage farm that grows everything from cardamom and ginger to avocados, oranges, peaches, mangoes and tea. The cottage ceiling is covered with silk, the simple bedrooms are bright with Sikkimese fabrics and family photos, and bathrooms are spotless and new. Check out the traditional Buddhist altar room where you can meditate should the mood take you. There's a communal sitting room indoors and a courtyard where you can sit in the sun. The food is superb and vegetables organically grown – try the local dishes that incorporate nettles, ferns and bamboo. (Other Indian food is served, too.) Thendup and Pema can show you some great walks, including those to a rhododendron forest, an aristocratic Lepcha house and a Buddhist monastery – quiet and remote. When the clouds clear, the views to Kanchenjunga are spectacular. Plant a sapling before you leave! *Treks & tours.*

Price	Full-board Rs4,200. Singles Rs3,000. Plus 10% tax. Peak season: January–June; September–November.
Rooms	4: 3 doubles, 1 cottage suite.
Meals	Full-board only.
Closed	Rarely.
Directions	2km down from Rinchenpong. Airport: Bagdogra (4 hours). Train: New Jalpaiguri (125km, 4 hours).

Ethical Collection: Food.
See page 264.

Price band: B

**Mr Thendup Tashi &
Ms Pema Chuki Tsechutharpa**
Yangsum Farm Homestay, Yangsum
Farm, Rinchenpong, West Sikkim, 737111

Tel	+91 (0)9434 179 029
Email	yangsumfarm@yahoo.com
Web	www.yangsumfarm.com

Bamboo Retreat

A meditative east-meets-west sort of place, with (mostly) low beds, bright rugs and cushions and all the vibrancy of Sikkimese culture. The building is classic, monastic, built of solid stone, grey marble and bamboo, with stunning views. The bedrooms too are calming, each painted to represent a different element; indeed, the whole place has been designed according to feng shui principles. Helen from Switzerland and her dedicated team have a passion for ecology, as is reflected in this serene place. They grow vegetables and herbs organically in the lovely terraced garden; their village homestay programme, too, deserves praise. Fresh fern, wild yams, stinging nettle, fermented mustard leaves, even orchids are a selection of the ingredients used; pizzas, also delicious, flow from the wood-fired oven. You also get a beautiful meditation room, a library, a new craft shop and herbal bathing room. In three acres of ox-ploughed paddy fields with breathtaking mountain views, Bamboo Retreat seems a world away from bustling Gangtok. Special. *Workshops in Mandala painting, meditation, Tibetan Buddhism & cookery on request.*

Price	Half-board Rs4,200–Rs4,500. Singles Rs3,600–Rs3,900. Peak season: March–May; September–November.
Rooms	12: 3 twins, 7 doubles, 2 singles.
Meals	Half-board only. Lunch Rs200–Rs300.
Closed	Rarely.
Directions	From Gangtok 19km along Rumtek road to Sajong village. Call to announce your arrival so staff can help with luggage.

Helen Kämpf
Bamboo Retreat, PO Box 20, Head Post Office, Gangtok, East Sikkim, 737101
Tel   +91 (0)3592 252 516
Web   www.bambooresort.com

Ethical Collection: Environment; Community. See page 264.

Price band: B

The Hidden Forest Retreat

A plant nursery with a guest house thrown in — this retreat has a fresh, green and wholesome feel. It's a good steep walk up into the bustling town but you are close enough not to feel isolated. Kesang, her family, and dog Georgie, are friendly, down-to-earth, green-fingered enthusiasts who may well invite you for a cup of tea and a chat. You eat what the family eats each evening, and it's as fresh and as delicious as you'd want it to be. On these verdant acres are cow sheds and greenhouses, a large organic vegetable patch for guava, kiwi and oranges, bonsai trees in the tea room and orchids a-go-go. Birds twitter, butterflies shimmer, cicadas hum and the views reach across the valley to the Ranka Runtek hills; perch on a forest bench and admire. The guest accommodation is built into the terraced hillside on split levels, the cottage suites (with sitting rooms) being the newest and largest. These functional bedrooms have floors and ceilings of teak and alnus, spotless shower rooms and a balcony each; bring woollies in winter! Let the peace and the nature wash over you. Stay at least two nights.

Price	Rs2,000. Full-board option. Plus 10% tax.
Rooms	12: 3 doubles, 6 twins, 3 cottage suites.
Meals	Breakfast Rs150. Lunch & dinner Rs250.
Closed	Rarely.
Directions	From Gangtok market right past stadium, left at district court; opp. wide bend. Airport: Bagdogra (124km, 4 hours). Train: New Jalpaiguri (125km, 4 hours).

Price band: A

Kesang Lachungpa
The Hidden Forest Retreat,
Lower Sichey Busty, Gangtok,
East Sikkim, 737101

Tel/fax	+91 (0)3592 205 197
Email	kesang27@gmail.com
Web	www.hiddenforestretreat.org

Samthar Farmhouse

On the edge of a Lepcha village, framed by forests, terraced fields and snow ranges, this wood and stone farmhouse has an intimate feel and awesome views. Pine-panelled bedrooms are furnished in simple comfort; go for the ones in the house you'll get the sunrise views. Samthar is basic, rustic, remote and exceptional, thanks to the spry gentleman who runs it. General Jimmy Singh has initiated a remarkable and ambitious social development programme: a vibrant village school, a homestay project down the hill and a clinic with doctors from Canada. After a day's trekking, bliss to return to the terraced garden, rich with azaleas, to swing in the hammock and enjoy a foot bath on the veranda while sipping the local tipple, chang, through a bamboo straw (it guarantees a good night's sleep). There's solar lighting inside and out, a wood-fired Bhukhari for hot showers, drinking water from the spring, hot water bottles at night. For decoration, hand-woven cushion seats and yak-skin rugs, Lepcha musical instruments and Buddhist thankas. Food may be Indian, Nepali or Tibetan. *Owner runs Gurudongma Tours & Treks.*

Price	Full-board Rs4,500. Singles Rs3,800. Plus 10% tax. Peak season: February–April; October–December.
Rooms	6: 2 doubles, 4 cottage suites.
Meals	Full-board only.
Closed	Rarely.
Directions	80km from Kalimpong in remote village; do not try to get here by yourself! Airport: Bagdogra (110km, 3.5 hours). Train: New Jalpaiguri (110km, 3.5 hours).

General Jimmy Singh
Samthar Farmhouse, c/o Gurudongma
Tours, Gurudongma House,
Hilltop Road, Kalimpong, 734301

Price band: B

Tel	+91 (0)3552 255 204
Email	gurutt@bsnl.in
Web	www.gurudongma.com

Gurudongma House

Up the hill above Kalimpong lies the modest private home of General Jimmy Singh – HQ for the renowned Gurudongma trekking company. The General now lives at Samthar Farmhouse where he oversees a successful cooperative village educational 'homestay' operation. Gurudongma is charming, intimate and personal: family snapshots and military memorabilia on the walls, heirloom furniture and the ever-smiling Catherine keeping an eye on things domestic. It's the perfect place to cool your heels after a long hiking expedition, and guest quarters are simple, comfortable and feel like home. There are two rooms in the main house and one lovely wood-panelled cottage in the flower-scented garden. Views are panoramic, the service is informal yet efficient and the food a delectable blend of Indian, Nepali, Chinese, Sikkimese and western: Catherine is an accomplished cook. Spend evenings comparing notes of mountains conquered, take advantage of your host's encyclopaedic knowledge, when he's there, or just kick back in the swing chair on the veranda and watch the clouds form over Kanchenjunga, the world's third highest mountain.

Price	Full-board Rs4,000. Cottage Rs4,500. Plus 10% tax.
Rooms	3: 2 doubles, 1 cottage suite.
Meals	Full-board only.
Closed	July/August.
Directions	Directions on booking.

General Jimmy Singh
Gurudongma House, Hilltop Road,
Kalimpong, 734301

Tel	+91 (0)3552 255 204
Fax	+91 (0)3552 255 201
Email	gurutt@bsnl.in
Web	www.gurudongma.com

Price band: B

Windamere Hotel

This is pure, ureconstructed Raj — yet Jan Morris wrote of it as a latter-day paradise. The Windamere is a buoyant reminder of a more leisured age, one which treated travellers with ceremony. Terraced flower beds greet you as you approach up the steep drive through pines; there's a small garden with shady sit outs and a big terrace at the back from where you can take in the impossibly beautiful mountain view from a swing chair. Irresistibly personal service, a hot water bottle for each foot and a real fire for your bedroom… the brass sparkles, the silver gleams, the logs glow and all is wholesomely clean. The plumbing is old but superb, the bathrooms have enamelled Victorian tubs and modern showers and the bedrooms are marvellously old-fashioned. Dinner here was always an event in Darjeeling society, and still is: you might get bread and butter pudding or steak and onion pie. It is all owned by one remarkable Tibetan family and though they are generally absent, they employ an excellent staff. The best way to arrive is, of course, by the slow 'toy' railway — completing this mellow, Edwardian dream.

Price	Full-board Rs8,850–Rs14,000. Singles Rs6,650–Rs12,500. Suites Rs9,100. Plus 15% tax. Peak season: March-May; September-December.
Rooms	40: 20 doubles, 18 suites, 2 cottages.
Meals	Full-board only.
Closed	Never.
Directions	Just above Chowrasta, the main square, on Observatory Hill. 2km from Darjeeling Toy Train.

Mr S Tenduf
Windamere Hotel, Observatory Hill,
Darjeeling, 734101

Tel	+91 (0)3542 254 041
Fax	+91 (0)3542 254 043
Email	reservations@windamerehotel.net
Web	www.windamerehotel.com

Price band: C

Entry 11   Map 6

Dekeling Resort at Hawk's Nest

Waking to heart-thumping views of snow-capped Kanchenjunga makes up for the steep pull to this Raj summer retreat that hangs, semi-hidden, above town. Retaining a distinct Britishness – Victorian tiled fireplaces, polished wooden floors – public rooms have been brightened with little touches. Norbu will greet you, all smiles and openness, and settle you in; the family live in the town. Fabulous old colonial-style suites are vast with sturdy furnishings and the odd elegant chair or wardrobe. Glowing wood panelling and delicious log fires (two per suite) warm you in winter; Tibetan rugs and paintings give colour. This is somewhere for unpretentious trekkers; you almost feel you're staying in Norbu's own home. Good simple meals – Indian, Chinese, Tibetan, continental – are shared around the dining table, wonderful Darjeeling tea is on tap and reception is ever-ready to help you. After a day's trekking or sightseeing – colonial buildings, Tibetan monasteries, Himalayan culture – return to the garden gazebo or the all-window sitting room with huge views. You'll feel on top of the world!

Price	Rs2,900. Plus 10% service charge. Peak season: mid-March to June; mid-September to mid-January.
Rooms	4 suites.
Meals	Breakfast Rs175. Lunch & dinner Rs275.
Closed	Rarely.
Directions	Taxi to Bose Road; sign on left 200m up steep hill. House at top of path. Airport: Bagdogra (90km, 3 hours). Train: Darjeeling Toy Train (2km, 20 mins).

Mr Tshering Norbu Dekeva
Dekeling Resort at Hawk's Nest,
2 AJC Bose Road, Darjeeling, 734101

Tel	+91 (0)3542 254 159
Fax	+91 (0)3542 253 298
Email	dekeling@sify.com
Web	www.dekeling.com

Price band: B

Glenburn Tea Estate

Husna-Tara, a woman of vision and flair, has created a dream – effortlessly stylish and wickedly indulgent. In 1860 a Scottish tea company established the estate, enticed by the luxuriant hillsides and cool climes; today they supply Harrods. As perfect as the teas are the sundowners on the terrace and the immaculate lawns, and the bedroom suites are the loveliest in the world. Great walks downhill – then they drive you back up! – huge teak beds, almost difficult to get into, hand-printed fabrics from Delhi, cupboards delicately etched with Himalayan flowers, open fires… the new rooms in Waterlily Bungalow are spectacular. Gaze from a wicker chair on inspirational views, dine by moonlight on exquisite foods (much vegetarian), let Sanjay and Neena spoil you… old school luxury. Camp out at their 'lodge' down on the river where sumptuous picnics are presented on linen beneath the gaze of the misty Kanchenjunga: lashings of homemade jam and honey doled out with homemade bread and washed down with pots of Glenburn. Tricky to get to but worth every rut and bounce. *Massage, Darjeeling tea tours, fishing, trekking.*

Price	Full-board Rs18,000. Singles Rs12,000. Extra bed Rs2,500. Activities, transfers & laundry included.
Rooms	8: Waterlily Bungalow: 4 suites. Burra Bungalow: 4 suites.
Meals	Full-board only.
Closed	Never.
Directions	Airport: Bagdogra (3 hours). Train: New Jalpaiguri (2.5 hours). Pick-up from either. Or call for directions.

Mrs Husna-Tara Prakash
Glenburn Tea Estate, Darjeeling, 734101

Tel	+91 (0)3322 885 630
Fax	+91 (0)3322 883 581
Email	info@glenburnteaestate.com
Web	www.glenburnteaestate.com

Price band: D

Fairlawn Hotel

Heinz ketchup on the tables, posters advertising Somerset, Assam tea, old furniture (much of it repainted), brown floral curtains and bric-a-brac – the Fairlawn Hotel is an oasis in Kolkata, the cultural centre of India. It is devoted to the past and determined to hang on. The the rooms are big and airy, you are served banana custard for lunch and the gong is sounded to summon you to dinner, served by devoted staff who have been there for ever wearing white gloves and cummerbunds. There are several lounges, a large, green and pleasant garden and you should feel immensely at home. The single rooms have been updated and now feature windows, but do bring your own mosquito repellent. There's a rooftop garden on the annexe, chairs and tables on the main roof and space to be yourself. It is all rather wonderful, a place to be calm, to create, to paint or write a novel. The atmosphere is 'family' and people come back year after year. Quaff Pimms in the evening heat: the bar is a watering place for expatriates of every hue and for locals intent on a gossip. They probably find it.

Price	Rs2,600-Rs3,000. Singles Rs2,100-Rs2,500. Extra bed Rs1,000-Rs1,500. Plus 11%-13% tax. Peak season: October–March.
Rooms	20: 13 doubles, 2 singles, 5 triples.
Meals	Lunch & dinner Rs280.
Closed	Rarely.
Directions	Next to the Indian Museum, opposite the Salvation Army. Airport: Kolkata (20km, 1 hour). Train: Howrah (5km, 30 mins).

Mrs Violet Smith
Fairlawn Hotel, 13/A Sudder Street,
Kolkata, 700016

Price band: B

Tel	+91 (0)3322 521 510
Fax	+91 (0)3322 521 835
Email	fairlawn@cal.vsnl.net.in
Web	www.fairlawnhotel.com

Entry 14   Map 6

Himachal Pradesh, Ladakh & Punjab

Johnson Hotel & Jimmy Johnson Lodge

You're close to Manali – nudged by the busy road but away from the rush. The peaceful wooded Nehru Park is opposite, the Dhungri Temple is up the hill and as you enter the well-choreographed gardens you could be entering the grounds of a private club. Special care has gone into the bedrooms of the hotel. Bright, fresh and warm, the best are on the first floor with mountain views (particularly wonderful from room no. 9) and the smallest are at the top (possibly warm in summer). Bathrooms display posies of garden flowers, walls local art. The three self-catering cottages – Jimmy Johnson Lodge – are older but equally good, in an English farmhouse-cosy way. The café/restaurant plans to specialise in Indian as well as French and Italian cuisine, and the ever-popular trout will remain on the menu; the food here has quite a reputation. Johnson's may be too sociable to be classified as a 'hideaway' but it's tranquil and famously laid-back, thanks to Piya and her good-humoured team, and the popular, funky bar; we hear good reports of the strawberry margaritas.

Price	Rs1,500–Rs2,000. Cottages Rs4,000–Rs4,500.
Rooms	12 + 3: 12 doubles. 3 cottages for 4.
Meals	Lunch & dinner from Rs350.
Closed	Never.
Directions	Left at Nehru Park; sign for Johnson's Restaurant. Go to Johnson Lodge Reception.

Price band: A

Jimmy & Bala Johnson
Johnson Hotel & Jimmy Johnson Lodge,
Circuit House Road, The Mall (top of
Mall Road), Manali, Kulu

Tel	+91 (0)1902 253 023
Fax	+91 (0)1902 245 123
Email	johnsonshotel@gmail.com
Web	www.johnsonhotel.in

Negi's Hotel Mayflower

Handsome, unpretentious and comfortable – and a great place to escape to in poor weather. There are log fires in your room and chairs to draw up and settle into. There is even cold-weather 'comfort' food, such as grilled trout and jam and sponge pudding! Hot water – in bathfuls – and an open fire in the dining room too, where you are surrounded by a wood-lined rustic simplicity reminiscent of the Alps. The smell of pine is redolent and the veranda is wide, comfortable and attractive. The backdrop is of tall pines and you may glimpse the snowy peaks. The garden restaurant terrace is on the other side and in close proximity to the gladed forest. (You can hear the road and its miscellaneous noises in the day, but not at night.) Wood-cosseted bedrooms are simple but amply comfortable, with good lighting, rough cotton-weave curtains and slightly elderly bathrooms that are immaculately clean. (A few rugs are UK-pub-style – but spotless.) The staff are delightful and the food is excellent and cooked to order. The owner runs Himalayan Adventures; if you wish to go trekking, you are in good hands.

Price	Rs2,200. Plus tax.
Rooms	19 doubles.
Meals	Breakfast Rs250. Lunch Rs550. Dinner Rs650. Plus tax.
Closed	Rarely.
Directions	From Manali Town, straight up towards Old Manali village for 1km.

Mr Dharmendra Minajagi
Negi's Hotel Mayflower, Old Manali
Road, Manali, Kulu, 175131

Tel	+91 (0)1902 252 104
Fax	+91 (0)1902 253 923
Email	reservation@mayflowermanali.com
Web	www.mayflowermanali.com

Price band: B

Entry 16   Map 2

Chonor House

Tibetan culture will never be lost while places like this continue to inspire. Everything matters, everything is respectful – from the way you are received to the flawless interiors. Tibetan murals on bedroom walls, hand-embroidered cushions and hand-knotted carpets, appliqué fabrics, a vibrant and elegant exterior. Each bedroom depicts some aspect of Tibetan life in bold wall paintings around which each room is individually furnished and named. The aesthetic voyeur in you will long to see each room; the artistry comes courtesy of the Norbulingka Institute. Bathrooms are dark, functional, with stone tiling and western-style loos. There's a library and cosy sitting room too, a restaurant on the terrace that serves delicate Tibetan food and scrumptious pastries, and a sun-dappled courtyard with marble-topped tables and wrought-iron chairs set among bushes and trees. One last, unexpected, bonus: an internet café, Cyber Yak. Your money goes to the charity that owns Chonor, Norling Guesthouse and the Norbulingka Institute, and it's wise to book early. Sometimes celebrities stay.

Price	Rs2,300–Rs3,500. Suite Rs3,500. Plus 10% tax.
Rooms	11: 10 doubles, 1 suite.
Meals	Breakfast Rs225. Lunch & dinner Rs350. Plus 4% tax.
Closed	Never.
Directions	Walking from Temple Road, take hairpin left–turn up Thardoeling Road.

Dechen Namgyal Maja
Chonor House, Near Thekchen Choling
Temple, McLeod Ganj, Dharamsala,
Kangra, 176219

Tel	+91 (0)1892 246 406
Email	guesthouse@norbulingka.org
Web	www.norbulingka.org

Price band: B

Norling Guest House

In the green and lovely Kangra Valley, an oasis of Buddhist culture. The Institute to which the guest house is attached is built in traditional Tibetan style following a ground plan based on the Avalokiteshvara – the Bodhisattva of Compassion. It rises up the hillside from the entrance gate to the temple, through terraced gardens of bamboo and water, past workshops and museum, and a gift shop of irresistible temptations. It is a fascinating place and its backdrop is the Himalayas; not yet two decades old, it feels rooted. The guest house has a similar charm, with spotless bedrooms and a 'refectory' feel to the cool upstairs, its corridor dotted with potted plants and cane chairs. All is simple, colourful, thoughtful, restful and serene. The first-floor bedrooms with their high ceilings and Himalayan views are simple spaces of traditional furniture, beautiful paintings and bright wall-hangings from the Institute. Delicious food is served in the restaurant/café; eat in the garden or on the rooftop. Trees are festooned with prayer flags – it is meditational and very peaceful.

Price	Rs1,550. Suites Rs2,500. Plus 10% tax. Peak season: March–June; September; November.
Rooms	11: 8 doubles, 3 suites.
Meals	Breakfast Rs150. Lunch & dinner Rs250.
Closed	Never.
Directions	In valley 6km below Dharamsala.

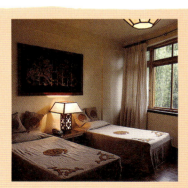

Dechen Namgyal Maja
Norling Guest House, PO Sidhpur,
Dharamsala, Kangra, 176057

Tel	+91 (0)1892 246 406
Fax	+91 (0)1892 246 404
Email	guesthouse@norbulingka.org
Web	www.norbulingka.org

Price band: A

Entry 18   Map 2

Country Cottage

Hemmed in by towering pines 5,000 feet up in the western Himalayas, just shy of the summer snow and above an army cantonment, the Sarin family's huddle of blue stone cottages is a marvellous base for exploration. The first person to establish trekking proper in Himachal, Mr Sarin Senior is a fount of outdoor know-how and, with his son Navin, runs his own trekking company; he has some fascinating stories. Their passion for honest simplicity is reflected in the basic design of the huts and cottages, which contain all you need and no more. With stone walls and slate roofs, wooden cladding and sisal floors, these snug dwellings sit among peach, plum and pine trees with tantalising glimpses of mountains and tea gardens. Flowers abound. The more basic Forest and Eucalyptus huts are one step up from camping, with a hot water bottle thrown in for chilly winter nights. The food is fresh, deliciously spiced and entirely local – you get what's available and dishes are based on family recipes. There's naturapathy and yoga at Kayakalp, and a boutique with souvenirs in the offing. *Trekking, camping, birdwatching & fishing.*

Price	Rs2,600–Rs3,000. Hut Rs2,100. Plus 10% tax.
Rooms	6: 4 cottages for 2, 2 huts for 2.
Meals	Breakfast Rs180. Lunch Rs340. Dinner Rs370.
Closed	Rarely.
Directions	1km from Palampur on road to Kulu; left thro' large cantonment gate; then road to Chandpur; left below helipad, then right. Cottage 800m down road.

Mr Karan Sarin
Country Cottage, Chandpur Tea Estate,
Palampur, Kangra, 176061

Price band: B

Tel	+91 (0)1894 230 647
Fax	+91 (0)1894 230 417
Email	info@countrycottageindia.com
Web	www.countrycottageindia.com

Taragarh Palace Hotel

A bevy of gardeners keeps the 15 acres of pine, oak, camphor and rhododendron shipshape, there's a polo field and a stables (choose your horse), badminton, tennis, an outdoor pool and a charming spa. Built in 1931 as a summer residence for the Nawab of Bahawalpur, the palace is now part of the WelcomHeritage Hotel chain and is run by the current Maharaja – devoted to the community and a big polo fan. Uniformed staff take your bags on arrival and usher you to reception up white marble stairs, and bedrooms beyond. We loved the Heritage Wing, creaky and quirky, with fancy floors and opulent ceilings, private dressing rooms and antiquated geysers – a place to catch a glimpse of how Indian royalty lived. The Palace Wing, in bright contrast to the rest, trumpets black marble floors inlaid with white, richly embroidered bedspreads on snazzy beds and bathrooms big enough to swing a tiger in. Tibetan heritage sites are a mere hour's drive; return to a long cool veranda or a quiet room for bridge. In the hushed, gilded and carpeted dining hall you are served tasty Northern Indian fare, much of it home-grown.

Price	Rs4,500–Rs5,500. Suites Rs6,100. Plus 14% tax.
Rooms	26: 18 twins/doubles, 8 suites.
Meals	Breakfast Rs350. Lunch Rs600. Dinner Rs600.
Closed	Rarely.
Directions	Taxi pick-up from Kangra airport (1 hour). Train: Pathankot (125km, 2.5 hours).

Yuvvraj Vikramaditya Singh
Taragarh Palace Hotel, V & PO Taragarh,
Kangra Valley, Kangra

Tel	+91 (0)1124 643 046
Fax	+91 (0)1124 692 317
Email	reservations@taragarh.com
Web	www.taragarh.com

Price band: C

Darang Tea Estate

The 70-acre plantation, the first in the region to be planted by an Indian, has been in the family for 150 years — you can drink all the tea you like! And the food is a joy: mouthwatering mutton, dhal and spicy salads, mango chilli relishes, fruit and veg from the garden, their own milk, butter, yogurt, lassi and raita, and chocolate cake to die for. Mr and Mrs Bhandari are equally special, full of anecdotes and stories and grow almost everything themselves. Behind the house, the cottages and the gardens are the hills; beyond, mountains capped with snow… it's very beautiful, very peaceful, interrupted only by the pylons marching through. Darang is the perfect homestay and you will soon feel part of the family. Be charmed by grandmother's brass and copper cooking pots and grandfather's hookahs, faded rugs and carpets, old swords and shields, pot plants, family photos and touches of chintz. Cottages have sitting rooms and verandas, small comfy bedrooms, snug bathrooms, shelves of books. Off the beaten track but not far from Dharamsala. We long to return.

Price	Rs2,500–Rs4,000.
Rooms	5: Main House: 1 double.
	Middle Cottage: 2 doubles.
	Upper Cottage: 2 doubles.
Meals	Breakfast Rs190.
	Lunch & dinner Rs350.
Closed	Rarely.
Directions	Airport: Dharamsala (21km).
	Train: Pathankot (100km).
	Coach: Delhi (530km).

Ethical Collection: Environment;
Community; Food.
See page 264.

Price band: B

Neera & Naveen Bhandari
Darang Tea Estate, PO Darang,
Darang, Kangra, 176060

Tel	+91 (0)9816 312 333
Email	darangtea@gmail.com
Web	www.darangteaestate.com

The Judge's Court

Cobbled Pragpur is beautiful, 1,800 feet up in the Kangra Valley and with views of the snow-tipped Himalayas. It's a designated 'heritage' village, of which Vijai, who sits on the board of the Heritage Association, is proud. There's a strong whiff of aristocracy here, or ancestry. Justice Sir Jai Lal was educated in England and the house was built for him by a proud father. Vijai is his grandson and returned to his roots with a passionate commitment to rebuilding the house. It is eclectic and surprising: butler service with pyrex dishes, touches of post-war affluence, cocktails before dinner, musicians from the village. All the staff are villagers and are learning the ropes. The bedrooms, divided between main house and new guest house, are comfortable, even elegant; bathrooms are huge and the top suites stunning. If you are lucky enough to find Vijai and Rani at home you will find a house full of bonhomie. The garden, with croquet lawn, outdoor terrace for candlelit dining and lovingly labelled trees, is a sweet retreat. And there's much to do in this countryside, so fecund and fruitful.

Price	Rs4,000. Suites Rs4,800. Plus 10% tax.
Rooms	20: 17 doubles, 3 suites.
Meals	Breakfast Rs250. Lunch Rs350. Dinner Rs450.
Closed	Never.
Directions	Directions on website. Train to Una (overnight), then 60km by road.

Mr Vijai Lal
The Judge's Court, Heritage Village,
Kangra Valley, Pragpur, Kangra, 177107

Tel	+91 (0)1970 245 035
Fax	+91 (0)1970 245 823
Email	info@judgescourt.com
Web	www.judgescourt.com

Price band: B

Thanedar Retreat

The views are among the most beautiful in this book. Steep valley sides ribboned with ancient terraces, farmhouses with slate roofs and carved balconies, pine forests climbing the mountain. Host Prakash longed to return to the Sutlej valley (a three-hour haul from Shimla) and now he is here, surrounded by apple and cherry orchards (his "labour of love"), living among family, staff and guests in a large spic and span house and two snug log cabins. Perfect harmony. People come to hike in the hills, retreat from the world and savour the wonderful Himachal food. Flat pancakes, palak paneer, home preserves and seasonal fruits are served in an octagonal dining room with vast views. As the sun sets through the spruces, evenings are spent snuggling up around the camp fire, swapping tales and listening to Prakash's delightful stories. Avid naturalist and trekker, a walking encyclopedia of botany and local history, your host is one of the reasons to come here. Retire to a simple spotless bedroom with dhurries on the floor and flip flops for the shower – and lashings of lovely hot water.

Price	Full-board Rs4,400.
Rooms	10: 6 doubles, 2 family suites, 2 log cabins for 2.
Meals	Full-board only.
Closed	Rarely.
Directions	Directions on booking. 80km from Shimla.

Price band: B

Rajesh Ojha & Ajay Sud
Thanedar Retreat, Banjara Camps & Retreats, Thanedar, Shimla

Tel	+91 (0)1126 861 397
Fax	+91 (0)1126 855 152
Email	info@banjaracamps.com
Web	www.banjaracamps.com

Entry 23   Map 2

Chapslee

If you have pottered up the mountainside in that splendid little train, filled with expectations of Shimla, you may have been underwhelmed by the town. Its glorious past and its parochial present are at odds. But to find yourself in Chapslee is a treat, undisturbed by mobiles, internet or TV. One of the oldest houses in town (1835), it was the summer residence of the late Raja Charanjit Singh of Kapurthala; the present owner is his grandson. The walls are festooned with swords and sabres, Raj-era paintings and embroideries; there are some marvellous rooms including a good old-fashioned library, and the staff are immaculately attired. Bedrooms are immensely comfortable and the suite is spoilingly sumptuous: good reading lights, paintings and prints, elegant white doors, writing desks, perhaps a Victorian pitcher and bowl… sparkling bathrooms, too. The sitting room is in hunting-lodge style, the garden is smothered in nasturtiums, the resident retrievers stroll and a 1930s Fiat in working order stands outside. It's more English than England, a flawless snapshot of another age. *Lawn tennis & croquet.*

Price	Half-board Rs15,000–Rs20,000. Singles Rs12,000.
Rooms	5: 4 doubles, 1 suite.
Meals	Half-board only.
Closed	January/February.
Directions	Next to Aukland House Senior School, between Lakkar Bazaar & Longwood.

Mr Kanwar Ratanjit Singh
Chapslee, Elysium Hill, Shimla, 171001

Tel	+91 (0)1772 802 542
Fax	+91 (0)1772 658 663
Email	chapslee@vsnl.com
Web	www.chapslee.com

Price band: F

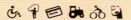

Sangla Valley Camp

Nearly 3,000 metres up and a short drive from Chitkul, the last village on the old trade route, is Sangla: truly remote. Reached by roads liable to landslides, surrounded by towering mountains, crouched among apple orchards scattered with October's marigolds (a sweet sight) on the banks of the surging Baspa river, its 'tents' are cosier than you could imagine. And now there's a sympathetic new chalet block, with big balconies for views. From each tent's wicker-furnished porch a flap opens to a most comfortable and comforting space: Rajasthani fabrics enclose you, rugs lie underfoot, there are dressing tables, cosy beds, heaters and hot water bottles; note the south-facing tents get the most light. A second flap opens to a private bathroom with tiled floor, stone sink, western loo and hot-water bucket shower. Public areas extend from thatched dining tent to picnic tables for barbecues to hammocks by the fire. Batseri village and temple are a 15-minute walk away, jeep safaris can take you further. The Sangla Valley is reputed to be the most beautiful in the Indian Himalaya. Natural splendour – and comfort.

Price	Full-board Rs5,500–Rs6,500.
Rooms	25: 12 doubles, 13 tents.
Meals	Full-board only.
Closed	November–March.
Directions	Directions on booking. 236km (8 hours) from Shimla.

Rajesh Ojha & Ajay Sud
Sangla Valley Camp, Banjara Camps &
Retreats, VPO Batseri, Sangla, Kinnaur

Tel	+91 (0)1126 861 397
Fax	+91 (0)1126 855 152
Email	info@banjaracamps.com
Web	www.banjaracamps.com

Price band: B

Hotel Shambha-La

Shambha-La, in Buddhist philosophy, means 'heaven on earth'. This comes close. A discreet entrance leads you into a green, tranquil garden. Hammocks swing under soaring poplars, white chairs and tables are grouped on the grass and prayer flags flutter. The owners are Pintoo and Tsering Narboo. He's Ladakhi and knowledgeable about the area (he was once a minister for tourism); she is Tibetan. They're relaxed, immensely kind and are usually here all summer. Bedrooms are cosy and unpretentious with modern furniture, bathrooms are functional, and balconies overlook the kitchen garden with views to the mountains. But the best place from which to drink in those snowy peaks is the terrace; wonderful to sit out here by moonlight, gazing across the valley and listening to the stream below. The garden brims over with organic vegetables and herbs, and the meals, mostly Indian or Chinese, are good, wholesome and very cheerfully served. They can pack picnic baskets too, for sightseeing days. It's all so peaceful – one of the plusses of being just out of Leh (a five-minute taxi ride, a 25-minute walk).

Price	Full-board Rs3,800–Rs5,000. Singles Rs3,000.
Rooms	28: 24 twins/doubles. New wing: 4 twins/doubles.
Meals	Full-board only. Picnics available.
Closed	November–April.
Directions	5-min taxi ride from Leh centre, or call hotel for pick-up.

Mr & Mrs Narboo
Hotel Shambha-La, Skarra Road,
Leh, 194101

Tel	+91 (0)1982 251 100
Fax	+91 (0)1982 252 607
Email	ladakh@hotelshambhala.com
Web	www.hotelshambhala.com

Price band: B

Mrs Bhandari's Guest House

Definitely not for sybarites but, for those happy to rough it a bit, this place is fun. It owes its merry, relaxed atmosphere to the warmth of Mrs Bhandari Junior and her family. The house is 1930s and unassuming, in a quiet area a rickshaw-ride away from the centre of town, not far from the magical Golden Temple. Small, plain, dim-lit and basically furnished bedrooms vary in size and colour and each has a heater for winter. The bed linen is spotless and the no-frills bathrooms are clean. A cupboard full of books in the sitting room ensures that you don't run short of reading material. Mrs Bhandari serves excellent Punjabi food – she's quite likely to ask what you fancy for your three-course dinner – and you're welcome to go into the big kitchen and watch meals being prepared. The family's green credentials are impeccable, the mango pickle is superb, and everything is organic and home-grown. There are large, pleasant gardens, water buffalo in the central yard and you do get the odd lizard. There's also a pool, and a small lawned area for a tent or two. Many of your fellow guests will be backpackers.

Price	Rs1,600–Rs1,900. Singles Rs1,300–Rs1,600.
Rooms	12: 5 doubles, 2 singles, 4 triples, 1 quadruple.
Meals	Breakfast Rs250. Lunch Rs400. Dinner Rs500.
Closed	Rarely.
Directions	Airport: Amritsar (8km, 30 mins). Train: Amritsar (2.4km, 10 mins).

Price band: A

Mrs Ratan Bhandari
Mrs Bhandari's Guest House,
10 The Cantonment, Amritsar, 143001

Tel	+91 (0)1832 228 509
Fax	+91 (0)1832 222 390
Email	bgha10@gmail.com
Web	bhandari_guesthouse.tripod.com

Ranjit's Svaasa

Seven generations of the family have owned this charming place and you sense that each in turn has loved it dearly; a display of photos in the gallery shows them all. The house is 250 years old and constructed in the colonial style. Once a rather grand British guest house it is now a small hotel, well-restored, decorated in bright, clear, classic colours and filled with pretty Victorian pieces. The family's three sons act as managers, and delightful staff welcome you with cool towels, herbal tea or fresh juice. Meals, served in the wood-panelled restaurant, are a tasty mix of Indian and western (and include comforting toasted cheese sandwiches). Each bedroom has its own colour scheme, some with jolly fabrics, others more demure, bathrooms in the new wing are immaculate, others are very old-fashioned; the best rooms are those with a balcony. There's also a superb spa with a host of treatments – try the vigorous salt scrub massage – and wicker chairs on verandas for basking in the sun. This is a quiet residential area two miles from the sacred domes of Amritsar: ask the hotel to organise a guide.

Price	Rs6,000. Singles Rs5,500–Rs7,500. Suites Rs8,000–Rs12,500.
Rooms	17: 8 doubles, 9 suites.
Meals	Lunch & dinner Rs500.
Closed	Rarely.
Directions	Airport: Amritsar (12km, 25mins). Train: Amritsar (2km, 5 mins).

The Mehra Family
Ranjit's Svaasa, 47-A The Mall,
Amritsar, 143001

Tel	+91 (0)1832 566 618
Fax	+91 (0)1835 003 728
Email	spa@svaasa.com
Web	www.svaasa.com

Price band: C

Uttar Pradesh & Uttarakhand

Ganges View

The roof terrace overlooks the great Mother Ganga and all those rituals of washers, bathers, buffalo herders and marigold sellers – what a setting for breakfast! This is a family-run guest house with a colonial feel and dark, cool rooms that are decadent and richly coloured; two resident murallists work around the clock. The rooftop rooms are the most inspiring because of the views, but are the hottest in summer. Your cultured host could not be kinder and provides a lobby full of books and an array of cultural events: traditional Indian music, talks from scholars. This is a special retreat away from the Shiva energy of Varanasi that can be overwhelming during festival time. You are on Assi Ghat so expect ghat pandemonium: wailing dogs, pilgrims chanting, drumming at all hours of the day… magical to take a row boat down the river at dawn. Nearby is the leafy area of the Benares Hindu University, popular with students of music and philosophy. The area teems with *chai* shops, round the corner is a good bookshop and, a few blocks away, the funeral pyres – life and death outside the door.

Price	Rs2,500–Rs3,500. Plus 10% tax. Peak season: October-March.
Rooms	14 doubles.
Meals	Breakfast & lunch Rs200. Dinner Rs300.
Closed	Rarely.
Directions	Rickshaw ride from station approx. Rs70. Airport: Varanasi (26km). Train: Varanasi (7km).

Mr Prakash Kumar
Ganges View, B 1/163 Assi Ghat,
Varanasi, 221005

Tel	+91 (0)5422 313 218
Fax	+91 (0)5422 369 695
Email	hotelgangesview@yahoo.com

Price band: B

Entry 29   Map 5

Carlton's Plaisance

In five acres of orchards and gardens where salvias and fuchsias bloom, this 'place of peace' on the Mussoorie hillside sits dwarfed by towering pines. The whole area once belonged to the British East India Company, one of whose officials built the house after falling in love with a French-Indian woman who persuaded him to stay. Anu and Ajit have left much of the Victorian architecture and period furniture intact; the stables below, the shoe-scrapers and the bear rugs are small signs of an existence that has been all but lost. Famous feet have walked these corridors (read Sir Edmund Hilary's comments in the guest book) and aspiring writers, artists and thinkers still come to stay. The area is stuffed with places to visit and things to do – temples, churches, birdwatching and great walks – about which the delightful Anu and Ajit are well versed. A quirky, rickety but comfortable place to stay, far from the madding crowd and with snow-clad mountain views. And possibly the only place in northern India where you can find French sausages and Mississippi Honey Chicken. *Overnight trekking to elephant sanctuary.*

Price	Rs3,000. Suites Rs5,000. Cottage suite Rs5,000. Peak season: May–June.
Rooms	9: 5 doubles, 3 suites, 1 cottage suite for 2.
Meals	Breakfast Rs250. Lunch & dinner Rs275–Rs450.
Closed	Rarely.
Directions	From Library Bazaar (Gandhi Chowk) take road to Happy Valley. On right, down signed driveway. Airport: Dehra Dun (55km, 1.5 hours).

Mrs Ajit & Anu Singh
Carlton's Plaisance, Near the LBSNA Academy, Happy Valley Road, Mussoorie, Dehra Dun, 248179

Tel	+91 (0)1352 632 800
Email	carltons@rediffmail.com
Web	www.geocities.com/carltonhotels_india

Price band: B

Kasmanda Palace

One of the oldest buildings in Mussoorie, this Anglo-French house became in 1915 the summer retreat of the royal family of Kasmanda. Built in 1836 as part of the Christ Church complex, it became a sanitorium for British forces, then a school, a private house and, in 1992, a splendid and characterful heritage hotel. Today territorial geese keep watch over its three acres of pine forest, gardens and lawns up on one of Mussoorie's highest points – the hotel jeep takes the strain out of the climb back from town. The colourful Rajkumar Sahib and his wife still live upstairs and bless you with their regal company over dinner (upon request). Bedrooms are the staging ground for a silent battle between the antique and the modern: flash yet 'old school'. Tiger skins speak of the past; today's thrills come from sports offered here. Towering log fires fend off the winter chill, whitewashed stone walls keep the summer heat at bay, food is good, staff are charming and the gardens, a rarity in the mountains, are stunning and terraced. Live like a king for the day. *Rafting, trekking, paragliding & birdwatching.*

Price	Rs4,000–Rs4,600. Suites Rs6,000. Plus 5% tax. Peak season: March-August.
Rooms	24: 17 doubles, 7 suites.
Meals	Breakfast Rs200. Lunch & dinner Rs350.
Closed	Rarely.
Directions	From main road, opp. Padmini Nivas; cont. up hill; pass church on left. Kasmanda signs on hill. Airport: Dehra Dun (55km, 2 hours); Train: Dehra Dun (35km, 1 hour).

Mr Dinraj Pratap Singh
Kasmanda Palace, The Mall Road,
Mussoorie, Dehra Dun, 248179

Tel	+91 (0)1352 632 424
Fax	+91 (0)1352 630 007
Email	kasmanda@vsnl.com
Web	www.kasmandapalace.com

Price band: C

Entry 31   Map 2

Padmini Nivas

Blessed with views over the Doon Valley to the Ganga on a clear day, in an enviable spot to catch the winter sun, Padmini Nivas is a half-eco, half-regal 1860s house built during the British Raj. Beautiful, antiquated, passed down from the Maharaja of Rajpipla, the guest house was built in British colonial style. Mrs Worah, a warm and generous host with a regal touch of her own, passionately recycles and has put in solar panels to catch a little of the Himalayan sun. She runs a nursery with hundreds of varieties; the garden is famously lovely. Imagine flowery verandas and balconies, lily gardens and rose bowers – perfect spots for lazing with books and tea, drinking in the scents and colours, with big hairy Meru the dozing Himalayan Bhutia dog for company. Mrs Worah and family are deeply involved in the local scene; daughter Sejal dashes between India and Africa for the WWF, weaving in local eco-tourism projects with wider work on environmental sustainability. Bathrooms have had a recent makeover and the suite in the old staff house is stunning. *Cookery classes.*

Price	Rs2,200–Rs6,500. Plus 5% tax.
Rooms	26 suites, cottage suites & singles.
Meals	Breakfast Rs125. Lunch & dinner Rs165.
Closed	Never.
Directions	Half-way between the library bus/taxi stand & the ropeway, a 5-min walk from the library. Airport: Dehra Dun (55km, 1.5hours).

Price band: C

Mrs Harshada Worah
Padmini Nivas, Library, The Mall,
Mussoorie, Dehra Dun, 248179

Tel	+91 (0)1352 631 093
Fax	+91 (0)1352 632 793
Email	harshada@vsnl.com
Web	www.hotelpadmininivas.com

Himalayan Hideaway

Up a twisting road that hugs the River Ganges, and slip deep into the forest to perfect peace and greenness. Melting into the Himalayan foothills, this is a hideaway that combines luxury with adventure. Kindly staff are experts at arranging activities, and if owner Yousuf is around, he'll entertain you round the camp fire with his adventures. Pioneer of white water rafting in the region, he also offers kayaking, trekking, climbing, river-swimming and fishing. For young families there are nature walks and birdwatching. The stepped gardens, landscaped with indigenous species, flow into the forest; pheasants, deer and porcupine trot along the paths. Rooms are quietly grouped overlooking forest or river; natural stone, tiled floors and high ceilings create an airy simplicity; colourful rugs, block-printed quilts, rosewood writing desks and teak blanket boxes add a cool colonial feel. Shower rooms are stunningly bold and big. Chill out with outdoor yoga and massage, then prepare for hearty dinner: homemade breads, home-grown vegetables, sometimes a barbecue. Dream on your balcony, as the river plays and darkness falls.

Price	Rs4,650–Rs5,400. Plus 10% tax.
Rooms	10 twins/doubles.
Meals	Breakfast Rs250. Lunch Rs300. Dinner Rs350.
Closed	Never.
Directions	Train: Haridwar (30 mins). Airport: Dehra Dun (45 mins). Pick-up optional.

	Ganeve Rajkotia
	Himalayan Hideaway,
	Rishikesh, Dehra Dun
Tel	+91 (0)1126 852 602
Email	info@himalayanriverrunners.com
Web	www.hhindia.com

Price band: C

Wild Brook Retreat

On the boundary of the undersung Rajaji National Park, an exhilarating drive from Rishikesh, is Wild Brook; leave worldly worries behind. Here are four spartan cottages and four spacious tents set on river rock plinths, scattered amid old agricultural terraces now thick with flowers: the feel is rustic and blissfully remote. From the hammam hot water for the basic (but clean) bathrooms to the limited solar electricity, the 'back-to-nature' slant is deliberate; Manoj, your jocular, encyclopedic host, is a passionate conservationist, and Wild Brook is the culmination of his life as scientist and activist. Meals are organic, fresh, wholesome – breakfasts on your veranda, picnics packed for your game drive, fireside dinners under the stars. Forget your phone (there's no signal), marvel at the calls of hornbill, parakeet and peacock instead. Skip the hot shower and bathe in the brook. Wander downstream and meet the sadhu living in a small temple on a forested ridge. If trips into the jungle to spot elephant, leopard, tiger and 400 species of bird sound too energetic, try some instructed yoga or read in absolute peace.

Price	Full-board $220. Singles $145. Price includes one safari.
Rooms	9: 5 cottages for 3, 4 tents for 2.
Meals	Full-board only.
Closed	15 August–30 September.
Directions	Train: Haridwar (24km, 45 mins). Airport: Delhi (229km, 6 hours).

Price band: C

Manoj Kulshreshtha
Wild Brook Retreat,
Bukundi Village, Pauri Garhwal

Tel	+91 (0)1412 604 570
Email	wildbrook@gmail.com
Web	www.wildbrookretreat.com

Kalmatia Sangam Himalaya Resort

Snow on the Himalayas blinks down on the scattered whitewashed houses with slate roofs and bright painted doors in the valleys below. The terraces produce wheat and vegetables, buffalos graze with goats, the women wear startling colours. Yet it is not remote – Almora (and its market) is close. Geeta inherited this hilltop estate and, with Dieter from Germany, opened a perfect Indo-European retreat. The steep garden is stunning, the views are spellbinding, the staff are impeccable and Geeta and Dieter are a joy. You can light a fire in your bedroom and sleep in a cottage; the newest, a honeymooner's haven at the top of the hill, faces south; the views will take your breath away. The rest are scattered among the pine trees, each with views and space galore, big beds and duvets, stone walls, good bathrooms, Scandinavian rugs on the floor. Practice yoga, be soothed by reflexology or massage, meditate on a special terrace. The Reebs have a strong eco policy so take a walk among the trees they have planted and labelled, and pick herbs and mushrooms in season; the food is indescribably good. *Trekking.*

Price	Rs6,800. Plus 8.75% tax.
Rooms	10 cottages: 4 for 2, 5 for 2-3, 1 for 3.
Meals	Breakfast Rs350. Lunch Rs600. Dinner Rs800. Plus 12.5% tax.
Closed	Never.
Directions	Upper Binsar road towards Kasar Devi temple; 1km before temple, on right. Airport: Delhi (380km). Train: Kathagodam (2.5 hours). Pick-up possible.

Ethical Collection: Environment; Community. See page 264.

Price band: C

	Dieter & Geeta Reeb
	Kalmatia Sangam Himalaya Resort,
	Kalimat Estate (near Kasar Devi),
	Post Bag 002, Almora, 263601
Tel	+91 (0)5962 233 625
Email	manager@kalmatia-sangam.com
Web	www.kalmatia-sangam.com

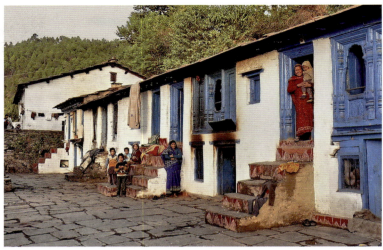

Kalmatia Sangam Village Trek

If, while staying at Kalmatia Sangam, the lure of Nanda Devi and the Kumaon range becomes irresistible, have a word with Dieter; he has used his intimate knowledge of the area to put together a gentle six-day trek. Starting from the old hill station of Almora, walks to suit all ages take you through some of the most beautiful landscapes in India. First Chittai Bell Temple and the Binsar Wildlife Sanctuary to adjust to the altitude; then, following ancient trails along terraced fields, pass waterfalls and gurgling streams; then pine, cedar and rhododendron forests – which, in February and March, explode with colour. Along the way you are treated to 1,200-year-old temples and picnic lunches beneath the austerity of snow-capped peaks. But what makes this trek really special is where you stay. Dieter has carefully tweaked designated village houses en route so you can experience authentic Kumaon village life, meet the people and discover their hospitality. Creaky stone houses with thick slate roofs and intricately carved doors, hot bucket baths and welcoming family dinners… Unforgettable.

Price	Full-board for 6 days: 3-day trek & 3-day stay at Kalmatia Sangam, Rs34,500 p.p. (minimum two people). Plus 8.75% tax.
Rooms	Overnight stays in village homes on 6-day trek.
Meals	Full-board only.
Closed	Rarely.
Directions	Upper Binsar road towards Kasar Devi temple; 1km before temple, on right. Airport: Delhi (380km). Train: Kathagodam (2.5 hours). Pick-up possible.

Dieter & Geeta Reeb
Kalmatia Sangam Village Trek,
Kalimat Estate (near Kasar Devi),
Post Bag 002, Almora, 263601

Tel	+91 (0)5962 233 625
Email	manager@kalmatia-sangam.com
Web	www.kalmatia-sangam.com

Price band: C

Camp Forktail Creek

Leave the strip of lodges behind, ford the river, meet the guide, let the 4x4 steer you steeply up the track, tramp 500m through vegetation… and you're there, in the heart of the deciduous Sal Forest. Ritesh and Minakshi – happy, savvy, humorous and well-travelled – settle you in by the bar, the hub of this charmingly rustic, unusually secluded camp. Paths snake through the undergrowth, hammocks hang from labelled trees, wind chimes tonk in the breeze, and there's a look-out/library up in the branches. The hint of thatched roof or canvas indicates a hut or a tent… expect slate-floored verandas, solar-charged lights, top-quality mattresses and shower-and-bucket bathrooms. The tents are equally good, with baths awaiting the other side of the zip – rustic perfection! Wake to a raucous dawn chorus and a big buffet breakfast that includes fresh Kumaoni pickles and jams. Spend days exploring the famous Corbett Tiger Reserve (fishing, birdwatching, elephant riding), return to futon-style sofas beside knotted-root tables and stories around the fire as the smoke spirals into a night sky thick with stars.

Price	Full-board Rs5,200. Singles Rs3,700. Ask about safari packages.
Rooms	9: 6 huts for 2, 3 tents for 2.
Meals	Full-board only.
Closed	Rarely.
Directions	Train: Ramnagar (23km).

Ritesh Suri & Minakshi Pandey
Camp Forktail Creek, Corbett Tiger
Reserve, PO Mohan (via Ramnagar),
Bhakrakot, Almora, 244715

Tel	+91 (0)5947 287 804
Email	info@campforktailcreek.com
Web	www.campforktailcreek.com

Price band: B

Entry 37   Map 2

Camp Corbett

Watch out for migratory elephants as you wander the garden: it doesn't pay to argue with ellies for right of way. Camp Corbett, the first in the area, lies in the very heart of Jim Corbett's old stomping ground and is still run by the delightful, hospitable, knowledgeable Anands who took great care, back in 1987, to create a small-scale jungle camp in harmony with the setting. Birdsong competes with the road (the birds win), pretty lawns are dotted with sun umbrellas, gravel paths are lined with flowers and the crystal-clear swimming waters of an old canal are a short walk downhill: bliss. In the circular thatched dining house, welcoming with uplighters, central fire and comfortably furnished veranda, Mr and Mrs Anand join in the fun and will regale guests with stories of their remarkable lives. Here, in the remote foothills of the Himalayas, the cottages are well finished and furnished, their grass roofs giving good insulation in all weathers; ask for one of the newer ones. Surinder the Nepalese guide is the cherry on the cake and the guest book overflows with praise. Relaxing for families.

Price	Full-board Rs2,800 per person.
Rooms	15 cottage suites.
Meals	Full-board only.
Closed	Rarely.
Directions	Left at Corbett Museum at Kaladhungi onto Nainital road. After 5 mins, on left. Airport: Delhi (260km, 5 hours). Train: Ramnagar (31km, 40 mins).

Price band: B

Suman Anand
Camp Corbett, Corbett Nagar,
Kaladhungi, Nainital, 263140

Tel	+91 (0)5942 242 277
Fax	+91 (0)5942 242 188
Email	campcorbett@yahoo.com
Web	www.campcorbett.net

The Ramgarh Bungalows

The valley drops away, the eye skims across orchards of apricots to the slopes on the other side. At night, only a few distant lights breach the darkness. Below these cottage bungalows, built to house officers and their wives, is a little school that awakes you with its chant and chatter. The split-level suite in Rose Cottage (with private terrace) is inviting, and the Writer's Bungalow (two suites) is lovely; you could live here for months. A communal veranda drops to a patch of grass, wicker chairs and secret corners vibrant with flowers. A brick path winds up to the dining room, a long whitewashed space decorated with prints and plain colours; Indian music and scents mingle with the French mood to make this a delightful place for tasty meals. Breakfast is European, with homemade local jams. Ashok Vatika, on a small hill above the other cottages, is the newest and snazziest but shares the same heritage. The set up is a little unkempt but the aesthetic is appealing and the views are a joy. It is a place to spend several days so sit, read, write, walk, eat, soak up the peace – far from the bustle of India.

Price	Rs3,000-Rs4,750. Suites Rs5,000-Rs6,250. Plus 5% tax. Peak season: 1 April-10 July.
Rooms	17: 16 doubles & suites in 6 bungalows; 1 cottage suite for 2-5.
Meals	Breakfast Rs200. Lunch Rs300. Dinner Rs350.
Closed	Rarely.
Directions	20km from Bhawali town. Take train from Delhi to Kathagodam, then 1.5 hour taxi ride.

Mr K S Mehra
The Ramgarh Bungalows, Malla,
Ramgarh, Nainital, 263137

Tel	+91 (0)5942 281 156
Fax	+91 (0)5942 281 137
Email	sales@neemranahotels.com
Web	www.neemranahotels.com

Price band: C

Himalayan Village Sonapani

Gentle Ashish Arora has two passions – to serve his community and to preserve the environment. Sonapani is his creation and his vision. Follow the path to this glorious 20-acre smallholding, its terraces thick with fruit trees and unbroken views. Named after a healing spring close by, Sonapani is 2,000 metres up in the Himalayas, surrounded by wild rhododendrons, oaks and pines. A scattering of cottages is connected by pathways and divided by vegetable plots, orchards of apple, apricot and plum, and brimming flower gardens and herbs. The well-insulated cottages are constructed of compressed blocks of earth, with mud-plaster interiors and tin roofs, and are very snug inside, comfort coming from new mattresses on pine beds, bright bed linen and hot 'en suite' showers. Your music is a cacophony of birds, your entertainment the view. Be a hermit by day, a socialite by night – there are campfires and communal eating and a lovely friendly feel (but you must provide your own alcohol). The buffet meals are varied and wholesome, and they bake divine cakes. Simple perfection. *Guided walks to villages & jungle treks.*

Price	Full-board Rs3,400–Rs3,800. Peak season: March–June; September–November.
Rooms	12 cottage suites: 10 for 2, 2 family suites.
Meals	Full-board only.
Closed	Rarely.
Directions	69km from Kathagodam; pick-up can be arranged. From drop-off point, 25-min walk along sandy path.

Mr Ashish Arora
Himalayan Village Sonapani,
Village and PO Satoli, Mukteshwar,
Nainital, 263138

Tel	+91 (0)9719 005 900
Email	ashish@himalayanvillage.com
Web	www.himalayanvillage.com

Price band: B

Sitla Estate

Fruit orchards, snow-capped peaks and unparalleled peace. Vikram Maira, fascinating, worldly wise and a genuinely nice fellow, cooks all the food, is a gracious host, a wonderful raconteur and clearly loves meeting people; this is his father's estate. He has also set up a bespoke trekking sideline to Nepal, Ladakh and Corbett he's keen to promote; he's an avid trekker, a qualified paramedic, knows everyone and ships in the whole shebang: chefs, kit, tents, transport and guides. As you take afternoon tea beneath the ancient plum tree, drink in the breezes and gaze on the peaks, a sense of oneness with the world will envelop you. Simple, beautifully kept bedrooms have splashes of colour from wall hangings, curtains and throws; Himalayan views add majesty. Ceilings are beamed, brick walls are white, mattresses are comfortable, hot water bottles add warmth, and bathrooms have simple luxuries. A dining room, sitting room and glassed-in veranda – built between the 150-year-old pillars of the shady courtyard – have recently emerged. Mealtimes are sociable and food is as Indian or as European as you like. Superb.

Price	Full-board Rs4,000-Rs4,700. Suites Rs5,500.
Rooms	6: 4 doubles, 2 suites.
Meals	Full-board only.
Closed	Never.
Directions	2 hours from Kathagodam, 8 hours from Delhi; pick-up can be arranged.

Mr Vikram Maira
Sitla Estate, PO Mukteshwar,
Mukteshwar, Nainital, 263138

Tel	+91 (0)5942 286 330
Email	maira_40@yahoo.co.uk
Web	www.sitlaestate.net

Price band: B

Delhi & Haryana

Ahuja Residency: Golf Links

A colonial refuge, a peaceful oasis far from the madding crowd. Delhi Golf Club is next door; Khan Market is a putt away. Marble staircases with wrought-iron railings twist through the six floors of this Fifties' giant, notable for its white trestle frontage. Rooms vary in size and view; we'd choose one overlooking the beautifully tended park – typical of this area. Walnut furniture is new, floors are tiled, walls are white and bathrooms are stocked with lovely Khadi potions and lotions. Newly refurbished bedrooms are busy with patterns rich in hue, WiFi runs throughout and, most surprising, there's a wonderful collection of Indian art, including a lovely well-lit buddha's head in the building's heart. Carpets of creepers cling to the brickwork of the spectacular high-walled garden, lovingly tended by Rashmi's mother. There's a homely feel and yet this is all run with an assured professionalism; Rashmi knows her stuff and has been taking in guests since the Asian Games in 1982. The family live on the ground floor but join you for breakfast. Book early: it's always full!

Price	Rs5,100. Singles Rs4,500. Plus 12.5% tax.
Rooms	11 doubles.
Meals	Lunch & dinner Rs250-Rs300.
Closed	Never.
Directions	In a small colony close to Khan Market. Call from Delhi for pick-up. Airport: Delhi (20km, 40 mins). Train: Nizamuddin Rey (2km, 10 mins).

Mrs Rashmi Ahuja
Ahuja Residency: Golf Links,
193 Golf Links, Delhi, 110003

Tel	+91 (0)1124 611 027
Fax	+91 (0)1124 649 008
Web	www.ahujaresidency.com

Price band: C

The Manor

Before you march headlong into the full Indian experience, unwind in a city oasis with an acre of garden. The Manor, Japanese-architect-designed, started life in the 50s as a jungle-fringed hotel; now it finds itself in the city's smartest suburb. In spite of the beige boutique suites and the international feel, it has far more character than other luxury addresses, and exudes a minimalism that is never austere: lovely wall hangings in the corridors, stunning mosaic floors with inserts of amber and a welcoming tone. The oft-quoted promise "nothing is too much trouble" is genuine here. Nor can you fault the chef, whose delicious food is Indian or fusion. Dine anytime, anywhere: in the restaurant, on the upstairs terrace or at a table on the lawns. The tranquil garden is colonial in feel, a sweet spot for a fresh lime soda, a blissful respite from booming Delhi. Be pampered by delicious showers with ayurvedic products and huge cosy towels. Book in for an excursion to the modern Lotus Temple, morning yoga or a rejuvenating massage – a 15-minute taster is included in the price, a typically generous gesture.

Price	Rs7,500–Rs18,000. Plus 12.5% tax & 10% service charge.
Rooms	15 suites.
Meals	Lunch Rs800–Rs1,500. Dinner Rs1,000–Rs2,500. Plus tax.
Closed	Never.
Directions	Airport: Delhi (20km, 45 mins). Car rental facility available at the hotel.

Price band: F

Samrat Banerjee
The Manor, 77 Friends Colony West,
Delhi, 110065

Tel	+91 (0)1126 925 151
Fax	+91 (0)9873 950 091
Email	info@themanordelhi.com
Web	www.themanordelhi.com

Entry 43   Map 2

Delhi Bed & Breakfast

One night at this guest house gets you closer to the real India than a month at Delhi's finest hotel. Pervez and Lubna gather you into their family (two young children and grandma) with a passion. A quiet retreat this is not! Pervez (who is from a hotelier family) is raconteur, entertainer and information guide wrapped in a bundle of joviality. Lubna is a dream cook who will take you to market and share her kitchen secrets. The three-storey house, in a smart suburb of south Delhi, is comfortable and colourful, overflowing with batik wall hangings and patterned rugs, bright cushions and carved sofas, knick-knacks and Bollywood DVDs. Spotlessly clean bedrooms contain vast new plasma screens, but you're more likely to linger with a book on a plant-filled terrace or in one of the two lounges… and you will scarcely get a page read before Pervez charms you with the latest Delhi gossip. He will happily point you in the direction of the city's sights, some of which – Humayun's tomb, Red Fort, Lodhi Gardens – are only 20 minutes away. Warmth and fun family living, Indian style.

Price	Rs3,000-Rs3,500. Peak season: September-April.
Rooms	3: 1 double, 2 twins. Extra beds available.
Meals	Lunch & dinner Rs350.
Closed	Rarely.
Directions	Aashram Crossing, then State Bank of India, behind petrol pump. In lane adjacent. Airport: Delhi (20km, 40 mins). Train: Nizamuddin Rey (2km, 10 mins).

Padma, Lubna & Sheik Pervez Hameed
Delhi Bed & Breakfast, A-6 Friends
Colony East, Delhi, 110065

Email	delhibedandbreakfast@gmail.com
Web	www.delhibedandbreakfast.com

Price band: B

Master

The luxury of having somewhere so small is that you can lavish attention on every corner. Avnish and Ushi's guest house is an expression of their principles and especially of their spiritual leanings – all encased in an unremarkable building in suburban north Delhi. Each room – choose from Mughal, Krishna, Ganesh – has been decorated with spiritual calm in mind, the placing of every object carefully measured according to principles of balance and harmony. Ushi is a reiki master and Avnish is a genial, hospitable man who spent years working for Taj Hotels. He now runs his own radio show offering hot business tips. The two rooms on the roof open onto a shaded, plant-scattered terrace where creepers climb the bamboo fence and spring evenings are easily lost to good conversation and books. The family live downstairs and occasionally eat with guests – Avnish and Ushi talk fondly of past travellers who have become friends. Welcome relief from the mayhem of Delhi (population 20 million) – a 20-minute ride by rickshaw. *Owners run Offbeat Tours in & around Delhi.*

Price	Rs2,500–Rs3,000. Plus 12.5% tax. Peak season: July–April.
Rooms	5 doubles.
Meals	Restaurants 1km.
Closed	Rarely.
Directions	Near the crossing of Shankar Road & Ganga Ram Hospital Road. 4km from Connaught Place. Entrance from the side of house.

Avnish Puri
Master, R-500 New Rajinder Nagar,
New Delhi, New Delhi, 110060

Price band: B

Tel	+91 (0)1128 741 089
Email	avnish@masterbedandbreakfast.com
Web	www.masterbedandbreakfast.com

Shanti Home

Step into the marble- and air con-cool reception – delicious! Immediately you are made to feel at home, in among the coordinated cushions and the beautiful sofas, the big sandstone Jaisalmer fresco and the chairs crafted from Rajasthani ox carts. The house was built in 2006 to the owners' exacting requirements, then joyously filled with statues of gods, contemporary sculptures and antiques from all over the country. Rajat is a raconteur and entrepreneur, Sanjana a charming and gregarious perfectionist, both know their onions and can organise anything you can come up with; loyal staff have almost telepathic attentiveness. Every peaceful bedroom is special in its own way – a gold-plated elephant head-dress or a Bollywood poster, a small balcony, a swish wet room, top mattresses. There's a sitting room for each floor, a library, a spa, and a rooftop restaurant whose washed bamboo shields the view west of the metro but opens up east over suburbs and trees. A five-course menu flows from the (ever-open) kitchen, with an exceptional chef and a brand new tandoor. Irresistible, stylish, laid back.

Price	Rs6,000–Rs8,000. Singles Rs5,000–Rs7,000.
Rooms	17 doubles.
Meals	Dinner, à la carte, from Rs300.
Closed	Rarely.
Directions	300m from Janak Puri-West Metro station. Airport: Delhi (13km).

Rajat & Sanjana Verma
Shanti Home, A-1/300 Janakpuri,
New Delhi, 110058

Tel	+91 (0)1141 573 366
Fax	+91 (0)1125 619 418
Email	contact@shantihome.com
Web	www.shantihome.com

Price band: D

Entry 46   Map 2

The Estate - Bed and Breakfast

Down a tree-lined street on a gated estate, peace and calm reign. You are minutes from the metro that ferries you into the city, and close to the airport, too… hard to imagine a better situation, or a more serene place to stay. Cross the manicured lawn, ascend the steps to the impressive modern house and there are Chetan and Mamta, courteous and engaging, their smiles welcoming, their English flawless. No wonder guests return — the owners and their uniformed staff combine warmth with professionalism. The guest annexe was finished in 2007 and its rooms are named after flowering shrubs and trees, the most secluded being on the second floor next to a stunning roof garden. All have balconies, top of the range mattresses, and furniture made by local craftsmen; rugs and well-placed pieces of tribal art add personality; wonderful bathrooms have earthy hues. Breakfasts are wholesome, there's an honesty bar in the dining room, Ramesh the cook produces good traditional dinners — do book — and the lit-up garden makes an enchanting backdrop to barbecues on balmy evenings. The nearby Qutb Minar is unmissable.

Price	Rs3,900–Rs4,900. Singles Rs3,500–Rs4,500. Extra bed RS1,000–Rs1,500.
Rooms	8 twins/doubles.
Meals	Lunch & dinner Rs350–Rs450.
Closed	Rarely.
Directions	Directions on booking.

Price band: C

Mamta Sharma
The Estate - Bed and Breakfast,
29 Sultanpur Estate, Mandi Road,
Mehrauli, New Delhi, 110030

Tel	+91 (0)9811 169 692
Email	contact@theestatebnb.com
Web	www.theestatebnb.com

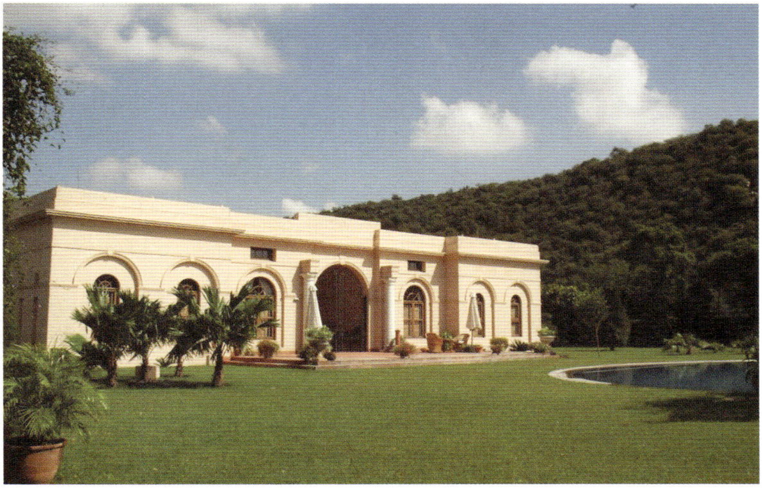

Tikli Bottom

The perfect soft landing into India. Martin and Annie are true Delhi-ites, with a profound knowledge of India (in 2008 they set up a primary school, a triumph of intelligent creativity) and give the warmest welcome you could wish for – cool lime sodas on arrival, delicious food and conversation later. Their new bougainvillea-strewn, Lutyens-style farmhouse, an hour outside the craziness of Delhi, displays impeccable taste. It is at once English and Indian – in winter a log fire in the study; in summer, a book-filled living room where only the dormant fan is a reminder of where you are. Each elegant bedroom opens onto a veranda'd courtyard and in summer you can sleep on the *charpois* (rope-strung beds) in the gardens. These, encircled by the only real hills around the capital, are a labour of love – immaculate tiered lawns, beds bursting with colour and a half-moon pool, birds dipping into the water alongside. Martin will walk you round his organic farmstead, where citrus fruits flourish and vegetables grow in neat rows; they keep pigs and buffalos too. Sublime!
Resident masseuse & reflexologist.

Price	Full-board Rs12,000. Singles Rs7,500.
Rooms	4: 2 doubles, 2 twins.
Meals	Full-board only. Drinks included.
Closed	20 April–30 June.
Directions	Airport: Delhi (33km, 45 mins). Train: Delhi (50km, 1.25 hours). Collection from Delhi station or airport possible.

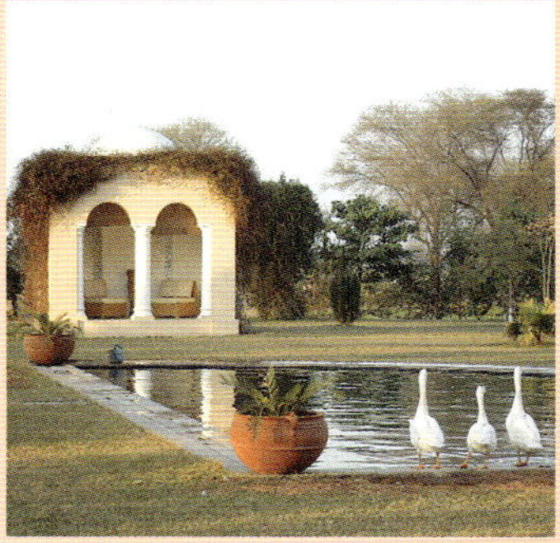

Martin & Annie Howard
Tikli Bottom, Gairatpur Bas, PO Tikli,
Gurgaon, 122101

Tel	+91 (0)1242 766 556
Email	honiwala@tiklibottom.com
Web	www.tiklibottom.com

Price band: C

Rajasthan

The Piramal Haveli

Of the famous frescoed mansions that punctuate the Shekhawati, Piramal Haveli must have been one of the most gracious. Once past the imposing entrance tower, built to honour the visit of the Maharaja of Jaipur in 1928, and beyond the wisteria-trailed façade, you enter a private world whose grandeur is tempered by disrepair. Eight bedrooms with heavy doors and massive padlocks surround pillared courtyards decorated with friezes of flying cherubs and gods in motorcars. Rooms are large and dark against the heat, decorated with 1930s colonial furniture and ageing portraits of British royalty; beyond the chipping paintwork and the faded bathrooms, the house still hints at the life of a Marwari merchant in the Thirties. Facilities and services are basic, and language can be a bar, but staff are friendly. Meals take the form of platters of vegetarian thali and you can dine outside, serenaded by distant burping cows! Or watch the peacocks prancing among the balustrades. It's a pretty long trip to get here – so come with a group of friends. *Picnics in the Thar desert.*

Price	Rs1,500–Rs2,000 p.p.
Rooms	8 twins/doubles.
Meals	Lunch Rs250. Dinner Rs300.
Closed	Never.
Directions	In the main gate of Bagar. Haveli on left, set back from the road, beyond the gardens.

Mr Dheeraj
The Piramal Haveli, Bagar,
Juhnjhunun, 333023
Tel   +91 (0)1592 221 220
Email   sales@neemranahotels.com
Web   www.neemranahotels.com

Price band: A

Entry 49   Map 1

Hotel Mandawa Haveli

And so to bed. Heavily studded double doors clunk and creak; lower your head and step over the sill into a mysterious and magical interior largely unadapted – though they have managed to sneak in an up-to-the-minute bathroom. Rooms on each floor lead off the richly decorated central courtyard; many have windows to the streetside, small and low, but the quietest are at the back. All are refreshingly uncluttered. Cultivated, delightful Dinesh seems tireless in his appreciation of his wonderfully preserved 1890s merchant's haveli, the first frescoed building en route into the old town; he knows all the history. You approach up steps, through a formal garden, then more steps… the garden is lovely. Choose a pretty corner, drink in the scents, practise your croquet skills, take a dip in the pool. The whole house is relaxing, seductive, and, floodlit, makes a magical backdrop to dinners beneath the stars. Buffet meals are local, traditional, with organic produce from Dinesh's Pushkar farm. And there's ayurvedic massage on an authentic wooden Kerala table. A heavenly haveli with a homely feel. *Camel rides & jeep safaris.*

Price	Rs1,950. Singles Rs1,250. Suites Rs3,250. Plus 8% tax. Peak season: October–February.
Rooms	20: 12 doubles, 2 singles, 2 suites, 2 family suites, 2 rooftop tents.
Meals	Breakfast Rs225. Lunch Rs250. Dinner Rs400.
Closed	Rarely.
Directions	From central bus stop in Mandawa, towards castle; hotel set back from the road up steps. Airport: Jaipur (2 hours).

Price band: A

Mr Dinesh Dhabai
Hotel Mandawa Haveli, Near Sothaliya Gate, Mandawa, Juhnjhunun, 333704

Tel	+91 (0)1592 223 088
Fax	+91 (0)1592 224 060
Email	hotelmandawahaveli@yahoo.com
Web	hotelmandawa.free.fr

Apani Dhani Eco-Lodge

Here your conscience and your corpus can be at peace. The principles are 'eco' and 'low impact', rooted in Ramesh's deep concern for the disappearing local heritage and the damaging effects that tourism can have. Ramesh lives here with his extended family, the sounds and smells of their lives providing a gentle backdrop to this beautiful and tranquil setting. The rooms are a cluster of traditional huts with mud-rubbed walls, thatched roofs and earthy colours. Wooden furniture and intriguing *objets* in russet-toned alcoves create an understated feel; bathrooms have gleaming white tiles and polished chrome. Everything you need is here though luxuries are few, and alcohol plays no part. Fabulous vegetarian food (seasonal, and from the organic garden) is served on leaf plates under a bougainvillea-clad pagoda in the circular courtyard that's the hub of the place. Visitors delight in Ramesh, a pleasant, well-travelled man of principle, who believes in the importance of harmonious living. Cookery classes, artisan workshops and guided treks, too. *5% room rate to community projects.*

Price	Rs850–Rs1,095.
Rooms	8: 3 doubles, 5 twins.
Meals	Breakfast Rs150. Lunch Rs225. Dinner Rs275.
Closed	Never.
Directions	Near Kisan Chatrawas off Nawalgarh bypass, on road from Sikar to Jhunjhunu. Train & bus: Delhi & Jaipur. Bus: Bikaner & Jodphur.

Mr Ramesh C Jangid
Apani Dhani Eco-Lodge, Old Jhunjhunu Road, Nawalgarh, Sikar, 333042

Tel	+91 (0)1594 222 239
Email	enquiries@apanidhani.com
Web	www.apanidhani.com

Ethical Collection: Environment; Community; Food.
See page 264.

Price band: A

Neemrana Fort-Palace

If the hordes descending on this maze of stepped palaces hadn't had a good sense of direction, the inhabitants might never have been defeated. Spread over eleven layers, built over six centuries, the architecture reveals a cornucopia of styles; innumerable corners and hidden courtyards, ramparts, walkways, turrets and stairs. A sensitive, modest yet beautiful restoration of near ruins, this 'non-hotel' is a powerful example of the triumph of pure good taste over standardised luxury, where bedrooms and suites of all sizes have blossomed and grown organically. A new wing houses further suites – plus a restaurant, a rooftop terrace, a delicious spa. Some rooms have *jharokha* balconies facing out onto plains peppered with bright mustard; others have bathrooms open to the skies. You can sleep in the old royal court or in a tent on the top of the highest turret. Expect peacocks, birds and chirruping crickets, ayurvedic massage and afternoon tea, flickering candles in hanging gardens and sundowners to the musicianship of local troupes. Beautiful, unusual, intriguing. *Yoga, camel cart rides, ballooning & 'zip flying' from battlements.*

Price	Rs3,000–Rs7,000. Singles Rs2,000-Rs2.500. Suites Rs6,000-Rs11,000. Family rooms Rs15,000. Plus 10% tax. Peak season: September-March.
Rooms	55: 33 doubles, 4 singles, 2 family rooms for 4, 16 suites.
Meals	Lunch Rs700. Dinner Rs800.
Closed	Rarely.
Directions	2 hours south-west of Delhi along NH8 to Jaipur. Turn right at signs in Neemrana village.

Mr Ramesh Dhabhai
Neemrana Fort-Palace, Neemrana, Alwar, 301705

Tel	+91 (0)1494 246 006
Fax	+91 (0)1494 245 005
Email	sales@neemranahotels.com
Web	www.neemranahotels.com

Price band: C

Entry 52   Map 2

The Hill Fort Kesroli

The massive walls of this delightful, multi-level, 14th-century fort perched imposingly above the plain enclose pretty flowered courtyards; inside has the feel of an intimate, impeccably restored castle, a retreat from the world outside. Beautifully decorated rooms and suites have matching Anoki bedspreads and curtains and white painted brick walls, giving rooms a cool feel against the heat; there's a great feeling of privacy. Traditional wooden Rajasthani furniture has been collected over the centuries; traditional paintings of women and gods are embellished with fabric and sequins. From the blue-and-white ceiling of one room swings a seat that overlooks sunrise at dawn; another suite hides in one of seven turrets. As dusk falls, drinks are served and guests congregate for local folk music, where a man sings and plays and children in traditional dress dance. Take tea on your arched veranda among the swooping parakeets, dine within the ramparts in the glow of the setting sun – the sound of distant voices is the only reminder of village life below. Beautiful. *Sariska Tiger Sanctuary & Siliserh Lake nearby.*

Price	Rs2,250–Rs3,750. Suites Rs3,250–Rs6,250. Plus 10% tax. Ask about off-season discount.
Rooms	21: 7 doubles, 14 suites.
Meals	Lunch Rs350. Dinner Rs500.
Closed	Never.
Directions	Train: Alwar (12km). Airport: Delhi (3 hours).

Satish Bhargav
The Hill Fort Kesroli, Near MIA, Post Office Bahala, Kesroli, Alwar, 301030

Tel	+91 (0)1468 289 352
Fax	+91 (0)1468 289 352
Email	sales@neemranahotels.com
Web	www.neemranahotels.com

Price band: B

Entry 53   Map 4

Fort Dhamli

Real Rajasthan: rural, remote and off the tourist trail. A dusty track leads to Inder's house next to the Fort. (In the 18th century, Inder's family was given the village, plus 11 others, by the Maharaja of Jaipur for bravery in battle.) Renovated by a Canadian friend Margaret Reid – she fell in love with the area and started a girls' school – the creamy building with its carved doors and decorative windows is a welcoming family home. Bedrooms surround the inner courtyard, simple yet comfortable with marble floors, carved wooden beds and colourful Indian quilts. It's homely and cosy. Meals – organic produce, much from Inder's farm – are in the light-filled dining room with its murals and village photographs. Inder's wife keeps a traditionally low profile but Inder and Margaret may join you. Charming and cultured Inder is passionate about his estate and Marwari horses; energetic Margaret, who spends half the year here, has thrown her heart into improving the local economy. Go riding, visit local villages or just relax on the rooftop terrace. A genuine homestay experience, rich with local life. *Riding safaris.*

Price	Rs2,550–Rs2,850.
	Singles Rs2,200–Rs2,500.
Rooms	12 doubles.
Meals	Breakfast Rs150. Lunch Rs250.
	Dinner Rs350.
Closed	Rarely.
Directions	Directions on booking.

	Inder Singh & Margaret Reid
	Fort Dhamli, Dhamli, Pali, 306501
Tel	+91 (0)1412 711 468
Email	fort.dhamli@gmail.com

Price band: B

Sri Niwas Country Homes

Surrounded by carefully tended, parrot-thronged greenery, this rural guest house 30 minutes from Jaipur is Candy Singh's dream home. After years of sharing army quarters she craved light and space, so this roomy house, a decade old, is whitewashed inside and out. Light pours through large windows illuminating Rajasthani dark wood sofas and beds and Candy's light touch is all over, from the individually decorated bedrooms to the lamp bases made from printing blocks. The two largest rooms have ornate four-posters, locally printed bedspreads, marble bathrooms. There are long views from swing seats on the roof terrace, and shady nooks in the large lawned garden. Breakfast ranges from a traditional rice and chilli 'poha' to a fry-up. Request lunch or candlelit dinner, vegetarian or meaty, and Candy will produce three delectable courses – eat en famille or à deux. In the comfortable sitting room you may meet her husband and their two 20-something children. The Singhs love spending time with their guests and Candy welcomes you as a friend – impossible not to feel at home here. *Cookery demonstrations & tours.*

Price	Rs3,500. Singles Rs3,200.
Rooms	4: 1 double, 1 single, 2 four-poster rooms.
Meals	Lunch & dinner Rs300–Rs350.
Closed	Rarely.
Directions	3km off the Jaipur/Ajmer highway, near Sirsi village. Turn off main road towards Bhatrokta. Airport/train: Jaipur (24km, 35 mins).

Mrs Candy Singh
Sri Niwas Country Homes,
Sirsi Bhankrota Link Road,
Sirsi, Jaipur, 302012

Tel	+91 (0)1412 240 380
Email	sriniwascountryhomes@gmail.com
Web	www.sriniwas.net

Price band: B

Entry 55   Map 4

Barwara Kothi

A royal welcome means just that. In her quietly dignified way, Mrs Ombala Singh will guide you through her family's history, beginning with the building of the white colonial villa in the 1930s as a mighty gift from the Maharaja of Jaipur, guardian to her father-in-law, Raja Man Singh (or 'Rabbit' to his majesty). Across the gardens, an erstwhile outbuilding – turned guest house – benefited from similar largesse: walk into the marble foyer with a winding staircase in the corner and face a beautifully carved miniature wooden temple. The drawing room is aristocratic, while the dining room flaunts elaborately carved silver chairs (and excellent cooking); sitting on the veranda around pretty wrought-iron tables you too may appreciate why the caged birds sing. The bedrooms are splendid, with attractive stained glass in the master shedding light on sumptuous paintings of copulating couples; but all the rooms have balconies which look out onto the lawn (and let in the city), as well as lovely old desks for penning postcards that describe a peaceful heritage stay in a chaotic heritage city.

Price	Rs3,500. Suites Rs4,000-4,500.
Rooms	8: 3 doubles, 5 suites.
Meals	Lunch & dinner Rs350.
Closed	Rarely.
Directions	Directions on booking.

Price band: B

Deepali Singh
Barwara Kothi, 5 Jacob Road,
Civil Lines, Jaipur, 302006

Tel	+91 (0)1412 222 796
Email	dsingh@barwarakothi.com
Web	www.barwarakothi.com

Bissau Palace

Faded photos of past and present British royals take pride of place in the impressive, wooden-floored sitting room where old weapons and vast portraits of steely-gazed ancestors remind you that peaceable Jaipur has seen more unruly days. The old palace is tucked away down an inconspicuous backstreet, off which a large driveway leads to its austere facade. Slightly scuffed around the edges, Bissau has a informality that appeals to travellers in their teens and twenties – you can sit quaffing a cold beer in the living room without fear of upsetting etiquette, and feel unusually free of the old-world stuffiness that is synonymous with some heritage places. You can snack in the new coffee bar, but main meals take place on the roof terrace, clean and tidy and with amazing views of the multiple layers of Jaipur. Bedrooms and bathrooms, sombre and faded, have beautiful murals and sometimes tilework, and soft furnishings in bright shiny fabrics. The library has beautiful old leather furniture, the restaurant some fabulous mosaics, and plastic sunloungers crowd around the old pool. *Lawn tennis. Camel safaris.*

Price	Rs3,000–Rs4,500. Suites Rs6,000. Plus 10% tax.
Rooms	51: 36 doubles, 15 suites.
Meals	Breakfast Rs240. Lunch Rs400. Dinner Rs495.
Closed	Rarely.
Directions	Out of Chandpol Road & turn right. Keep right; hotel set back on left.

Mr Sanjai Singh of Bissau
Bissau Palace, Outside Chandpole Gate, Jaipur, 302016

Tel	+91 (0)1412 304 371
Fax	+91 (0)1412 304 628
Email	bissau@sancharnet.in
Web	www.bissaupalace.com

Price band: C

Entry 57   Map 4

Hotel Meghniwas

The old Colonel is a genial soul with a twinkle in his eye and a bear-like handshake – a man happy with his lot. Having spent many years with the Indian army, he has returned to the roost to do what he loves most. The building is Forties-modern, not fancy, and sits gleaming white in gardens that are neat but not fussy. Established 20 years ago as a functional, friendly place from which to explore Jaipur and the surrounds, the hotel is just this. Bedrooms are smartly, sedately furnished and come with all mod cons (including good lighting – a treat in India); ask for one on the peaceful lawn side. It is, however, the Colonel and his gentle wife, Indu, who make 'the house of the clouds' special – they love meeting new people and helping visitors uncover the hidden corners of fascinating Jaipur. Delicious food is sourced from their farm in Pushkar, and the gardens are green, floral, walled and lovely. A pool is sunk into the grass, at the back of which the Colonel's cosy travel bureau lies. The Meghniwas is run with all the trimmings of a western hotel yet has a family feel.

Price	Rs2,500-Rs3,000. Suites Rs3,800. Plus 10% tax. Peak season: October-March.
Rooms	21: 17 doubles, 4 suites.
Meals	Breakfast Rs275. Lunch & dinner Rs375.
Closed	Rarely.
Directions	Half-way down Jai Singh highway, opp. ATM booth. Airport: Jaipur (16km, 30 mins). Free pick-up from bus & train station.

Price band: B

Colonel & Mrs Indu Singh
Hotel Meghniwas,
C-9 Sawai Jai Singh Highway,
Bani Park, Jaipur, 302016

Tel	+91 (0)1412 202 034
Email	email@meghniwas.com
Web	www.meghniwas.com

Entry 58   Map 4

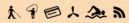

Hotel Madhuban

A prancing elephant fresco, and probably one of their four dogs or two children, greet guests to the Singhs' home. As they say, "Madhuban is not luxury. It is a comfortable way of life". You're about a kilometre from the old town, in a pretty, quiet, leafy residential area; there's a swimming pool in the sheltered garden and the occasional partridge or peacock strutting between the tables and chairs dotted about the lawn – a good place to write and read. Digvijay, 'Dicky', is thoroughly at home with westerners, and understands their preoccupation with cleanliness and their desire for cornflakes and milder meals from time to time; his wife Kavita is helpful and hands on. The style here is quite sedate and proper: the sitting room is elegant, the restaurant brightly lit; bedrooms have traditional wooden furniture, heavy brocade curtains and covers, marble-chip floors and spotless bathrooms; go for the Royal Suite. Some rooms give on to a pleasant rooftop area with potted plants and easy chairs in the shade. A thoroughly reliable place – with free basic yoga sessions, from sunrise, in the next door ashram.

Price	Rs1,600-Rs2,200. Suites Rs2,700-Rs3,200. Plus 8%-10% tax. Peak season: October-March.
Rooms	26: 20 doubles, 6 suites. Extra beds.
Meals	Breakfast Rs175. Lunch & dinner from Rs275. Plus 12.5% tax.
Closed	Never
Directions	2km from train station & bus stand. Free pick-up service from train & bus station.

Mr Dicky Singh Patan
Hotel Madhuban, D-237 Behari Marg,
Bani Park, Jaipur, 302016

Tel	+91 (0)1412 200 033
Fax	+91 (0)1412 202 344
Email	madhuban@usa.net
Web	www.madhuban.net

Price band: B

Hotel Shahpura House

One sighs with relief in India when sinking into a bed that is not like a marble plinth. Shahpura House has memorably soft beds. The home of the head of the Shekhawat clan of Rajputs, the building stands in a residential enclave surrounded by high walls. It is relatively modern but has managed to avoid the worst of Fifties' architecture by strictly following old architectural practices. Mughal and family influence are mixed in the shape of hand-painted walls, stained-glass doors and skylights, and blown-glass lamps – all set against pristine walls and swathes of delicately inlaid marble. The place is immaculate and uncluttered, the bathrooms spotless, and the pool lined with sunloungers. Many of the old royal retainers are still around – not exactly rushed off their feet – and the original horse-drawn carriage waits at the front, available for guests who plan a sightseeing tour. People settle in for days, though the atmosphere is more hotel than family guest house. And the candlelit dinners, held outside under a draped tent, sometimes accompanied by musicians, are delicious.

Price	Rs3,000–Rs3,500. Suites Rs3,500–Rs5,000. Peak season: August; October–March.
Rooms	34: 20 doubles, 14 suites.
Meals	Breakfast Rs250. Lunch Rs600. Dinner Rs600.
Closed	Rarely.
Directions	In residential area of Bani Park, to west of Chandpol Gate. Airport: Jaipur (24km, 45 mins).

Price band: B

Mr Surendra Shekhawat
Hotel Shahpura House, D-257 Devi Marg, Bani Park, Jaipur, 302016

Tel	+91 (0)1412 202 293
Fax	+91 (0)1412 201 494
Email	reservation@shahpurahouse.com
Web	www.shahpurahouse.com

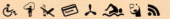

Umaid Bhawan

Krishna dances through the halls and rooms of Umaid Bhawan, playfully delighting milk maids, decently of course. Equally heartening is that you'll find pennies remaining in your pockets after a stay here, a good-value choice of base for discovery of India's picture-book face, Jaipur. Richly enamelled furniture in rooms is lightened by glass ceilings, Venetian mirrors and sweet *jharokha* balconies that look out onto the tiny but beautiful pool; the garden is small but perfectly formed. The sandstone pink-red building was first renovated in 1956 before becoming a hotel in 1993, yet three generations of the Rathore warrior clan have lived here since the turn of the last century. Military photographs line the walls but the current owner is far from ferocious and will delightfully give you the low-down on all that's worth seeing. From the rooftop restaurant all you hear are distant horns; the old city is a five-minute ride away. Surmounting the building are antique guard posts softened by cushions and low tables; lazy spots to enjoy a city sunset, or superb chicken tikka served by delightful Nepalese waiters.

Price	Rs2,400. Singles Rs2,000. Suites Rs3,500. Plus 15% tax. Peak season: October–March.
Rooms	35: 28 doubles, 7 suites.
Meals	Lunch & dinner Rs350.
Closed	Rarely.
Directions	Airport: Jaipur (15km, 20 mins). Train: Jaipur (0.8km, 5 mins).

Mr Karan Rathore
Umaid Bhawan, D1-2A, Behind Collectorate,
Behari Marg via Bank Road, Bani Park,
Jaipur, 302016

Tel	+91 (0)1412 206 426
Email	email@umaidbhawan.com
Web	www.umaidbhawan.com

Price band: B

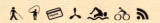

Entry 61   Map 4

Dera Rawatsar

Come face-to-face with history: Grandma Laxmi Chandawat was the first woman in Rajasthan to break with purdah; she is a remarkable lady. Set around neat lawns, with a charming new swimming pool fringed by ashoka trees, Dera Rawatsar is a stylish place, soothingly white and crowned with a balcony. The quiet comes as a joyous surprise given that this residential area is within strolling distance of the main bus station. The ladies of the house run things here, and the rooms have an understated elegance, light in feel and uncluttered. A gauze veil curtains off some of the bed areas, which are vast and silkily comfortable, and the bathrooms have big white bath tubs, a rarity in India. Mother and daughter-in-law Veena and Mandvi have a charmingly relaxed manner, run a happy staff and are helpful when it comes to Jaipur orientation. The family can trace its origins back to the Rawatsar clan, pre-eminent in the Bikaner region, and claim to offer an authentic Rajput experience: huge servings of food served by candlelight don't disappoint and you'll be taking Grandma's biography to bed.

Price	Rs2,400–Rs4,500. Plus 8%–10% tax. Peak season: October–March.
Rooms	17: 13 twins/doubles, 4 suites.
Meals	Breakfast Rs170. Lunch & dinner Rs350. Plus 12.5% tax.
Closed	Never.
Directions	Airport: Jaipur (11km, 25 mins). Train: Jaipur (3km, 5 mins). Behind Sindhi Camp bus station.

Price band: C

Veena Chauhan & Mandvi Ranawat
Dera Rawatsar, D-194/C Vijay Path,
Bani Park, Jaipur, 302016

Tel	+91 (0)1412 206 559
Fax	+91 (0)1412 360 717
Email	service@derarawatsar.com
Web	www.derarawatsar.com

Entry 62   Map 4

Savista Retreat

Behold the Indian pastoral: acres of wheat fields, twittering birds, gardens, and hammocks swinging from shady fruit trees… then the old house itself, elegantly light and cooled by the breeze. Savista has its own adventurous storyline: 300 years ago, the heir to the Kacchawa throne ran away to set up his own kingdom here. Performances are encouraged, often musical with so many instruments to hand, and held on the amphitheatre steps. Old, rescued artefacts account for much of the furniture, while uncluttered bedrooms – Jasmine, Lapis Lazuli – are named according to their colours. A well-stocked gym and library stretch different muscle groups before a candlelit dinner (of your request) in the company of your wonderful, warm, cultured hosts. Bhanwar and his wife are deeply environmentally conscious, encouraging guests to share a car (which they will provide with driver), employing and buying locally, composting, water harvesting… Even the pool, set among palms and a beautifully twisted tree stump, is an irrigation resource. This is special in every way.

Price	Rs6,500–Rs7,500. Plus 10% tax.
Rooms	16: 13 doubles, 3 suites.
Meals	Lunch Rs400. Dinner Rs450.
Closed	Never.
Directions	Directions on booking.

Bhanwar Rishyasringa
Savista Retreat, Ajmer Road,
Post Office Thikaria, via Bhankrota,
Sanjharia, Jaipur, 302026
Tel   +91 (0)9829 214 453
Email   info@savista.com
Web   www.savista.com

Ethical Collection: Environment; Community.
See page 264.

Price band: C

Ranthambhore Bagh

This couple are gems, full of humour and charm. And this is the ungentrified jungle experience that you don't get at the posher camps: higgledy-piggledy with part-tended gardens perfect for kids. He is a wildlife photographer and she a sculptress, there's a huge sense of fun and an artistic mood. Weird and wonderful objects are strewn about, floors are a lovely jade green, sitting areas are scattered – a great place to meet others and share safari stories. The building, on the outskirts of town, is around two small courtyards of concrete and stone, enlivened by plants and 'ethnic' decorations. The rooms are basic but have been upgraded (expect crisp white linen, new floors and repainted walls), the wildlife maps are brilliant, and the game drives are the main topic of conversation. The tents are charming, cosy rather than immaculate, with rugs on stone floors and showers at the back. Jeep safaris head out before breakfast or you can take a larger vehicle and book a day or two ahead, but note that the railway station is near and there are bikes for hire. Food is Rajasthani buffet style – and delicious!

Price	€43. Tents €53. Peak season: October–April. Safaris extra.
Rooms	23: 10 doubles, 1 family room, 12 tents.
Meals	Breakfast Rs175. Lunch Rs275. Dinner Rs325. Plus 12.5% tax.
Closed	July–September.
Directions	From Sawai Madhopur station take Ranthambhore Road towards National Park; 4km. Airport: Jaipur (175km, 3 hours).

Aditya & Poonam Singh
Ranthambhore Bagh, Ranthambhore Rd,
Sawai Madhopur, 322001

Tel	+91 (0)7462 221 728
Fax	+91 (0)7462 224 251
Email	tiger@ranthambhorebagh.com
Web	www.ranthambhorebagh.com

Price band: B

Dev Vilas

A delight to breakfast outside, overlooking the pool and the distant hills. And on winter nights there are candles, braziers and a great fire to keep you warm… a fine spot for swapping stories with other guests, Indian or European. Thanks to numerous staff all is accomplished with grace and good humour, including the early wake-up safari call! This you cannot miss – the Ranthambhore National Park, the most famous tiger reserve in India, is minutes away. (October to April is the time to visit.) Your entertaining host Mr Singh is passionate about nature and conservation, and a font of knowledge. There are tiger paintings and luxurious sofas in the bar, big bedrooms with super balconies and a safe décor, and nicest and newest of all, seven stylish safari tents with bathrooms that flourish big white towels and lashings of water. Food is Indian and tasty, with a limited choice. Gardens glow with bright butterflies and flowers; there are vegetable gardens, a good pool, a giant sculpture of deer and, in the far corner, the family pet – an elderly elephant who still gives rides. *Ayurvedic massage.*

Price	Full-board $225-$250. Safaris extra. Peak season: October–March.
Rooms	28: 14 doubles, 5 twins, 2 suites, 7 tents.
Meals	Lunch & dinner Rs450.
Closed	July–September.
Directions	Fork left shortly before Khilchipur village; hotel on the left, within sight. Airport: Jaipur (180km, 3.5 hours). Train: Sawai Madhopur (7km, 15 mins).

Balendu Singh
Dev Vilas, Ranthambhore Road, Village Khilchipur, Sawai Madhopur, 322011

Tel	+91 (0)7462 252 168
Fax	+91 (0)7462 252 195
Email	devvilas@datainfosys.net
Web	www.devvilas.com

Price band: C

Entry 65   Map 4

Khem Villas

Nestling beside the tiger sanctuary of Ranthambhore National Park, Khem Villas luxuriates in a wilderness of its own. For 20 years, ecologist and doctor Goverdhan Singh (son of an Indian tiger expert) reclaimed the land with indigenous trees and created a 12-acre haven of jungle, grassland and lakes. Then he added the luxury: thatched cottages, Rajasthani tents and colonial villa, designed with contemporary elegance. Granite floors, tented ceilings and indoor/outdoor bathrooms in the cottages; sunshine colours, bamboo and dark wood in the tents; sleek furnishings and window seats in the villa. Light and uncluttered, rooms are an extension of the green outdoors. Watch nature from veranda or roof terrace, take a guided walk around the grounds, spot jackals, hyenas, crocodiles and trillions of birds. Relax in the plunge pool or take a massage while gazing over the Bagh Hills. Dinners are gourmet vegetarian and home-grown — eaten around lake or camp fire with charming Goverdhan's conservation stories. Run on strong ecological principles (recycled water, alternative energy) — it's eco luxury at its best.

Price	Full-board Rs9,000. Tents Rs13,000. Cottages Rs16,000. Safaris extra.
Rooms	15: 4 doubles, 6 cottages, 5 tents.
Meals	Full-board only.
Closed	Rarely.
Directions	Directions on booking.

Ethical Collection: Environment;
Community; Food.
See page 264.

Price band: C

Usha & Goverdhan Singh Rathore
Khem Villas, VPO Sherpur, Kutalpura
Village, , Khilijipur, Sawai Madhopur,

Tel	+91 (0)7462 252 219
Email	khemvillas@anokhi.com
Web	www.khemvillas.com

Shahpura Bagh Palace

Shahpura Bagh would look very different if ancestor Rajadhiraj Nahar Singh had not mortgaged the jewels to build earth dams and bring water to his people. There would be no pastures, mustard crops or evergreens and the 19th-century family home, a neat right-angle of limestone, would not be surrounded by lushness. Columns rise to staggered levels of vast flagstone terraces, great for yoga. Carpets are Kashmiri, brocades are jewel-bright, lamps are Art Deco. At the top of the house, bedrooms – some of the loveliest we've seen – are served by light and cool walls and bathrooms with old claw-foot tubs. Eat together, beautifully, in the dining room. The family (exceptionally hospitable) will entertain you with hilarious anecdotes of Rajasthan's most "colourful characters" and royal life pre-Independence. Something of the past remains here: Shah Jehan's handprint for one, but most of all Uncle Indrajit, who continues a tradition of care as a homeopath. And there's a new square pool, flanked by sunloungers and four-poster day beds. A perfect place. *Cookery classes & tours.*

Price	Rs5,000-Rs7,700. Suites Rs6540-Rs10,900. Plus 10% tax. Peak season: October-April.
Rooms	10: 4 doubles, 6 suites.
Meals	Lunch Rs500. Dinner Rs600.
Closed	May/June.
Directions	Between Jaipur & Udaipur on NH79. Airport: Jaipur (220km, 3.5 hours). Train: Bijainagar (50km, 1 hour).

Mr Jai Singh & Mr Sat Singh
Shahpura Bagh Palace,
Shahpura, Bhilwara, 311404
Tel   +91 (0)1484 222 077
Email   res@shahpurabagh.com
Web   www.shahpurabagh.com

Price band: C

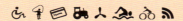

Fort Seengh Sagar

When the rains come, the moat transforms into a shimmering lake which you cross by boat, serenaded by cow bells and birds. The thick stone walls have seen 300 years of history but battlements are now sit-out areas and the rocky grounds and waterfall pools are yours for relaxing. Step through ornate stone arches to a marble-floored dining area and Bond-style bar, lanterns lighting antique art and unfussy Rajasthani décor. A leafy central court harbours a fountain and staircase spiralling to a dramatic rooftop – clamber up for 360 degree views of wild surroundings. Spidering off the courtyard are bedrooms in which the maharaja housed his harem, no less luxurious now: beds of ruby silk and soft white muslin; terracotta tiles topped by patterned rugs and antiques. Some have miniature temples, one has a small fountain, another a jacuzzi and rock garden; all get balconies and bathrooms in carved stone and mosaic. With just four rooms it's intimate – perfect for a celebration – but you can use nearby Deogarh Mahal's facilities and join excursions, or ask the chefs over to cook up a feast. Gorgeous. Fantastic.

Price	Rs12,000–Rs13,800. Plus tax.
Rooms	4 suites.
Meals	Breakfast Rs350. Lunch Rs550. Dinner Rs650. Plus 12.5% tax.
Closed	Rarely.
Directions	Airport: Jodphur (150km, 2.5 hours), Udaipur (135km, 2 hours). Train: Jaipur (280km, 4.5 hours), Deogarh (0.5 km).

Price band: E

Veerbhadra Singh
Fort Seengh Sagar, Deogarh Madaria,
Rajsamand, 313331

Tel	+91 (0)2904 252 777
Fax	+91 (0)2904 252 555
Email	info@deogarhmahal.com
Web	www.deogarhmahal.com

Deogarh Mahal

Built in 1670, huge and rambling, high and cool, Deogarh Mahal has an eccentric spirit and exuberance at every turn. It's also the most fairytale palace in Rajasthan. Step into the courtyard (replete with WWII jeep used for safaris) and you sense the scale and joyfulness of the place. Staff are courteous and kind, the head cook is full of smiles, the princely brothers are charming and entertaining. Cauldrons of burning wood at night help keep winter chills at bay as you recline on the courtyard's wicker chairs. In summer, there's a bursting lotus-shaped pool; here the elephants once stood. Lose yourself in the bustling streets of the little town, join a bullock-cart procession to the family's hunting lodge in the rugged hills, return to spacious, elegant and opulent rooms, one with a polished antique swing, another with a luxurious divan, all with fabulous views. Everything shimmers, from mosaic jacuzzis to peacock windows to inlaid mirrored glass. Dinner is high on the terrace walls; breakfasts are feasts. A heritage hotel that's held onto its soul, held by Delhi-ites in high regard.

Price	Rs7,000–Rs8,050. Singles Rs6,000–Rs6,950. Suites Rs9,000–Rs13,800. Peak season: October–March.
Rooms	50: 20 doubles, 30 suites.
Meals	Breakfast Rs350. Lunch Rs550. Dinner Rs650. Plus 12.5% tax.
Closed	Rarely.
Directions	Airport: Udaipur (135km, 2 hours), Train: Deogarh (0.5km, 5 mins). Jodhpur (150km). Jaipur (280km, 4.5 hours).

Veerbhadra Singh
Deogarh Mahal, Deogarh Madaria,
Rajsamand, 313331

Tel	+91 (0)2904 252 777
Fax	+91 (0)2904 252 555
Email	info@deogarhmahal.com
Web	www.deogarhmahal.com

Price band: D

Kankarwa Haveli

This is heritage as it should be. There is nothing superfluous, no tat, no plastic, no hassle; it is a romantic, laid-back, lakeside guest house run by delightful people. And the rooms are 'to die for', intelligently renovated to show the simple majesty of the architecture, many with heavenly views. Cushioned *jharokhas* hang over the Lal Ghat steps, delicate lace-work curtains stretch across the arched windows, and block-printed bedspreads and cushions provide splashes of colour. The old building is a handsome structure in which it would have been sacrilege to go for fuss: simplicity is the hallmark and the essence. There is a refreshing absence of mirror-work, glass inlay or coloured walls that can go so 'wrong', and all is beautifully maintained. Soak up the stupendous lake views with delicious vegetarian thalis on the glorious roof terrace. Your host is an intelligent man, relaxed and extremely helpful, his one weakness glossy magazines; those who return each year (having happened upon a place so close to ideal) often add to the pile. Wonderful value, in ever-bustling Udaipur.

Price	Rs2,800–Rs3,3850. Singles Rs2,390. Plus 8% tax. Peak season: July–April.
Rooms	15 doubles.
Meals	Breakfast Rs200. Lunch Rs150–Rs250. Dinner Rs150–Rs250.
Closed	Rarely.
Directions	Right in the Lal Ghat. Airport: Dabok (25km, 30 mins). Train: Udaipur (10 mins).

Price band: B

Mr Janardan Singh
Kankarwa Haveli, 26 Lal Ghat,
Udaipur, 313001

Tel	+91 (0)2942 411 457
Fax	+91 (0)2942 521 403
Email	kankarwahaveli@hotmail.com
Web	www.indianheritagehotels.com

Lake View Villa

English gardens, a terracotta bridge, 80s kitsch – yet this is still the real India, living with a family in what Mr and Mrs Singh love to call 'a cosy home from home'. It's right in the heart of romantic Udaipur too and, from beneath Rajput arches on the terrific rooftop terrace, you can visually plan your day's itinerary, starting at the famous Fateh Sagar Lake. 'India down the centuries' might be the best way to describe the decoration, the furniture in the bedrooms taking you on a colour-coded journey, beginning with 200-year-old Rajasthani and tumbling into the present. Go for the suite, with its big indoor terrace, sofa with lion arms, bongo drum table, view of the lake and sensuously feminine sink. Enter the living and dining rooms to find a profusion of ornamentation; most notable are some vivid porcelain pieces, a cuckoo clock, a huge fish tank and some funky chandeliers. None of this would work if it were not for the wonderful Singhs, whose bright energy, social conscience and advice are best savoured by joining them for dinner; and then it all makes sense. *Cookery lessons available.*

Price	Rs1,800–Rs3,000. Suite Rs4,000. Plus 10% tax.
Rooms	5: 4 doubles, 1 suite.
Meals	À la carte menu available. Lunch Rs400. Dinner Rs400.
Closed	Never.
Directions	Directions on booking.

M P Singh
Lake View Villa, 774, OTC Scheme, Rani Road, Udaipur, 313001

Tel	+91 (0)2942 430 561
Email	mps.villa@yahoo.in
Web	www.lakeviewvilla.in

Price band: B

Entry 71   Map 3

Devra Udaipur

Wraparound verandas and a sweeping roof terrace give exquisite views of the countryside yet ancient Udaipur is beguilingly close. Across Lake Pichola the City Palace glints; on a nearby hill stands the Monsoon Palace. Inspired by her family home, Jyoti has designed a modern building and tucked in a garden strewn with statuary, capturing the warmth and intimacy of a private house and adding a swish of class. Lounges — more than strictly necessary — are scattered with big wicker armchairs, low tables and earthy-toned cushions. Plenty of space to be alone or share sightseeing stories with other guests. Family photos and fresh flowers give an informal feel and this continues into the bedrooms, stylish contemporary spaces of four-posters, bright fabrics, cream floors and bed linen as white as the bathrooms' tiles. Delicious meals are created by Jyoti from produce from their much-loved garden or their organic farm. Chill out TV-free and let the Major — Jyoti's husband — arrange yoga, fix a drink, suggest tomorrow's birdwatching trip. Warm, professional and cultured, this couple delight all who stay.

Price	Rs4,000. Peak season: October–March. Whole house can be rented May/June.
Rooms	8: 4 doubles. New block: 2 twins, 2 family rooms.
Meals	Lunch & dinner Rs350.
Closed	May/June (when whole house becomes available).
Directions	Airport: Udaipur (32km, 40 mins). Train: Udaipur City (13km, 20 mins).

Major Durga Das
Devra Udaipur, Sisarma–Burja Road,
Kalarohi, Udaipur

Tel	+91 (0)2942 431 049
Fax	+91 (0)2942 431 049
Email	devra2004@india.com
Web	www.devraudaipur.com

Price band: B

Entry 72   Map 3

Hotel

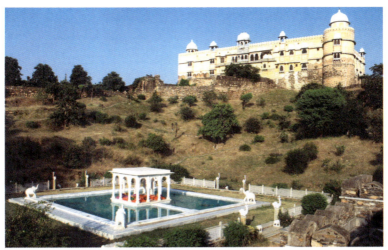

Karni Fort

The terraced gardens of the 300-year-old fort slope down to one of the most romantic swimming pools in India. Peacocks strut, birds trill, frogs serenade and sunsets can be seen from every window. The 1710 Sisodia outpost is a maze of upstairs and downstairs, balconies, terraces, corridors, courtyards, turrets, domes and arches. The comforts are princely and the cheerful young staff cannot do enough for you; towels are laid out by the pool, massages with aromatic oils are all yours. High up above Bambora, with views to the rolling Aravalli hills, this is a deeply rural spot. Picnic by the reservoir, alive with tree-pies and bee-eaters, kingfishers, swallows and kites; cool off in the marble pool, complete with island. Inside, gold furniture and stained glass abound. The bar, with fake gas lamps, is regal; the bedrooms are luscious with mosaics and silks. Meals are buffet style or you dine on your balcony; many rooms have one. When the pampering palls, there's the village bazaar to browse and local tribes to visit: book a horse safari. Udaipur, dominated by the labyrinthine City Palace, is 50 kilometres away.

Price	Rs5,300–Rs5,900. Singles Rs3,850–Rs4,150. Suites Rs6,700–Rs7,300. Plus 8% tax. Peak season: October–March.
Rooms	30: 18 doubles, 12 suites.
Meals	Breakfast Rs300. Lunch Rs425. Dinner Rs500. Plus 12.5% tax.
Closed	Never.
Directions	Airport/train: Udaipur (35km, 1.5 hours).

Th. Chanderveer Singh
Karni Fort, Bambora, Udaipur
Tel +91 (0)2942 398 283
Fax +91 (0)2942 398 220
Email karnihotels@satyam.net.in
Web www.karnihotels.com

Price band: C

Entry 73   Map 3

Udai Bilas Palace

A splendid surprise at the end of a 'road to nowhere'. Lying on the banks of the Gaibsagar Lake – paradise for birds – this palace, still a royal residence, has a supremely serene setting and a deliciously faded grandeur. Nature intermingles with nostalgia; sweep away the palms to find a swimming pool with a sunken bar and fountain-elephants; resident Great Danes and hunting dogs meander. The palace bursts with arches, vaulted windows, tiles and frescos among the finest examples of their kind. No less exquisite are the suites, each with its own character, from traditional and floral to Art Deco, all with balconies, plump pillows and sumptuous divans. Big marble bathrooms reveal handmade soaps and luxurious towels. Guests come together for dinner at a marble dining table with a scented pool at its centre; exotic hunting trophies line the Africa Room and the feel is reminiscent of a 1930s Scottish lodge. Staff are as attentive as you'd expect; more so. Massages and manicures are available, there's boating on the lake and the family's 13th-century palace Juna Mahal awaits discovery.

Price	Rs5,100. Singles Rs4,050. Suites Rs6,300–Rs15,000. Extra beds Rs1,200. Plus 8% tax. Peak season: October–March.
Rooms	23: 4 doubles, 2 singles, 17 suites.
Meals	Breakfast Rs300. Lunch Rs500. Dinner Rs575. Plus 12.5% tax.
Closed	Never.
Directions	120km from Udaipur; 175km from Ahmedabad.

M K Harashvardhan Singh
Udai Bilas Palace, Dungapur, 314001

Tel	+91 (0)2964 230 808
Fax	+91 (0)2964 231 008
Email	contact@udaibilaspalace.com
Web	www.udaibilaspalace.com

Price band: C

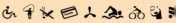

Chhatra Sagar

A chance to star in your own Indian epic. The savannah unfolds from across the banks of a 100-year-old family-built reservoir, home to over 250 species of migratory birds, while antelope graze on the bank. All this makes for an amazing view from the nearby hill on top of which two of the white Shikar tents perch – worth the sharp climb if only for the reward of a "summit sundowner" courtesy of Stetson-wearing owner, Harsh. Or relax in your own sit-out and watch the wildlife perform. Smartly contained within a rigging of white canvas and furnished in elegant Rajput style, bedrooms teeter on the edge of tent-reality, while marble and slate 'bathrooms' transport you to another – indoor – dimension completely. Toast and tea are delivered to your tent before breakfast, pillows are of softest down. A honeymoon can easily be imagined here as you are warmed by camp fires and dine in style by candlelight. All is exemplary, from lessons on village lore to surely the freshest and most delicious food in the region. Head to bed by torchlight – to discover hot water bottles tucked between the sheets. *Rural jeep excursions.*

Price	Full-board Rs18,000. Singles Rs16,000. Plus tax. Jeep & birdwatching tour included.
Rooms	13 tents.
Meals	Full-board only.
Closed	April-September.
Directions	2 hours from Jodhpur & Ajmer on Ajmer-Jodhpur highway.

Nandi & Harsh Vardhan
Chhatra Sagar, Nimaj, Pali, 306303
Tel   +91 (0)9414 123 118
Email   harsh@chhatrasagar.com
Web   www.chhatrasagar.com

Price band: D

Inn Seventh Heaven

Escape the hustle of Pushkar bazaar (or the raucous annual camel fair) for this: an airy elegant whitewashed atrium, leafy hanging plants, a delicate tree, a trickling fountain. The old haveli has been faithfully rebuilt with layered galleries encircling the central court and beautiful swing seats overlooking it all. Rooms branch off from each corner in neat simplicity: no fancy frills, just plain colourful fabrics and traditional furnishings. The higher the room the smarter it is and the better the view; but you can always climb up – and up – to share the restaurant's sweeping vistas. Watch your vegetarian meal (no alcohol) being hauled up in a basket, then tuck in on couches at low tables; owner Anoop, and perhaps his wife and young daughter, are often around for a chat. Learn about the culture of this special part of Rajasthan; Hindus believe that Pushkar was where Brahma dropped a lotus flower to earth, creating a sacred lake now ringed by 52 pale-blue ghats: steps for pilgrims to reach the water. A place of harmony on a most hallowed site – and great value for those who appreciate simple pleasures.

Price	Rs450–Rs2,000.
Rooms	12 doubles.
Meals	Breakfast Rs300.
	Lunch & dinner, à la carte, from Rs90.
Closed	Never.
Directions	Directions on booking.

Anoop
Inn Seventh Heaven, Next to the Mali Ka Mandir (Temple of the Gardeners), Chotti Basti, Pushkar, Ajmer, 305022

Price band: A

Tel	+91 (0)1455 105 455
Email	anoop_loves_you@yahoo.co.in
Web	www.inn-seventh-heaven.com

Fort Barli

The women of the dusty village still cook over open fires, as they did when brave Darbar Lal Singh ruled 300 years ago. He would be pleased with Anirudh Rathore's restoration, recalling the halcyon days of royal Rajasthan. Seated beneath the fabulous ceiling of the dining room, guarded by portraits of five generations, you can appreciate how this was the court where warriors met over matters of state, even as you sample garden-fresh meals made to delicious recipes served by a charming staff. Here stands a water bottle carried into the desert by successive rulers, but large and breezy bedrooms, captivating with chandeliers, are within easier reach. Disturbed only by distant prayer, you may yet extol such faraway charm when stretched over gorgeous silk, or while floating in the exquisite infinity pool. Why not play at being queen in your frescoed chambers, spying on guests through purdah windows of a private terrace – or the movie star when, couched in velvet on a bullock cart, you progress through the village (not for the shy), to the great curiosity of the locals. Few travellers make it this far: a rare treat.

Price	Rs6,000. Singles Rs5,000. Suites Rs10,000.
Rooms	8: 6 doubles, 2 suites.
Meals	Breakfast Rs175. Lunch & dinner Rs300–Rs400. Plus 12.5% tax.
Closed	Rarely.
Directions	Airport/train: Jaipur (180km, 3 hours).

Mr Anirudh Rathore
Fort Barli, Barli, Ajmer
Tel   +91 (0)1412 200 770
Email   reservations@fortbarli.com
Web   www.fortbarli.com

Price band: C

Phool Mahal Palace

By the old city gates and beneath its fort, this lakeside palace feels like a grand and quirky domicile. It appears in paintings of the Kishangarh Miniature School and is home to India's version of the *Mona Lisa* (a beguiling 18th-century painting of sharp-profiled Radha). The Maharani is as passionate about her hotel venture as she is about local arts and culture; small study groups come here to paint and draw, in the style of Indian miniatures. Massive bee hives drip from the battlements, water chestnut harvesters toil in their dinghies, public rooms display family portraits and deep sofa'd opulence. Bedrooms have all the essentials plus ornate fabrics and murals reflecting the history and the wildlife (post monsoon, the lake is a twitcher's paradise). The original rooms ooze authenticity and the suites are truly romantic but the new rooms across the courtyard are more comfortable. Kishangarh is off the standard tourist trail, but a wander around the medieval town and the market, where silversmiths and sweet-makers rub shoulders, is something rare and special – and the tours of the fort are amazing.

Price	Rs3,500. Suites Rs4,500. Plus 8% tax. Peak season: September-March.
Rooms	20: 18 doubles, 2 suites.
Meals	Breakfast Rs200. Lunch & dinner Rs370.
Closed	Rarely.
Directions	On the lakeside by the gates into the old city beneath the fort.

Mr D D Purohit
Phool Mahal Palace, Kishangarh,
Ajmer, 305802

Tel	+91 (0)1463 247 405
Fax	+91 (0)1463 247 505
Email	phoolmahalpalace@yahoo.com
Web	www.royalkishangarh.com

Price band: B

Entry 78   Map 4

Roopangarh Fort

We can't promise you the delights of a 17th-century court but we can promise you the luxury of space. Most bedrooms are bigger than those of your wildest fantasies, and are furnished with an individuality in defiance of modern design. This was the abode of kings, a centre of culture and fine living and there is a lot to live up to; where to begin? The sheer splendour of the scale, of course, but it is the 'well-kept secret' feel that inspires attention. Decorated columns, green swards and courtyards, swathes of bougainvillea, cane chairs poised to receive you in marbled corners, a rooftop tennis court (why not?), bright red tables under decorated arches, a mad miscellany of marble in a bathroom... Then, lovely old mahogany desks against white walls, a suit of chain mail above dining tables, polo sticks above the bed, an exquisite double/treble bed floating on a sea of white marble – and on it goes. There are cracks in the façade and it is not luxury western style but the Queen's Suite is a marvel and historians will love it. Above it all looms the massive fort, a symbol of stability. *Complimentary camel rides.*

Price	Rs2,300–Rs3,600. Suite Rs5,000. Plus 8% tax. Peak season: October–February.
Rooms	19: 18 doubles, 1 suite.
Meals	Breakfast Rs200. Lunch & dinner Rs350. Plus 9% tax.
Closed	Rarely.
Directions	Turn off Jaipur-Ajmer highway at Kishangarh; north for 22km along NH 8. Into Roopangarh; fort entrance at far end of main street.

H H Maharaja Brajraj Singh
Roopangarh Fort, Roopangarh,
Ajmer, 305814

Tel	+91 (0)1497 220 444
Email	roopangarhfort@yahoo.co.uk
Web	www.royalkishangarh.com

Price band: B

Chandelao Garh

History has seeped into the dusky pink walls of this fort built in 1744 for the local thakur – a reward for serving the maharaja; it is still lived in by his descendants. In ornate Rajasthani style, it overlooks peaceful Chandelao village where women still gather at the wells. Beyond, the deserts of Rajasthan. Less hotel, more living museum, its walls are covered with ancestral portraits, ancient rattan armchairs beckon in the garden, tiger skins cover the floors. In the lounge, sofas ask to be sunk into and 1902 albums of grand tours to be browsed. Airy bedrooms are a comfortable mix of family furniture, Indian antiques and the odd newer piece. Locally printed fabrics in rich colours cover cushions and beds, bathrooms are shining temples of tile and marble. Pradhuman and his mother – warm and lovely – mix with guests and share meals (delicious) and stories about the village and their community projects (volunteer if you wish). This is tourist-free India: Pradhuman can arrange a camel-cart safari, and dining under the stars atop the fort's gateway in the light of flaming torches is pure fantasy.

Price	Rs2,300. Singles Rs2,000. Peak season: October–March.
Rooms	18: 17 doubles, 1 single.
Meals	Breakfast Rs200. Lunch & dinner Rs350.
Closed	Rarely.
Directions	Airport: Jodhpur (40km, 40 mins). Train: Jodphur (43km, 50 mins).

Ethical Collection: Environment; Community. See page 264.

Price band: B

Mr Pradhuman Singh Rathore
Chandelao Garh,
Chandelao, Jodhpur
Tel   +91 (0)2916 538 004
Email   chandelao@rediffmail.com
Web   www.chandelao.com

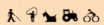

Indrashan Guest House

A small lush, flower-filled garden surrounds this neat, pretty house in one of Jodhpur's quietest neighbourhoods – you might walk by and wonder enviously who lives here. Your hosts are keen to emphasise this is a homestay, not a hotel; they take all meals with their guests and often join them on sightseeing expeditions. Bedrooms, a decent size, are spotless; much of the furniture belonged to Chandrashekhar's grandfather. Three of the rooms, one with its own entrance from the garden, would be ideal for families. Food is fresh, delicious and home-cooked to order by Bhavna, who wins the gong of 'Best Meal Eaten in India' from satisfied guests. But you're also encouraged to help yourself in the kitchen – and from a generously stocked bar in the living room. The Singhs' tour company, Rajputana Discovery, does something few others do, sending you on week-long tours through Rajasthan, staying with aristocratic relations of the family and being drawn into the heart of Indian households. The guest book bears testament to the magic of the trips. Genteel Indian hospitality at its finest – don't rush it.

Price	Rs1,500. Singles Rs1,300. Peak season: October–April.
Rooms	10: 6 doubles, 4 twins.
Meals	Breakfast Rs150. Lunch Rs325. Dinner Rs350.
Closed	Never.
Directions	Airport/train: Jodhpur (3km, 15 mins).

Mr Bhavna & Chandrashekhar Singh
Indrashan Guest House,
593 High Court Colony, Jodhpur, 342001

Tel	+91 (0)2912 440 665
Fax	+91 (0)2912 438 593
Email	chandraraoti@gmail.com
Web	www.rajputanadiscovery.com

Price band: A

Shahi Guest House

Small, original, atmospherically ramshackle and lovingly restored, Shahi Guest House attracts those seeking character and authenticity. It sits down a fascinating, cobblestoned alley in the heart of Jodhpur's Blue City, and its roof terrace has some of the finest views of the city. Your hosts are delightful people for whom nothing is too much trouble; interesting and fun, they have learnt to speak English from their guests. Bedrooms are great value, bathrooms are basic. In the family room (where the women of the house used to meet in purdah) is a sweeping mosaic floor and a sleeping gallery for children. The balcony room has 16 windows and the top two suites – the newest – are slightly larger and lighter than the rest, with windows on three sides and fabulous views. Shelves are filled with family curios, rose oil is sprinkled on curtains and you feast off platters of Anu's home-cooked thali from that glorious rooftop, the mighty Fort towering above. A favourite with backpackers, a happy household and a charming place to stay. *Palm reading, yoga, meditation & classes on Hindu traditions.*

Price	Rs700–Rs1,800. Peak season: October–March.
Rooms	6: 5 doubles, 1 family suite.
Meals	Breakfast Rs95. Lunch & dinner from Rs225.
Closed	Never.
Directions	In city centre, 2km from train station, 2.5km from bus station. Airport: Jodhpur (5km, 20 mins). Free pick-up.

Price band: A

Anu & Vishal Jasmatiya
Shahi Guest House, City Police Gandhi St,
Opp. Narsingh Temple, Jodhpur, 342001

Tel	+91 (0)2912 623 802
Email	shahigh@rediffmail.com
Web	www.shahiguesthouse.com

Entry 82   Map 3

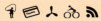

Devi Bhawan

There's no dishonour in sounding the retreat back to the garden sanctuary of Devi Bhawan. No need to don the saffron robes of old and ride out to a certain fate if your attempt to conquer Jodhpur's mighty fort has failed. Instead, relax by the pool or on lounge divans, take dinner in the gazebo or by candlelight in the garden. A series of cottage rooms runs discreetly through this lush and immaculate scene, those on the floors above with the best garden views. Some parts seem a mess of shrubs and plants overflowing from pots, half-hidden by neem trees; others are carefully ordered around trim lawns, an angel-shaped pond and a swing. Peacocks call, a dachshund dozes, bougainvillea shines. Uncluttered rooms have simple designs and teak furniture made by local craftsmen; bathrooms are clean and marble fresh. A young and delightful couple own the property, with noble connections to the royal family, not far away at Umaid Bhawan. Grandfather helps to look after the garden expertly. It would be hard to find a more serene setting ten minutes by rickshaw from Jodhpur; harder still to find better value for money.

Price	Rs1,200-Rs1,800. Singles Rs1,000. Plus 8% tax. Peak season: November-February.
Rooms	20 doubles & suites in 10 cottages.
Meals	Breakfast Rs100. Thali Rs150-Rs175. Buffet dinner Rs200.
Closed	Rarely.
Directions	Airport/train: Jodhpur (1.5km).

Rahesh Singh
Devi Bhawan, Ratanada Circle,
Def. Lab Road, Jodhpur,

Tel	+91 (0)2912 511 067
Fax	+91 (0)2912 512 215
Email	info@devibhawan.com
Web	www.devibhawan.com

Price band: A

Haveli Inn Pal

Outside swirls heady old Jodhpur, jostling with bazaars and the Blue City; inside all is grace and calm. This traditional, 18th-century haveli, two minutes from the Clock Tower, is the perfect cool and airy city retreat. Run by descendants of the Thakur of Pal, the first owner, it is awash with high ceilings, marble floors, arched tracery windows and golden light. Bedrooms are large, simple and uncluttered: some handsome beds, silk cushions, coloured glass lampshades, a scattering of rugs, perhaps a carved chair or a stained-glass panel to add a striking note. Inevitably, you're drawn to the glorious city views through vast windows. Even better are the views from the rooftop terrace restaurant: Jodhpur Fort on one skyline, Umaid Bhawan Palace on the other, Balsamand Lakes and the Blue City below. Relax here with a book and a drink or enjoy a candlelit dinner of Rajasthani dishes. There's also a lively café (same menu) around the corner. Owner Narpat, whose family owns the larger neighbouring hotel, is friendly, courteous and quietly proud of his heritage. He runs a happy, homey and hospitable ship.

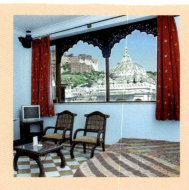

Price	Rs1,850–Rs2,350. Singles Rs2,150. Extra bed Rs500. Plus 10% tax.
Rooms	12 twins/doubles.
Meals	Breakfast Rs150. Lunch & dinner Rs350.
Closed	Rarely.
Directions	Free pick-up from airport or station.

Price band: B

Narpat Singh Rathore
Haveli Inn Pal, Opp. Lake Gulab Sagar,
Clock Tower, Jodhpur

Tel	+91 (0)2912 612 519
Fax	+91 (0)2915 101 401
Email	info@haveliinnpal.com
Web	www.haveliinnpal.com

Fort Pokaran

On an ancient Persian spice road in the Thar Desert lies Pokaran, its glorious 14th-century sandstone fort built by local Rajputs, illustrious forebears of the owner Param. Entering the citadel through castellated walls you are surrounded by courtyards, turrets and gardens, while a vanished age of opulence is conjured up in the palatial suites, which have their own internal courtyards. Ornate archways, silk bedspreads, plaster floors and wooden pieces glow in the jewel tinted light of stained-glass windows. The dining hall, its pale blue walls dotted with ancestors, is the old Durbar hall, where Rajputs held court. Breakfast is European – cereal, fruit juice, toast with Param's mother's guava jelly; at lunch and dinner, old family recipes inspire toothsome dishes. Param, keen for guests to love this place as much as he, leads walking tours of Pokaran and camel safaris to the salt flats, a twitcher's paradise. Roam the grounds, visit the fort's museum, curl up with a book in the sitting room or library, relax by the white marble pool. At day's end, take high tea in the turrets as the sun sets over the dunes.

Price	Rs3,500. Suites Rs7,000.
Rooms	19: 15 doubles, 4 suites.
Meals	Breakfast Rs300. Lunch & dinner Rs600.
Closed	Never.
Directions	On the road from Jaisalmer to Jodhpur: Jaisalmer 110km, 1.5 hours; Jodhpur 170km.

Param Vijay Singh
Fort Pokaran, Pokaran, Jaisalmer

Tel	+91 (0)2994 222 274
Email	reservation@fortpokaran.com
Web	www.fortpokaran.com

Price band: B

Shahi Palace Hotel

One of the nicest, most informal budget hotels in the area. Cheerful Jora and his brothers designed and built Shahi Palace to resemble a 500-year-old haveli. Much is new – beds and mattresses included – yet has stacks of character. Jora and his brothers visited hotels in different countries picking up tips and the attention to detail has paid off handsomely. Bedrooms are cheerful and comfortable – beds carved from stone or wood, sandstone floors, wicker chairs and soft uplighting – while bathrooms display polished sandstone and gleaming fittings. Ask for a room with a view. You dine on the roof terrace, dotted with a few pot plants, topped by a new roof and accompanied by stunning views of the fort (especially fabulous by night) where you are served vegetarian, multi-national dishes from a Nepalese chef. Should guests wish to eat with a family, then Jora will escort you to his village home for dinner with his. A superb budget option, and an environmentally conscious one – the hotel lies just outside the fast-subsiding walls of the Fort. *Camel & jeep safaris. Free pick-up from station.*

Price	Rs350–Rs1,850. Dormitory Rs100. Peak season: July-April.
Rooms	16: 15 doubles, 1 single. Dormitory also available.
Meals	Breakfast Rs100. Lunch & dinner Rs120–Rs300.
Closed	Never.
Directions	5-min walk from the Fort along Shiv Road. Train: Jaisalmer (2km). Free pick-ups from bus & train station.

Price band: A

Mr Jora Lal
Shahi Palace Hotel,
Opp. Government Bus Stand,
Shiv Street, Jaisalmer, 345001

Tel	+91 (0)2992 255 920
Email	shahipalace@yahoo.co.in
Web	www.shahipalacehotel.com

Entry 86   Map 3

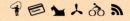

Hotel Monsoon Palace

In the backstreets of Jaisalmer where women beat their daily wash, you will be delighted to find – in spite of the name – a home not a palace. This is a 600-year-old Brahmin's home built of soft sandstone: ceilings are low, packed earth floors lend a welcome simplicity and space for two small bedrooms has been elegantly created through an awareness of light, colour and mirrored embroidery. Bathrooms are clean and modern. Lots of eating places in town, of course, but here you may cook your own dinner, then dine on your own roof terrace. Views reach across town to the outskirts and the land beyond, and at night time the stars are a glory. Note you can also ask the lady up the lane to cook for you, or dine at Fifu's, their sister hotel. Plan your desert safari from that cushioned rooftop terrace as a smiling Babu brings your breakfast and morning tea. The two Brahmin brothers make for gentle and endlessly hospitable company: multi-lingual Om (also known as Fifu) is curious about European culture, Jitu is an excellent cook, and gives classes. A sweet place perfect for two couples; you may have it all to yourself.

Price	Rs1,500-Rs2,650. Peak season: July-March.
Rooms	2 doubles.
Meals	Guest kitchen. Restaurants nearby.
Closed	Never.
Directions	Airport: Jodphur (300km, 5 hours). Train: Jaisalmer (2km, 15 mins). Free pick-up by rickshaw.

Om Prakash Kewalia
Hotel Monsoon Palace, On Fort,
Vyasa Para, Jaisalmer, 345001

Tel	+91 (0)2992 252 656
Email	monsoonpalacejsm@yahoo.com
Web	www.monsoonpalacejsm.com

Price band: B

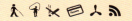

Hotel Fifu & Jasmine Haveli

Views to golden Jaisalmer Fort one way, the dunes of the Thar Desert the other, and a cool glass of banana lassi in your hand. Goodness, you might never leave the rooftop terrace of this elegant 'haveli'. Warm and homely, yet with 24-hour reception, the hotel, housed in a new but traditional building, lies in the town's outskirts; it is linked to Jasmine Haveli. A fun and youthful spirit runs throughout (as does a noisy stairwell!)… from the exuberantly friendly Om ('Fifu') and his staff to the compact and brightly furnished rooms. Tiled floors and stone walls are offset by vivid silks and cottons, carved niches, cushioned window seats and wrought-iron beds. Bathrooms are basic but clean and colourful. Walk ten minutes to Jaisalmer Fort, borrow the rickshaw to visit Jain temples, or let the owners help you organise a camel safari. Return to a vegetarian dinner in the joyful rooftop restaurant, the social centre of these houses, with its bunting and baubles and sunset views. No licence, no frills, but a cheerful and comfortable place to stay. *Cookery classes.*

Price	Rs2,050. Singles Rs1,850.
Rooms	15: 2 doubles, 10 twins/doubles. Jasmine Haveli: 3 doubles.
Meals	Breakfast Rs250. Lunch Rs350. Dinner Rs450.
Closed	Rarely.
Directions	Airport: Jodhpur (300km, 5 hours). Train: Jaisalmer (2km, 15 mins). Free pick-up by rickshaw.

Price band: B

Om Prakash Kewalia
Hotel Fifu & Jasmine Haveli,
Opp. Nagarpalika, Bera Road,
Jaisalmer, 345001

Tel	+91 (0)2992 254 317
Email	fifutravel@yahoo.com
Web	www.hotelfifu.com

Mirvana Nature Resort

There's desert as far as the eyes can see and a few farms growing mustard, cumin and millet; you are 50 minutes from Jaisalmer yet way off the beaten track. The thatch-roofed dining area is colourful and fun, there's a lovely pool in the maturing gardens and 106 acres free for farm, tents and cottages; hospitable Mr Rathore, his wife and two daughters are justly proud of their brand new resort. The most striking thing about the circular cottages is their size: they're huge! Adobe walls are pale cream, floors pale marble, beds are impressive and windows have dark shutters. Rajasthan embroidery and patchwork add colour, air conditioning adds comfort, and shower rooms are spacious. The smart white tents are decorated in similarly ship-shape fashion but note that only a few have air con. Wake to the sound of birdsong and garden sprinklers, then enjoy breakfast outside your room. Dinners are a treat and made almost entirely of home produce: rabbit curry, papaya, egg pakoras. There are camel rides on the dunes a jeep ride away (thrilling at sunset) and herbal spa treatments at the resort.

Price	Rs3,299–Rs3,799. Singles Rs2,799. Plus 10% tax.
Rooms	53: 15 cottage suites, 38 tents.
Meals	Breakfast Rs225. Lunch Rs400. Dinner Rs450. Plus 12.5% tax.
Closed	Rarely.
Directions	Train: Jaisalmer (55km, 50 mins).

Balveer Singh Rathore
Mirvana Nature Resort, RG Farms,
Sodakore, Jaisalmer

Tel	+91 (0)2997 200 128
Email	mirvananatureresort@gmail.com
Web	www.mirvananatureresort.com

Price band: B

Gujarat

The Beach at Mandvi Palace

A few miles out of the old port of Mandvi is a small-but-perfectly-formed collection of decadently decorated Rajasthani tents. Their verandas facing each other, they are snugly tucked away in amongst the dunes. You'll feel like minor royalty on a tiger hunt once inside; solid wooden furniture, low lighting and primary colours, even air-conditioning for those parched by the journey across the Kutch. The bathrooms are state-of-the-art, the service is impeccable. There's plenty to do in the area, from watching the dhow builders ply their 500-year-old skills to shopping for the famous Kutch embroidery, but the main focus of this place is the beach – an endless, pristine, scimitar stretch that curves off towards the sunset and the palace itself, visible above the palms. Beach umbrellas and loungers provide perfect daytime reading spots and in the evening the bamboo and thatch restaurant delivers excellent seafood and tandooris. This is a romantic setting and popular with honeymooners, but that doesn't mean the solo traveller won't appreciate a sunset stroll or a candlelit dinner on the shoreline under the stars.

Price	Full-board Rs6,000. Singles Rs5,000. Extra bed Rs2,000. Children under five free.
Rooms	10 tents for 2.
Meals	Full-board only.
Closed	Rarely.
Directions	Directions on booking.

Anil Mulchandani
The Beach at Mandvi Palace,
Vijay Vilas Palace, Mandvi, Kutch

Tel	+91 (0)2834 295 725
Email	reservations@mandvibeach.com
Web	www.mandvibeach.com

Price band: B

Shaam-e-Sarhad Ecotourism Resort

Step out of time and into Shaam-e-Sarhad: 'Sunset at the Frontier'. A straight 40km drive north of Bhuj, across windswept desert and scrub, is this tribal village-resort owned by the Banni and sculpted out of mud. Arrive to an entrance with painted motifs and an explosion of bougainvillea, a patchwork of fluttering handkerchiefs beneath a communal thatch, eight tents, three bhungas and various staff dwellings. Each bhunga, its conical roof supported by a central pole, is decorated with tribal dhurries, bedspreads and cushions, mozzie nets and western showers; tents are comfortingly colonial and there are planters' chairs for gazing on sunsets (which are heavenly). The Banni are friendly, proud, tall… watch deft fingers create amazing mirror work, embroidered footwear and costumed dolls, listen to songs about the beauty of the Kutch, experience dinners that are teetotal and vegetarian – homemade butter, rich pungent buffalo curd, tasty chapatis. The government is waking up to a brand of sustainable tourism that promotes cross-cultural understanding, and cultural and wildlife trips abound.

Price	Full-board Rs2,000-Rs2,600. Singles Rs1,800-Rs2,800. Bhungas Rs3,200.
Rooms	11: 8 tents (6 for 2, 2 for 4), 3 bhungas for 2.
Meals	Full-board only.
Closed	April-September.
Directions	Directions on booking.

Village Tourism Committee
Shaam-e-Sarhad Ecotourism Resort,
Hodka Village, Kutch, 370510

Tel   +91 (0)2803 296 222
Web   www.hodka.in

Price band: A

Entry 91   Map 3

Rann Riders

The sea receded a few hundred years ago and left this fascinatingly barren land of salt and desert: the Little Rann of Kutch. It's hard to imagine making a living here, but the area provides much of India's salt and the people bring survival skills and traditions from Rajasthan and as far away as Afghanistan; expect to see exquisite embroidered textiles, silver jewellery and pottery, and maybe a festival or two. There is also a vast and astonishing variety of bird and animal life: pelicans, flamingoes, nilgai, gazelle, wolves, jackals and wild asses. The huts were created in Kutchi style, of mud and with roofs of terracotta tiles or grass and nestled in a verdant paradise of pampas grass, neem and tulsi trees; a lake separates you from main road hum. Inside are paintings on the walls and mirror-work on the wooden beams or doors, many of which are ornately carved. There are cane chairs and a writing desk, rugs on the floor and ample space; bathrooms have open-air showers. The staff are formal, helpful and charming, and the surrounding area rich in interest and history. *Spend a night camping with a nomad community.*

Price	Full-board Rs6,400. Includes safari. Peak season: September-February.
Rooms	20 cottages for 2.
Meals	Full-board only.
Closed	Rarely.
Directions	Clearly signed just before entering Dasada. Airport: Rajkot (135km). Train: Surendranagar (35km).

Muzahid Malik
Rann Riders, Dasada,
Surendranagar, 382750

Tel	+91 (0)2757 280 257
Fax	+91 (0)2757 280 457
Email	rann-riders@usa.net
Web	www.rannriders.com

Price band: B

House of MG - Metro Heritage Hotel

Mr Mangaldas Girdhardas (hence the House of MG), a wealthy Ahmedabad philanthropist, built this grand townhouse in 1924 – an oasis in a crazy city. His grandson has realised his own vision and now the project is complete. This extraordinary Gujarati family house has been beautifully restored, and its ornamental Baroque-influenced façade preserved – along with Italian mosaic marble flooring, stained-glass windows and numerous courtyards and passages; it is a place with a surprise round every corner. The outdoor café serves Indian and continental delicacies while the open kitchen and the rooftop restaurant specialise in Gujarati cuisine; the food is authentic and delicious. There's also a banquet 'facility' and a lifestyle store, and a café and craft centre nearby – the Mangaldas ni Haveli. Also: a film and a reading club, a lovely indoor pool and a gym, and a cultural tour for walkers; borrow an iPod and go. The big smart bedrooms wrap themselves round an inner courtyard and come with plush bathrooms and every modern thing. Splash out on the Kanchangauri suite: it comes with its own swing.

Price	Rs5,990–Rs8,490. Singles Rs4,990–Rs10,990. Suites Rs10,990–Rs12,990. Apt Rs10,900. Plus 8.5% tax. Peak season: October–March.
Rooms	14 + 1: 10 doubles, 4 suites. 1 apartment for 2.
Meals	Lunch Rs325–Rs425. Dinner Rs345–Rs495. Plus 2.5% tax.
Closed	Rarely.
Directions	In central Ahmedabad near the Old Town, opp. Sidi Saiyed Jali. Airport: Ahmedabad (7km).

Abhay Mangaldas
House of MG - Metro Heritage Hotel,
Opp. Siddi Saiyad Mosque,
Lal Darwaja, Ahmedabad, 380001

Tel	+91 (0)7925 506 946
Email	customercare@houseofmg.com
Web	www.houseofmg.com

Price band: D

Entry 93   Map 3

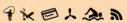

Arts Reverie

Up dusty alleys lined with ancient haveli and a cacophony of shopkeepers, children and cattle is a bright Jain temple and an as-vibrant arts centre/guest house just beyond. At dusk, its narrow façade is festooned with candles and twinkles like a birthday cake; expect to be greeted with a dab on the forehead and a garland of marigolds. Arts Reverie is unlike anywhere else you are likely to stay: funky yet traditional, airy yet claustrophobic, run by unfailingly attentive staff and a manager who has his finger on the city's pulse. Steep wooden stairs bannistered with silver-painted bars lead to a big open studio and gallery area, a second shared bathroom (the first is below) and bedrooms (just four) almost touching distance from those on the other side of the alley. The rooms are boho but basic, with stained-glass windows and shutters galore, firm mattresses and floral linen; bathrooms have beautiful soaps and strong showers; roof terraces are packed with flowers. The Reverie is part and parcel of the city's regeneration, linking rich heritage with contemporary creativity – and warmly succeeding.

Price	Rs3,950. Singles Rs3,500.
Rooms	4: 1 double, 1 twin, 2 singles.
Meals	Lunch Rs150. Dinner Rs250.
Closed	Rarely.
Directions	Opposite Jain Derasar, in centre of Dhal Ni Pol.

Anupa Mehta
Arts Reverie, 1824 Khijda Sheri,
Opp. Jain Derasar, Dhal Ni Pol,
Astodia Gate, Ahmedabad, 380001

Tel	+91 (0)7922 170 629
Email	info@artsreverie.com
Web	www.artsreverie.com

Price band: C

Entry 94   Map 3

Madhya Pradesh & Maharashtra

Ahilya Fort

Ancient Maheshwar is a sacred place, and Ahilya, perched high above the Narmada river where there's always a breeze, is an enchanting hotel. More home than fort, the building's pale stone floors, dark timbers and ancient shuttered doors have been exquisitely restored. Richard Holkar is the driving force behind Ahilya and the Holkars were the kings of Indore, though the family is more westernised today. Thanks to the Holkar Trust, the hand weaving for which Maheshwar was once famous is again thriving – you may visit the handloom centre nearby. Tranquil bedrooms have finely woven fabrics and views, an immaculate bathroom peeps through an arch, a white bloom graces a vase, and courtyards, gardens and pool drift serenely one into the other. Have buffet breakfast on the ramparts, lounge on silk cushions on the *jharokha* overlooking the water, dine on delectable home-grown food on the terrace, dream in the soft-lit magic. The two tents are as luxurious as the rest. Ahilya may not be cheap but it's a place to treasure, and is run by delightful staff. *Two-day river trips & organic farm trips.*

Price	Full-board Rs11,000-Rs31,400. Peak season: October to mid-April.
Rooms	14: 9 doubles, 2 twins, 1 single, 2 tents.
Meals	Full-board only.
Closed	Rarely.
Directions	Directions on booking. Ask for Maheshwar, then fort easy to find. Airport/train: Indore (95km, 2.5 hours).

Richard Holkar
Ahilya Fort, Ahilya Wad,
Maheshwar, Khargone, 451224
Tel +91 (0)1141 551 575
Fax +91 (0)1141 551 055
Email info@ahilyafort.com
Web www.ahilyafort.com

Price band: E

Rashid Kothi

The moment you leave the town's main road and pass through the gates, you enter a hidden sanctuary. The large, sturdy house, surrounded by lush forest, was built in the 1930s. It belonged to Anu's grandmother and is still the family home, simply and beautifully furnished with a subtle luxury. Anu, Ashish and their parents are courteous, warm, generous and good company: you're treated as an honoured guest here. Ashish teaches physics and Anu runs a nursery in the grounds; they know the area well and can help you plan your tour. Three lavish, exquisitely prepared vegetarian meals (no alcohol) are served each day in the gazebo or on the dining room's petal-strewn table – and there's the delightful ritual of afternoon tea with the family. The two bedrooms have books and flowers; one is a leafy summerhouse in the garden, both have ethnic bedspreads, pretty lamps and candles. Rainwater harvesting provides the showers. Frangipani and jasmine scent the air and the neem trees are revered for their revitalising properties – as we feel this house should be.

Price	Full-board Rs10,000. Singles Rs5,500.
Rooms	2: 1 twin, 1 cabin for 2.
Meals	Full-board only.
Closed	Occasionally.
Directions	From station to Rani Sati Gate. House next to motorcycle showroom, signed 'Playhouse Nursery'. Airport: Indore (8km, 25 mins). Train: Indore (2km, 10 mins).

Price band: C

Ms Anuradha Dubey
Rashid Kothi, 22 Yeshwant Niwas
Road, Indore, 452003

Tel	+91 (0)7312 545 060
Email	ashanu@hotmail.com
Web	www.ahilyafort.com/your_stay_indore.php

Entry 96   Map 4

Ivy Suites

It is the last house on this prosperous residential estate, at the end of a long, meandering, lakeside road. The 1980s-built ivy-clad home has been converted by its owners into a very welcoming, very homely hotel. Hospitality is second nature to Mr and Mrs Sharma who delight in engaging guests in conversation over tea or something more substantial – the food is amazing. Architecture, economics, the environment, food: all are subjects worthy of discussion. Indeed, you are encouraged to use their home as would a friend. Relax in the big airy sitting/dining room with its marble floor, brass statuettes of dancing goddesses, coffee table books and fish-tank bar; in the upstairs lounge with its smart settees, lush plants and WiFi; or on the roof terrace, a good spot for 8.30am yoga. And everywhere, big views through big windows of Bhopal's shimmering lake. Do ask for a room with a view; the best are most definitely upstairs, and two have their own sitting areas. (Note: bathrooms and baths are pretty simple.) Bhopal, on the other side of the lake, is a gentle green city full of lovely gardens and parks.

Price	Rs2,500–Rs4,500. Singles Rs2,100. Plus 10% tax.
Rooms	11: 4 doubles, 7 twins.
Meals	Dinner Rs300. Lunch Rs200.
Closed	Rarely.
Directions	Airport: Bhopal (12km, 20 mins). Train: Bhopal (5km, 15 mins).

Pramod & Manju Sharma
Ivy Suites, 26 A Nadir Colony,
Shamla Hills, Bhopal, 462001
Tel   +91 (0)7554 235 508
Fax   +91 (0)7554 235 508
Email   prashar26@yahoo.com
Web   www.ivysuites.in

Price band: C

Hotel Jehan Numa Palace

Up a hill steep enough for rickshaw wallahs to appeal to your sympathy and purse, Jehan Numa Palace comes as a Bhopal surprise. Turning away from Upper Lake, a bold white façade greets you with 1890s colonial decorum, while columns and balconies are unmistakably Renaissance in style. The result is a relaxed, open-plan layout of lawns, quads and swimming pool, gym and spa, all connected by covered walkways hung with violet bougainvillea. Teak furniture in marbled bedrooms is comfortably austere and large beds are covered with muted patterns. With ambient music as you bathe under swish showers, who could resist? Four restaurants and open-air barbecues cater for every taste, including one of India's best attempts at an Italian trattoria. General Obaidullah Khan may have built the palace, but it was not until 1983 that his grandsons reinvented Jehan Numa. Staff will happily list all the things to see and do in atmospheric Bhopal. They even have their own horse race track here… find out why the bars have equestrian names, while drinking beer from the first pumps to offer draught ale in Madhya Pradesh.

Price	Rs3,550–Rs12,000. Plus 15% tax. Peak season: July–April.
Rooms	101: 95 doubles, 6 suites.
Meals	Breakfast Rs300. Lunch Rs550. Dinner Rs650.
Closed	Never.
Directions	Airport: Bhopal (12km, 20 mins). Train: Bhopal (5km, 15 mins).

Price band: D

Mr Yawar Rashid
Hotel Jehan Numa Palace,
157 Shamla Hill, Bhopal, 462013

Tel	+91 (0)7552 661 100
Fax	+91 (0)7552 661 720
Email	jehanuma@bsnl.in
Web	www.hoteljehanumapalace.com

Entry 98   Map 4

Junglemantra

Without the owners – a young couple, passionate about the environment and wildlife – this place would be special. With them, it's a privilege to stay. Between the core forest and the buffer zones of the Bandhavgarh National Park, among acres of grasses and trees – mahua, banyan, peepal, ebony – is a magical setting, close to the elements and the animals. A large open-air shala, a dining room and a library create a happy hub around which cluster your romantic bamboo cottages. Some display marble floors, others red sandstone, all have space for big beds, easy chairs and Indian furniture from all over, heaps of towels for rain showers and organic ayurvedic toiletries: style in the jungle! The breads, biscuits and croissants are famously good and Rhea's dinners are full Indian banquets, served by smiling tribal staff (not fluent in English). The game drives are sublime. Track leopards and tigers on elephant back, return to great terraces and verandas, a big fire and sofas, exploration guides and ice-cold mocktails. Trekkers and sybarites, honeymooners and young families – all will feel at home here, such is the welcome.

Price	Full-board Rs18,500. Price includes 2 game drives.
Rooms	8 cottage suites for 2.
Meals	Full-board only.
Closed	July–September.
Directions	Directions on booking. Train: Umaria (1 hour).

Shailin & Rhea Ramji
Junglemantra, Tala, Rancha,
Bandhavgarh, Umaria

Tel	+91 (0)7627 280 547
Email	contact@junglemantra.com
Web	www.junglemantra.com

Price band: E

Entry 99   Map 5

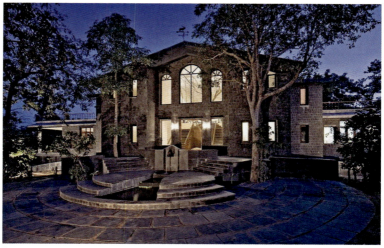

Singinawa Jungle Lodge

Few places actually move you during a stay, but this is one. Handsomely constructed of granite, slate and wood, set among 50 acres of regenerative land under their protection, Nanda and Latika's safari lodge is the realisation of a dream. It's easy to get caught up in their passion for tiger conservation and empowerment of local tribes, even as you immerse yourself in pulsating Kanha, looking for that break in the rhythm of the jungle and a breathless moment of pride and power. Safe inside your own vehicle, you are in sure hands, right down to the coffee and samosa of a jeep-bonnet breakfast. Back in your stone cottage, hushed and snug between double stone walls, slip into the unassuming luxury of sound beds, crisp cottons and bathrooms with rainwater showers. Food, mostly local or fresh from the garden, is the best of Indian and Nepalese, as is the conversation, enjoyed on the terrace by the fire, or beneath the lovely old banyan tree. Cocktails, hot water bottles, a stone pool are further treats. Take time to wander birdwatching trails, nestle into viewing hides and admire Nanda's stunning wildlife photography.

Price	Full-board Rs29,820. Singles Rs18,750. Includes 2 safaris & lodge activities.
Rooms	12 cottages for 2.
Meals	Full-board only.
Closed	June–October.
Directions	Directions on booking. Train: Gondia (140km, 3 hours). Airport: Nagpur (280km, 5.5 hours).

Nanda & Latika Rana
Singinawa Jungle Lodge, Village
Kokha, PO Baihar, Tehsil Baihar,
Balaghat, 481111

Tel	+91 (0)1244 068 852
Email	info@singinawa.in
Web	www.singinawa.in

Price band: F

Entry 102   Map 5

Shergarh Tented Camp

Wild grasses and jungly trees, and six lovely tents dotted around a plot of land on the edge of Kanha. Katie and Jehan have a deeply ecological vision for Shergarh and their enthusiasm is exhilarating. Deliberately keeping things low key – in spite of some luxurious bathrooms – the impact is hardly apparent and the feel is wonderfully natural. A romantic couple or a family of four is more than comfortably quartered under the canvas, while constant hot water is supplied by clean-burning LPG. After a morning's safari, where you may spot a tiger, everyone tucks into superb food on the lodge veranda; salads and continental lunches come from their organic garden, eggs from their hens and the banana bread flows. At night: delicious Indian banquets under the stars by the lake. No waste here either for Katie is queen of composts. Light pollution is kept to a minimum to encourage wildlife and being on the less-busy Mukki side of the park, all is quiet. Hard to imagine a more magical environment to bring up Kai and Ella, their young children, whose growth will be a reflection of Shergarh's own.

Price	Full-board Rs21,000. Singles Rs14,500. Safaris included.
Rooms	6 tents for 2-4.
Meals	Full-board only.
Closed	Mid-May to mid-October.
Directions	Located at Mukki Gate. Bus from Jabalpur to Kisli; 4x4 to Shergarh. Train: Gondia (140km, 3 hours). Airport: Nagpur (280km, 5.5 hours).

Jehan & Katie Bhujwala
Shergarh Tented Camp, Village Bahmini,
PO Kareli, Tehsil Baihar, Balaghat, 481111

Tel	+91 (0)7637 296 215
Email	enquiries@shergarh.com
Web	www.shergarh.com

Price band: D

The Verandah in the Forest

Deep in primary forest, reached only by foot, palanquin or horse, this small hotel is well named. The veranda is a fancy one, framed by white wooden balustrades and tiled in large flower shapes – perfect camouflage for the forest's pervasive red dust. Lounge on planters' chairs, lime soda in hand, and gaze out over the view. You dine here or indoors, at a very long table: a truly international occasion. The food is delicious (but if you prefer Indian you must order in advance). The airy drawing room echoes beneath its vaulted ceiling and is stocked with guides to the region. Hammock-chairs are strung from trees in the wonderful wild and wooded garden, there's a treehouse for children and a pond full of toads. Horse rides along dusty tracks can be arranged, and lovely dappled walks under the canopies of trees. Retire to a four-poster bed in a splendid big room and sleep soundly… be woken by monkeys on the rooftop at dawn. Matheran is the last pedestrian hill station in Asia; this house was built by a colonel to escape the Mumbai heat. Note: the journey to get here is not for the timorous!

Price	Rs2,500–Rs6,500.
Rooms	11: 8 doubles, 3 suites.
Meals	Lunch Rs450. Dinner Rs500.
Closed	Never.
Directions	150km from Mumbai.

Price band: C

Mr Surender
The Verandah in the Forest,
Barr House, Matheran, Raigad, 410102

Tel	+91 (0)2148 230 296
Fax	+91 (0)2148 230 811
Email	sales@neemranahotels.com
Web	www.neemranahotels.com

Goa

Fort Tiracol

You might expect a fort to be austere and empty; not this one. It's a national monument, with all the restrictions on change that that implies, and open to tourists from noon: there's a constant to-ing and fro-ing. It's romantic and super-chic and they have managed to repaint and refurbish every corner; the yellow and white walls and modish metal furniture create an elegant mood. There's no air con and not all bedrooms have TV but each has its own balcony and the best views in Goa: the building stands on a river estuary so you can gaze along the whole length of coast and to the ocean. Watch the fishermen at work on the sandbanks or visit the dolphins at sea; a snappy speedboat will take you off for sunrise breakfasts and picnics to remote beaches. From the rooftop restaurant/café are the same eye-stretching views and the food is exceptional; within the compound is an old chapel to which the townspeople still hold the keys and Mass is held on weekends and Wednesdays. The owners live away but the manager is friendly and helpful. A rare and special place, away from southern bustle.

Price	Half-board Rs7,600. Suites Rs9,600. Plus 10% tax.
Rooms	7: 4 doubles, 2 suites, 1 family room for 4.
Meals	Half-board only. Lunch $10–$20.
Closed	Rarely.
Directions	From Panaji head for Calangute, then Siolim, then Tiracol.

Price band: C

Mark Ferrao
Fort Tiracol, Tiracol, Perney,
North Goa, 403524

Tel	+91 (0)2366 227 631
Email	info@forttiracol.com
Web	www.forttiracol.com

Nilaya Hermitage

A star-spangled retreat on the crest of a tropical hill. The hotel was designed by Goan architect Dean D'Cruz; German designer Claudia added the final touches. Cosmically themed with fantasy elements, bedrooms have vibrant colours, white muslin, bathrooms of mosaic; all are large, cool, chic, and connect around a curving central pool. Be seduced by bowls of floating flowers, sun-shaped lamps, teak columns from a temple in Kerala… and views over paddy fields and wooded hills to a glittering sea. The stylish owners, Hari and Claudia, are not always present but young staff in blue kurtas and white saris look after the beautiful people – and that includes you! Food is a subtle blend of eastern and western flavours overseen by a French chef. There's no starched formality and the atmosphere is house party not hotel; dine in your sarong by the langorous decked pool, or in your room. Breakfast lasts as long as you like. Should you finally tire of the pleasures of the gym, steam room, sauna and ayurveda, the coast is a ten-minute drive. *Children over 12 welcome. Minimum stay three nights. Boat trips available.*

Price	Half-board €320.
	Christmas & New Year up to €490.
	Airport transfer included.
Rooms	14: 10 doubles, 4 tents for 2.
Meals	Half-board only.
Closed	Rarely.
Directions	Hotel staff will pick you up from Arpora airport.

Claudia Derain & Hari Ajwani
Nilaya Hermitage, Bhati, Arpora,
North Goa, 403518

Tel	+91 (0)8322 276 793
Fax	+91 (0)8322 276 792
Email	info@nilaya.com
Web	www.nilaya.com

Price band: E

Casa Colvale

Off the beaten track, up in north Goa, two stylish villas with views that soar downriver. You arrive at the upper one, your bags disappear and you are ushered to the terrace with a sundowner: lap up the luxuriant scene. The views from the infinity pool are more breathtaking still… later, meander downhill for a barbecue under the stars: dinner is on the elegant deck in dry season. Goan or western, it will be fresh, vibrant and tasty. More terraces for the rooms, each with a sit-out space overseeing the river or the islands. You might have a soft sofa, or a Goan artwork to illuminate the walls. There are simple bright linens and rugs on dark stone floors, and walk-in showers with floor to ceiling mirrors and scented candles. Look forward to long days lazing by two pools, serenaded by wildlife and spoiled by staff; the steep inclines and the steps and stairs will keep you fit and trim. Read, write, watch the mangoes ripen on the trees – nothing else matters. Join in yoga on the terrace. Plan a trip to the beaches: Mandrem, Vagator, Anjuna. Leave by speedboat – James Bond style. Bliss.

Price	Rs7,000–Rs9,000. Plus 10% tax.
Rooms	11 doubles.
Meals	Lunch & dinner from Rs500.
Closed	Never.
Directions	Directions on booking.

Price band: D

James Foster
Casa Colvale, Taliwado, Chiklim,
Colvale, Bardez, North Goa, 403211

Tel	+91 (0)9765 394 353
Email	reservation@casaboutiquehotels.com
Web	www.casacolvale.com

Coco Shambhala

A romantic hideaway, a family getaway or – if you take all four houses – a decadent pied-a-terre for friends. This villa collection is sequestered away in the untouched village of Nerul, a mile or so inland from Candolim Beach. With two floors, two bedrooms, a huge veranda and a state-of-the-art kitchen apiece, these tropical villas, in beautifully landscaped gardens, are the result of meticulous thought and careful planning. The striking angular architecture makes good use of light and space; the glass and the shutters are matched by exceptional interior design. Slate, steel, glass, bare wood and distressed paintwork mix with antique day beds, wicker sofas swathed in white cotton and old Goan fishing boat prows. Chic-sleek bathrooms of slate and contoured polished cement feature al fresco showers surrounded by fragrant frangipani. Make the most of your dedicated driver for day trips, throw extravagant dinner parties on your private terrace, walk to Coco Beach. Or hang out by the black-tiled pool after a late night out, pretend you're a rock star and cavort in the jacuzzi under the stars. *Minimum stay one week.*

Price	£1,185–£1,995 per villa. Prices per week. Daily maid service included.
Rooms	4 villas for 4.
Meals	Restaurant 100km.
Closed	June–September.
Directions	Directions on booking.

Giles Knapton
Coco Shambhala, Coco Beach, Nerul,
Bardez, North Goa

Tel	+44 (0)1202 484257
Email	info@shambhalavillas.com
Web	www.cocoshambhala.com

Price band: C

Entry 108   Map 8

Casa Palacio Siolim House

Much-travelled Varun Sood discovered the neglected 300-year-old villa on one of his travels, then transformed it into a cool, breezy and immaculately designed haven. Once belonging to the Governor of Macau, the *casa de sobrado*-style building has been properly renovated with walls of shell and lime plaster, and windowpanes of oyster shell. It's a spoiling place – seven big suites named after 17th-century trading ports, fabulous food, solicitous staff. Terracotta pots sit under shapely white pillars in the central courtyard with fountain and bougainvillea; more pots nudge the pool. Bedrooms, two on the top floor, some around the courtyard, have white walls, dark wooden or tiled floors, rosewood cupboards and wrought-iron beds hung with muslin. There are a sitting room and a library with chess, and a restaurant with glass-topped tables. Dine on caught-that-day fish: pomfret, snapper, bass, mussels, crab and the biggest prawns ever seen. Siolim is a small village with a large Catholic church (services are in English at weekends), bustling Anjuna is three kilometres away, Calangute beach ten. *Tailor-made tours.*

Price	Rs6,600–Rs13,250. Singles Rs4,950–Rs6,225. Plus 10% tax. Peak season: 20 December–10 January.
Rooms	7 suites.
Meals	Lunch & dinner $15.
Closed	Rarely.
Directions	1km down Chapora road from Siolim village crossroads.

Mr Varun Sood
Casa Palacio Siolim House, Waddi, Siolim, Bardez, North Goa, 403517

Tel	+91 (0)8322 272 138
Email	info@siolimhouse.com
Web	www.siolimhouse.com

Price band: E

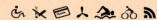

Hotel Bougainvillea/Granpa's Inn

It doesn't matter what you call this place, it's bliss – thanks to the ever-delightful Lucindo and Betina. He is a descendant of the family that built this old, Portuguese-styled Goan mansion and you can see the ancestral portraits inside; he'll tell you the history. The house has been modernised but the old terracotta tiles and lofty rooms remain. It's a cool, rustic hotel whose good-sized rooms are clustered around a beautiful colonnaded courtyard; light and airy, they have cheerful bedspreads and plants and open to the veranda. The air-conditioned poolside suites have private courtyards and extra outdoor showers. There's no-one to rush you, and the food is wonderful; on some days there are barbecues and a band. Cool off with a cocktail by the pool, lounge in the lush gardens under the wind chimes and the mangoes, drift indoors for a game of billiards. Then spin off on a bike to discover the heady, hippy delights of the coconut-palm-fringed beach – one of many glories in one of India's richest states. *Go-karting, elephant trails & dolphin trips.*

Price	Rs1,950. Suites Rs2,450–Rs3,250.
Rooms	21: 6 doubles, 15 suites.
Meals	Lunch Rs175–Rs250. Dinner Rs300.
Closed	Rarely.
Directions	1km from Anjuna church on Mapusa–Anjuna road; 7km from Mapusa town. Airport: Dabolim (50km, 1 hour). Train: Thivim (16km, 30 mins).

Lucindo & Betina Faria
Hotel Bougainvillea/Granpa's Inn, Gaun Wad, Anjuna, Bardez, North Goa, 403509

Tel	+91 (0)8322 273 270
Fax	+91 (0)8322 274 370
Email	granpas@hotmail.com
Web	www.granpasinn.com

Price band: A

Entry 110   Map 8

Laguna Anjuna

Lazy days! This funky architect-designed resort-hotel is the ultimate, laid-back place to stay. It sits in a coconut grove resplendent with bamboo, frangipani, banana and mango, there's an intimate central courtyard, a rustic-chic cottage to retreat to, and mud baths, massages and a meandering pool. The cavernous cottages differ in shape and size but all have whitewashed walls, wooden rafters, pillars, arches, domes and split levels. Furniture is wrought-iron, colours bright, materials natural. Bathrooms are hip, some with black baths, some with copper basins. Owner/manager Farrokh is as relaxed as can be, the staff are friendly but unobtrusive and guests are an eclectic mix: cool families with kids, Mumbai groovers and shakers. Views stretch from paddy fields to hills, and there's a sociable restaurant that has old-world style and outstanding cuisine. The whole place is perfect for Anjuna, Goa's hippy heart and, should you tire of the easy living here, the busy beach is a jog away. Ideal for those who thrive on informality and spontaneity. *Water sports, casino trips, yoga, birdwatching.*

Price	Rs5,500–Rs14,000. Peak season: 20 December–15 January.
Rooms	25: 19 cottages for 2, 6 cottages for 4.
Meals	Lunch & dinner Rs350.
Closed	Never.
Directions	Ask for directions in village.

Shamir Pereira
Laguna Anjuna, Soranto Vado, Anjuna, Bardez, North Goa, 403509

Tel	+91 (0)8322 274 305
Fax	+91 (0)8322 274 305
Email	info@lagunaanjuna.com
Web	www.lagunaanjuna.com

Price band: D

Yogamagic Eco Retreat

Spot the tents and flags from a distance – splashes of colour amid the palms, paddy fields and strolling buffalo. British Phil and Juliet greet you warmly – both are passionate about their natural retreat. In the restaurant – all bamboo, rammed-earth and palm leaves – relax on soft cushions and let the kingfishers, humming birds and bathing animals entertain you. Floating flowers, water candles, a Buddha statue, soft Indian music and delicious organic treats are here – from fresh juices and perfect eggs florentine to generous vegetarian buffets. The style combines rural India with contemporary minimalism, traditional local materials with solar-power and recycling. The peaceful and luxurious suite is inside, while the recently upgraded Rajasthani hunting tents, each lined with a different colour to represent one of the *chakras*, have comfy beds, wardrobes, terraces and composting loos. Flower- and tree-filled gardens and outside showers are a short stroll. There's yoga by day (should you choose it) and a pool; fires and musical performances by night. A small piece of paradise. *Daily yoga classes & workshops.*

Price	Rs5,000–Rs6,500. Suites from Rs5,000. Plus 8%-10% tax. Peak season: mid-December to mid-January.
Rooms	9: 7 tents for 2, sharing showers; 2 suites.
Meals	Dinner Rs340.
Closed	Mid-April to mid-November.
Directions	Train: Thivim (16km, 20 mins). Airport: Dabolim (48km, 1 hr).

Phil Dane
Yogamagic Eco Retreat, 1586/1 Grand Chinvar, Close to Bobby Bar, Anjuna, Bardez, North Goa, 403509

Tel	+91 (0)8326 523 796
Email	info@yogamagic.net
Web	www.yogamagic.net

Price band: C

Panchavatti

The choice of setting for 'Sacred Five Trees' is inspired and the 40m-long covered veranda is a place to sit and dream, amid the sweet scents of jasmine and frangipani. Unfussy decorative touches – copper pots, bowls of floating flowers, cane lampshades – soothe, as do the views of the river, the buffalos grazing and the distant forest. You breakfast on homemade strawberry jam, lashings of real coffee and Goan bread. Belgian by blood, Goa-born and convent-eductated in Surrey and Mumbai, Lulu's approach to guests is wise and warm; nothing is too much trouble and her new venture is a success. Only traditional materials have been used (apart from in the bathrooms): laterite stone, high wooden ceilings and tiled roofs. All the furniture, including divans and charpoys, has been copied from old designs in order to preserve traditional techniques; the décor is enchanting. Bedrooms, each with a private balcony, wrap around an inner courtyard where fountains play; there is a constant sound of flowing water. The serene swimming pool is the final treat. *Cookery courses, concerts & yoga.*

Price	Full-board from Rs10,000.
Rooms	4 doubles.
Meals	Full-board only.
Closed	June–September.
Directions	From Aldona, signs to Aldona Bridge for Corjuem Island. Left after bridge; 2nd road on left; 1st mud road on left; along wall, thro' gates. No signs! Airport: Dabolim (1 hour).

Price band: C

Ms Isla Maria 'Lulu' Van Damme
Panchavatti, Corjuem Island, Aldona,
Bardez, North Goa, 403508

Tel	+91 (0)9822 580 632
Fax	+91 (0)9823 026 447
Email	info@islaingoa.com
Web	www.islaingoa.com

Marbella Guesthouse

The house was built not so long ago, and resembles an old Goan mansion. Dian recycled the white roof borders, the pillars, the outdoor table tiles and some of the furniture; the flooring displays stencils from early 20th-century houses. The whole place is unashamedly romantic, its luxurious suites individually decorated and named (Bougainvillea, Moghul etc); the penthouse is especially fabulous, all marble floors and huge views. There's lots of space, and you can mingle with other guests in a beautifully lush central courtyard. Cats and dogs doze in and around, and the kitchen is open so you can watch the chefs prepare your meal; the food is amazing, even by Goan standards. Now Dian is joined by the delightful Suzanne, who has set up a beauty room offering fabulous facials. There's even a touch of the exotic at play, which may stem from Dian's half-German background and his passion for the guitar – rock, jazz and blues. The blissful Marbella sits down a lane, a ten-minute walk from a quiet beach, a good restaurant too, yet away from coastal mayhem. Come to be thoroughly spoiled.

Price	Rs1,500-Rs7,200.
Rooms	6: 3 doubles, 3 suites.
Meals	Breakfast Rs400. Lunch & dinner Rs600.
Closed	Rarely.
Directions	Left at Joe Joe's on main road towards Fort Aguada Beach Resort. Guest house 500m along, last on the right. Take a taxi.

Dian Singh
Marbella Guesthouse, Sinquerim-
Candolim, Bardez, North Goa, 403515

Tel	+91 (0)8322 479 551
Email	marbella_goa@yahoo.com
Web	www.marbellagoa.com

Price band: C

Panjim Inn & Panjim Pousada

These two are perfect if you want a taste of Panaji's (previously Panjim's) Portuguese past. They are both in Fontainhas, the throbbing heart of the Latin Quarter, an area of sleeping dogs and gonging chapels. The Inn is Goa's first and only official heritage hotel, a 300-year-old mansion built by the owner's family and graced with colonial rosewood furniture. Mr Sukhija has introduced new rooms at the back, with big Goan four-posters and curtains fluttering at wooden lattice windows. There's a smart new dining room too, with a furnished balcony from which you can watch Panaji life go by, and the food is tasty (Goan or international). The nearby Pousada – quieter than its neighbour – is an ancient Hindu house in a largely Catholic area, and renovated in a similarly elegant fashion. Downstairs rooms open to the garden and courtyard that doubles up as a local gallery – note the huge Ganesha – where you can rest awhile in a swing-chair in the shade of the spreading breadfruit tree. Upstairs rooms share a balcony overlooking the garden, and funky mosaic flooring runs throughout. *Dolphin watching & bird spotting.*

Price	Rs1,200–Rs4,500. Plus 8-10% tax. Peak season: 21 December-2 March.
Rooms	Inn: 24 doubles. Pousada: 9 doubles.
Meals	Lunch & dinner Rs200–Rs250.
Closed	Never.
Directions	In Fontainhas (the Latin Quarter of Panaji) opp. the People's High School.

Mr Ajit Sukhija
Panjim Inn & Panjim Pousada,
31st January Rd, Fontainhas, Panaji,
North Goa, 403001

Tel	+91 (0)8322 221 122
Email	panjimin@bsnl.in
Web	www.panjiminn.com

Price band: C

Panjim Peoples

Cobbled Fontainhas is a legacy of Goa's past; it's unlike anywhere else in India. And it's more lively than sleepy in the mornings when the neighbouring high school gets into swing. Panjim Peoples was itself a school and the big corner-shaped building keeps its colonial feel. Come to Peoples if you like to see how the locals live; the welcoming Sukhija family have been taking in guests for years. There's no sitting room, no garden and the house is not outstandingly cosy – it was a school, after all – but the red-tiled guest bedrooms are elegant, large and lofty, all equally lovely, and furnished with framed maps of the world and antique rosewood beds (among the finest we've seen, and most comfortable). Choose the quietest, at the back. Bathrooms are funkily mosaic'd, and have deep tubs and excellent fittings. There's also an impressive gallery below displaying contemporary art – you can browse for hours – and you have all the advantages of the Inn opposite with its friendly restaurant. Interesting, too, to live in Asia's only Latin Quarter. Very charming.

Price	Rs7,200–Rs9,000. Plus 10% tax.
Rooms	4 doubles.
Meals	Lunch & dinner Rs200–Rs250 at Panjim Inn.
Closed	Never.
Directions	In Fontainhas (the Latin Quarter of Panaji) next to the People's High School, opp. Panjim Inn.

Mr Ajit Sukhija
Panjim Peoples, 31st January Road,
Fontianhas, Panaji, North Goa, 403001

Tel	+91 (0)8322 221 122
Fax	+91 (0)8322 435 220
Email	panjimin@bsnl.in
Web	www.panjiminn.com

Price band: D

Coconut Creek

'Paradise', says the brochure, and paradise it is. These ten houses lie among swaying coconut palms near the sea; be lulled to sleep by the rustling wind. It is ineffably lovely: state-of-the-art, yet respectful of the environment and the essence of Goa. Lynn and Agnelo are a Scottish-Goan couple who have poured love and energy into creating Coconut Creek. It is a 'resort', so you may expect quiz nights, darts and pool, but it is exquisitely put together and some of the profits go to a local orphanage. Each house has two storeys; the ground-floor bedrooms are air-conditioned, those on the upper floors have ceiling fans and generous French windows; one bedroom has a mattress on a wide wooden platform and pale yellow walls with niched arches for candles and flowers. The style is minimalist yet exotic; bed linen is crisply white. You cross the lovely pool on wooden bridges, and the sea and Bogmalo's unspoiled beach are two minutes away. Lynn is a wonderfully friendly, down-to-earth hostess, on hand to help in any way, and the food is delicious.

Price	Rs5,500–Rs6,500. Peak season: October–April; Christmas & New Year.
Rooms	20: 16 doubles, 4 twins.
Meals	Lunch from Rs150. Dinner from Rs310.
Closed	Never.
Directions	At the north end of Bogmalo beach. Airport: Dabolim (3km, 5 mins). Train: Vasco da Gama (6km, 15 mins).

Price band: C

Lynn & Agnelo D'Cruz
Coconut Creek, Bimmut, Bogmalo,
South Goa, 403806

Tel	+91 (0)8322 538 100
Fax	+91 (0)8322 538 880
Email	joets@sancharnet.in

Joet's

Right on the beach at Bogmalo, with Coconut Creek a few yards down – owned by the same delightful people – is an unusual meeting of Scotland and Goa. The place is run by Agnelo's brother Selvy who goes to the fish market daily, so there is a constant supply of prime fish to the restaurant: prawns, shark, kingfish, crab; people come from far and wide to eat here. Joet's is a guest house, a Coconut Creek on a modest scale, and you may share the swimming pool if you tire of the sea. Café-bars play western music but Bogmalo is still a small-scale resort, and the guest house still stands among battered fishing boats and wind-bent palms. It's been a big success considering it started life as a fisherman's shack, and the beach is pretty much yours: a treat in Goa. The interiors are light and colourful, simple and charming: blue tiles in the restaurant, blue spreads on the beds, tiled floors, fans and mini-bars, tea and coffee trays and small balconies for the upstairs rooms. All have their own separate living room. The noise of giant waves tumbling onto the sands guarantees deep sleep.

Price	Rs3,500–Rs4,000. Plus 3–10% tax. Peak season: October–April.
Rooms	7 suites.
Meals	Lunch & dinner Rs350.
Closed	Never.
Directions	At the north end of Bogmalo beach. Airport: Dabolim (3km, 5 mins). Train: Vasco da Gama (6km, 15 mins).

Lynn & Agnelo D'Cruz
Joet's, Baillichad Ward, Bogmalo,
South Goa, 403806

Tel	+91 (0)8322 538 100
Fax	+91 (0)8322 538 880
Email	joets@sancharnet.in

Price band: B

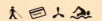

Entry 122   Map 8

Casa Susegad

Among the coconuts on the outskirts of Loutolim, one of Goa's prettiest villages, the Jodhpur Blue exterior and the fairy lights cascading from the terracotta roof are the first signs that you're in for something different. Norman and Carole greet you warmly and proudly show you around their 700-year-old dream house, a wonderland of colour, outstanding local and international art (much Cuban), richly embroidered Rajasthani upholstery and antiques… the attention to detail is immaculate and the renovation has been a labour of love. Complementary interests – for Norman, art and a three-quarter-size snooker table, for Carole, her exceptional cooking and jewellery (for sale) – come together with a shared passion for their garden and their guests. Four serenely well-designed bedrooms the colour of jewels face out onto the pool and a raucous festival of plant life, flowers and shrubs; relax in the shaded sit-outs. Watch out for deceptively strong sundowners at the sunset bar above – and Carole's infamous chocolate puddings. There's masses to do in the area but you won't be able to leave. Sweet staff, too.

Price	Rs5,170. Singles Rs3,685.
Rooms	4 doubles.
Meals	Breakfast Rs250. Lunch Rs450. Dinner Rs850.
Closed	Rarely.
Directions	South Goa, in village of Loutolim. Train: Margao (20 mins). Airport: Dabolim (25 mins).

Price band: C

Norman & Carole Steen
Casa Susegad, Orgao, Loutolim,
Salcette, South Goa, 403718

Tel	+91 (0)8326 483 368
Email	casasusegad@gmail.com
Web	www.casasusegadgoa.com

Vivenda dos Palhaços

Restored by the ebullient Simon and his charming sister Charlotte, this charismatic Hindu-Portuguese mansion is a jewel in Goa's tiara. With five boutique bedrooms in the house, a huge opulent tent and a cottage in the garden, all requirements are catered for, but it's the details that delight. There's a bar made from the painted tailgate of a Tata truck, antique dentists' chairs on the veranda, the thwump of colonial-style ceiling fans, huge comfortable four-posters, a big convivial dining table and a thunder box loo in the tent. Then there's the ozone-purified pool with decadent Romanesque folly, the cotton-swathed day beds under the palms and outstanding food and wines — all against the authentic backdrop of a traditional village backwater. It's the perfect retreat for a contemplative sojourn on your own, romantic enough to impress any partner yet has space enough for families with kids: it's peaceful and jolly all at the same time. You can sun-worship on some of Goa's best beaches, fish, dive, go clubbing, be cultural. *Tatler* has voted it one of the best hotels in the world.

Price	Rs3,500–Rs9,350.
Rooms	7: 5 twins/doubles, 1 tent, 1 cottage for 2. Camp beds for children.
Meals	Lunch & dinner Rs300–Rs850.
Closed	Never.
Directions	Airport: Dabolim (25 mins). Train: Margao (15 mins).

Simon Hayward
Vivenda dos Palhaços, Costa Vaddo,
Majorda, Salcette, South Goa, 403713

Tel	+91 (0)8323 221 119
Email	simon@vivendagoa.com
Web	www.vivendagoa.com

Price band: D

Entry 124   Map 8

Dwarka Eco Beach Resort

Dwarka, named after Krishna's birthplace, is an understated gem. You're met by the owner at the road and led down a bouncy track through the jungle to the sea; park, walk through a gap in the bushes and there they are: ten thatched cabins with verandas scattered along sandy palm-fringed terraces, linked by a footbridge across a private freshwater lagoon. Clemente discovered the spot when researching settings for fashion shoots... imagine you've walked into a Bounty commercial. The deliciously secluded solar-supplied huts, woven loosely from palm leaves to allow for a breeze, are flawlessly simple and carefully thought through; billowing cotton, glitter worked into floor polish, simple comfortable beds, hot en suite showers. And mosquito-free — no bites or whines! The cabins are deconstructed each monsoon so are continually evolving. Spend lazy days on the beach or sipping cocktails in the thatched restaurant. Chat with Clemente and Arlene under the stars as the staff happily serenade you with local songs. Back to nature, back to the basics, with several mod cons but as green as can be. *Electricity from 6pm only.*

Price	Full-board Rs4,500.
Rooms	10 beach cabins.
Meals	Full-board only.
Closed	May–October.
Directions	15km from Palaolem beach in South Goa.
	Airport: Dabolim (45km).
	Train: Madgaon (30km).

Price band: B

Clemente Edmond
Dwarka Eco Beach Resort, Mattimol, Canacona, South Goa,

Tel	+91 (0)9823 377 025
Email	dwarkagoa@gmail.com
Web	www.dwarkagoa.com

Hotel Oceanic

Rebuilt from scratch by the delightful Sheila and Les, the Hotel Oceanic brings a refreshing slice of the Med to the Goan hotel repertoire; their sense of joie de vivre is infectious. Expect whitewashed walls with cornflower blue detailing, patios and terraces tinkling with wind chimes, a breezy café with canvas sun umbrellas, good modern shower rooms and simple tile-floored bedrooms with balconies… even the menu features Mediterranean classics. Enjoy calamari delicately fried in garlic, or a knock-out tiger prawn salad. In this very Indian jungle of mango trees and coconut palms, complete with marauding monkeys and a startling dawn chorus, you are a short walk from Palolem beach – one of Goa's best; take a speedboat in search of dolphins and sunsets. Closer to home, there's a lively scene around the bar most evenings, and classical music on Thursdays, when the pool area is transformed into a magically bohemian setting with candles and incense; there are also two residential masseuses to ease away your cares. It's relaxed, romantic and remote, enjoyable for both families and young couples.

Price	Rs1,500–Rs3,500.
Rooms	6 twins/doubles.
Meals	Breakfast Rs40–250.
	Lunch Rs100–Rs300.
	Dinner from Rs100.
Closed	Rarely.
Directions	Airport: Dabolim (70km, 1.5 hours).
	Train: Canacona (3km).

Les & Sheila Medcroft
Hotel Oceanic, Timbawadu, Palolem,
Canacona, South Goa, 403702

Tel	+91 (0)8322 643 059
Email	info@hotel-oceanic.com
Web	www.hotel-oceanic.com

Price band: B

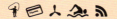

Entry 126   Map 8

Kerala & Lakshadweep

Neeleshwar Hermitage

Lining the deserted white sands of north Kerala are 16 fisherman's cottages – exquisite, newly built and designed according to Vaastu principles. The heart of this paradisiacally laid-back eco resort is its ayurvedic spa (lots of massage and yoga packages to choose from). Neeleshwar is named after Shiva, God of Transformation, but you may be as spiritual or as hedonistic as you like. We fell in love with it the moment we arrived: the infinity pool that gazes over the dunes to the ocean, the hyacinth-filled natural spring, the luxuriant gardens, the cottages that exude serenity, beauty and space. Frangipani trees grow through bathrooms half open to the sky, aromatic soaps top eco-friendly basins, Bose docks await guests' iPods, and views are to garden or sea. Dine (and drink) deliciously and organically in the palm-roofed hall, in the beach shack or under the stars. Come in high season and you may meet the cultural director, relaxed, delightful, with a passion for India. Neeleshwar is his labour of love and it's worth your last rupee. *Free consultation with spa doctor & beginners' yoga.*

Price	Rs7,950–Rs14,000. Plus 15% tax. Peak season: October–April.
Rooms	16 cottages.
Meals	Lunch & dinner from Rs1,000 p.p. Plus tax.
Closed	Never.
Directions	Airport: Mangalore (2 hours).

Altaf Chapri
Neeleshwar Hermitage,
Neeleshwar, Kasaragod

Tel	+91 (0)1244 010 072
Fax	+91 (0)1242 368 604
Email	reservations@neeleshwarhermitage.com
Web	www.neeleshwarhermitage.com

Price band: E

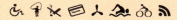

Kannur Beach House

Cancel your onward travel, loosen your belt a notch or two, let yourself sink into the real Kerala. Not the easiest place in the world to reach, but this only boosts the sense of blissful isolation. Sandwiched between creek and lagoon, and within earshot of the waves breaking on the sandy shore, this place is heaven for water babies. Rooms are spacious and simply furnished and all have balconies to the front. Rosie and Nazir are a warm-hearted, smiling, unflappable couple who are generous with their time, their food, and their knowledge of all things Keralan. Rosie is a magician in the kitchen and mealtimes are lively affairs, cherished by all; don't leave without jotting down a recipe. Take boat and binoculars down the river for some stunning birdwatching (Brahminy kites, kingfishers, bee-eaters); bag a hammock for a nap in the sun; wander for miles along the palm-fringed beaches without meeting another soul; follow Nazir on a midnight jaunt to a local Theyyam. Don't be surprised if you find you get 'stuck' here for a while; time has the habit of slipping away here.

Price	Half-board Rs1,800-Rs2,500. Peak season: November-March.
Rooms	6 doubles.
Meals	Half-board only. Lunch Rs125 p.p.
Closed	Rarely.
Directions	From main Thottada stop on NH17 connecting Kannur & Talassery, head to Thottada Beach. Please call before arrival. Airport: Kozhikode (110km).

Nazir & Rosie
Kannur Beach House,
Thottada Beach, Kannur

Tel	+91 (0)9847 186 330
Email	info@kannurbeachhouse.com
Web	www.kannurbeachhouse.com

Price band: A

Costa Malabari

If you seek somewhere off the tourist trail and are a fan of 'small is beautiful', you'll love Costa Malabari: hemmed in by cashew and coconut plantations it's an idyllic five-minute stroll from golden beaches and dolphins. Once a handloom shed, this unpretentious guest house – the more peaceful rooms in two houses close by – still has a lofty warehouse feel; don't come seeking luxury. Pastel walls soften the cavernous dining hall while a warm yellow washes the snug and simple bedrooms. Host Mr Kuriyan is intelligent and welcoming and his inventive twists on traditional recipes make each communal meal a feast… the tropical fruit ice creams are delicious. Ingredients are bought locally, staff are from the neighbouring village, and the guest house hasn't expanded in its 12 years. The result is a respectful, easy and unobtrusive relationship with the community; you may get invited to local events or weddings and are well placed to find out about Keralan festivals. A getaway in the best possible sense, wonderful people, a great ethos. Of the owner's various properties, this is the one we recommend.

Price	Full-board Rs2,500.
	Peak season: 15 October-14 February.
Rooms	4 doubles.
Meals	Full-board only.
Closed	June/July.
Directions	Near Adikadalayi Temple. Please call before arrival.
	Train: Kannur (8km).

Mrs Reena Joseph
Costa Malabari, Near Adikadalayi
Temple, Kannur, 670007
Email   touristdesk@satyam.net.in
Web   www.costamalabari.com

Price band: A

Harivihar Ayurvedic Heritage Home

Lush lawns tumble around this horseshoe-shaped house and if you can resist the charms of the natural bathing pond there are many shady spots under the jackfruit and mango trees. Inside, a sense of calm beguiles. Soft cotton sheets, teak furniture… you feel you have your own private butler; overall warmth, consideration and elegance pervades. Bedrooms are sober and charming, some with great garden views. A lofty dining room opens to the lawn and a meditation and yoga room on the top floor resides serenely over all. So tranquil is it that it's easy to forget you're in Kozhikode (previously Calicut) – and hard to believe that until the early 1980s almost 60 members of delightful Neethi's extended family called this home. Neethi has returned here with her husband Dr Srikumar and they have carved out this little sanctuary – a committed centre of treatment and learning. Book in for talks on Indian culture and philosophy; immerse yourself in ayurveda. The whole house is filled with sweet scented incense mists at sunset to repel mosquitos, adding an extra night-time sensory allure. And cuisine is melt-in-your-mouth European / Keralan.

Price	Full-board from €103. Singles from €75.
Rooms	7: 5 doubles, 2 singles.
Meals	Full-board only.
Closed	Mid-May.
Directions	Train: Kozhikode (15 mins).

Dr G Srikumar
Harivihar Ayurvedic Heritage Home,
Bilathikulam, Kozhikode, 673006

Tel	+91 (0)4952 765 865
Email	admin@harivihar.com
Web	www.harivihar.com

Price band: B

Tranquil - A Plantation Hideaway

Three thousand feet up in the Western Ghats, this wonderfully convivial guest house sits hidden among the coffee bushes and unspoilt rainforest of the Kuppamudi Coffee Estate. The 70-year-old plantation bungalow has been beautifully restored; enormous bedrooms have thick cotton sheets, patterned bedcovers and extremely comfortable beds. Expect hotel-smart furniture, TVs and floral curtains, huge bathrooms, thoughtfully scattered verandas and secluded terraces with fabulous forest views. Best of all are the two sturdy treehouses constructed from natural materials – bamboo woven walls, coffee roots for tables and shelves, branches growing inside; the newest has his and hers bathrooms. Victor, Ranjini, Ajay and Nisha sweep you into their lives – you may meet the grandchildren. There's a shady platform for a nap, and hammocks and pool-side loungers – a sense of calm pervades. Guests can enjoy Indian and continental buffet dinners around the big table; hill-top breakfasts and lovely plantation walks can be arranged. *Ayurvedic massage on request. Trekking & birdwatching in wildlife sanctuary.*

Price	Full-board €170–€236. Singles €130–€275. Suite €225–€315. Treehouses €225–€345. Peak season: December–March.
Rooms	10: 6 twins, 1 double + sofabed, 1 suite + sofabed, 2 treehouses.
Meals	Full-board only.
Closed	Never.
Directions	1.5km off Mysore-Kozhikode highway. Turn at Kolagapara Junction onto road leading to Edakkal caves; house signed on left.

V K Rajaram
Tranquil - A Plantation Hideaway,
Kuppamudi Coffee Estate, Kolagapara
PO, Wayanad, 673591

Tel	+91 (0)4936 220 244
Email	tranquilresort@gmail.com
Web	www.tranquilresort.com

Price band: D

Tharavad

Nearly all the agricultural land you pass on the route from Palakkad belonged to the Kandath family. Their impressive ancestral home was built in 1794 on part of the estate, of mud and teak. Much of the land has since been redistributed but charming Tharavad is unwilling to relinquish the splendour of its glory days. However, renovation has added creature comforts, and the presence of Mr Bhagwaldas and his family memorabilia lends it a homely air. Bulbous carved-teak pillars frame the colourful naturally dyed tiles of the raised *purathalum*, where Mr Bhagwaldas's grandfather perched to conduct his money lending. Little carved wooden doors draw you to a smaller *purathalam*, traditionally the female domain. Although only seven metres apart, not a sound can be heard between the two. Conversation is still important at Tharavad, where guests enjoy shared meals with your quietly intelligent host, perhaps round candlelit tables on the lawn. Guests speak highly of Mr Bhagwaldas, highly regarded in the village, and his fascinating home. Rooms vary; ask for one of the more spacious.

Price	Full-board Rs7,600.
	Peak season: October–March.
Rooms	4: 1 double, 1 twin, 1 triple, 1 suite.
Meals	Full-board only.
Closed	Rarely.
Directions	10km from Palakkad; call for pick-up.

Price band: C

Mr Bhagwaldas Sudevan
Tharavad, Kandath Tharavad,
Thenkurussi, Palakkad, 678671

Tel	+91 (0)4922 284 124
Email	tharavad15@yahoo.com
Web	tharavad.info

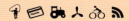

Olappamanna Mana

A remarkable, traditional and hospitable place to stay. In the 18th century this was a feudal lord's house with a Hindu family deity, a bathing tank and separate quarters for men and women. Over the years additional structures sprang up, and it became an important seat of learning for Kathakali (classical Keralan dance) and traditional Veda and Sanskrit. The main building is where you can watch the *puja*: dance, prayer and drumming around a giant sand painting of the goddess Kali. This is authentic culture par excellence with your own private Kathakali performances (ask for prices). Guests now stay in a newer, lighter building: three cheerful rooms, simple but lovely, furnished with antiques and sharing a kitchen and a wonderful big veranda. Mr Damodaran brims over with local and arts knowledge and is always available to make sure guests explore the richness of the surrounding area. He and his smiling wife Sreedevi live a five-minute stroll away though coconut palms. Their garden is stuffed with pineapples, papaya and mangos and they serve authentic and delicious south Indian vegetarian food.

Price	Full-board Rs4,500. Family room Rs6,000. Peak season: November-May.
Rooms	3: 1 double, 2 family rooms.
Meals	Full-board only. Packed lunches available.
Closed	Rarely.
Directions	From Palghat, 43km, take Kozhikode Rd (Cherepalchery route). Airport: Kozhikode (50km, 1.5 hours). Train: Palakkad Jn, Shoranur (25km).

Mr O N Damodaran
Olappamanna Mana, Vellinezhi,
Palakkad, 679504

Tel	+91 (0)4662 285 383
Email	olappamannadamodaran@gmail.com
Web	www.olappamannamana.com

Price band: B

Entry 133   Map 8

Mundackal Homestay

Down a bumpy winding track, you wash up at a superb Indian homestay on the edge of the Salim Ali Bird Sanctuary. Seeing no official boundaries, birds of every colour come to sing over breakfast: the only disturbance in a lush oasis. Daisy and Jose are a warm, educated and delightful pair who ensure you will not go hungry: dinners are lively and Daisy's food is generous, organic and delicious. The décor is unremarkable with splashes of kitsch, you sleep in plain but adequate bedrooms, and relax on a lovely long veranda. Beyond the lawn (white picket-fencing, ornate bridge over small stream) are spacious hammock'd grounds and plantation walks aplenty; the setting – secluded, green and with birds to excite twitchers – is superb, and they keep goats and hens too. Jose will tell you how rubber is tapped and turned into sheets, and show you where the spices grow. An engagingly Indian experience, particularly for anyone with ornithological or gastronomic leanings, and a rare chance to dip your toes into the lives of a working plantation family. *Kodanad elephant training camp nearby.*

Price	Full-board Rs7,500–Rs8,500.
Rooms	5 doubles.
Meals	Full-board only.
Closed	Never.
Directions	Kothamangalam is 57km from Kochi. Plantation House is 7km from Kothamangalam. You will need your own driver.

Price band: C

Jose & Daisy Mundackal
Mundackal Homestay, Mundackal
Estate, Pindimana PO, via Thrikariyoor,
Kothamangalam, Ernakulam, 686698

Tel	+91 (0)4852 570 717
Email	nestholidays@hotmail.com
Web	www.mundackalhomestay.com

Periyar River Lodge

The views from this simple teak-built lodge on the banks of the serene Periyar river soothe the soul. On the doorstep of the Thattekad Bird Sanctuary – home to some 270 bird species – the guest house has an exquisite simplicity. And you're in the midst of the rubber plantations, making this is a great place for people-watching and taking in village life. Inside is a sunken central courtyard where a leafy palm reaches for the sun. A small seating area with subdued cosy lighting and bamboo seats with stripy red and burnt-orange cushions lies on one side; a small kitchen and dining room lie on the other. A local lady cooks delicious south Indian meals, served by your attentive, eager-to-please host Paul. Several windows throw light into the bedrooms which have been designed with a stylish hand. Rattan blinds, decorated terracotta lamps, red and cream bedspreads on comfy beds – all look beautiful against the backdrop of rich teak walls. Best of all: open-air showers with pretty pebble floors. The birds will wake you, the insects will sing you to sleep. *Birdwatching & boat trips, bicycle tours & guided walks.*

Price	Full-board Rs3,500. Singles Rs3,000. Whole lodge Rs6,000.
Rooms	2 doubles.
Meals	Full-board only.
Closed	Never.
Directions	8km from Thattekad Bird Sanctaury. Airport: Kochi (50km, 1.5 hours).

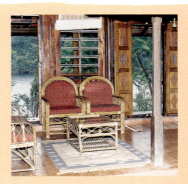

Mr Eldho Kuruvilla
Periyar River Lodge, Anakkayam,
Kuttampuzha PO, Kothamangalam,
Ernakulam, 686691

Tel	+91 (0)4842 207 173
Email	info@periyarriverlodge.com
Web	www.periyarriverlodge.com

Price band: B

Entry 135   Map 8

Green Lagoon Resort

Take a seven-acre tropical island on Kerala's largest lake, add a passionate eco-green owner and beautiful buildings, and dust generously with luxury: a recipe for success. Step from the speedboat transfer onto your private 'island' – one of three bridge-linked residences – to a personal welcome from Klaus and a kurta-clad staff. Traditional wooden houses (one 200 years old with original prayer room) have been revamped with infinity pools, verandas, jacuzzis, artworks and antiques; immaculate bath-gardens are half open to the sky and if anything's amiss a butler will fix it. Everything is timed to perfection (it's almost theatrical) and the details are exquisite, from individualised menus to antique cutlery from Berlin. Chat to the chef about his specialities, much organic or from the lake; then dine under the mango tree or by the pool (the fruit ice cream's to die for), surrounded by silence and stars. Admire Klaus's art collection, jog through luxuriant gardens, book a mud bath or call in a yoga master – be pampered all day long. Or speed across to Vaikom Temple and Fort Kochi, for history, spices and silk.

Price	€120–€640 for 2. Plus 15% tax. Transfers included.
Rooms	3 villas for 5.
Meals	Lunch €20. Dinner €30. Plus 12.24% tax.
Closed	Rarely.
Directions	Directions on booking.

Ethical Collection: Environment; Food.
See page 264.

Price band: F

Klaus Schleusener
Green Lagoon Resort, Island House,
Vettila Thuruthu, Eramalloor,
Ernakulam, 688537
Tel   +91 (0)4786 451 811
Email   island@green-lagoon.com
Web   www.green-lagoon.com

Entry 136   Map 8

Koder House

Once this striking house was a playground for presidents, viceroys and ambassadors.
Easy to imagine you're a head honcho too, as cold towels and fresh pineapple are presented
on arrival by unfailingly helpful staff. A heritage landmark near the Kochi waterfront, the
house was built in 1808 by Jewish merchants; converting it into a hotel, the owner
preserved the lavish feel, with original furniture and expanses of dark wood floor.
Extraordinarily spacious rooms have immense carved wood beds and white jacuzzi
bathrooms, and many have dressing rooms to boot; extra touches include bowls of cashews
and other treats. The servants' hall, now the Menorah Restaurant, serves American or
South Indian breakfasts; for lunch and dinner there's a sophisticated menu of Indian and
western dishes, Keralan seafoods and Jewish specialities – all delicious. In keeping with the
hotel's heritage, the festival of Hanukkah is celebrated each year, accompanied by a special
Jewish menu. All is perfect, from the service to the spa – and the small plunge pool in the
courtyard gives blessed respite from humidity and heat.

Price	Rs5,000–Rs17,940.
	Peak season: October–March.
Rooms	6 suites.
Meals	Lunch & dinner Rs450–Rs750.
Closed	Rarely.
Directions	In the centre of Fort Kochi, opposite the beach.

Vicky Raj
Koder House, Tower Road, Fort Kochi,
Kochi, Ernakulam, 682001

Tel	+91 (0)4842 218 485
Fax	+91 (0)4842 217 988
Email	koderhouse@gmail.com
Web	www.koderhouse.com

Price band: E

Trinity at Fort Cochin

The onetime Indian headquarters of the Dutch East India Company has become a voguish little bolthole exuding privacy and peace — ideal for families or groups of friends. It's a young offshoot of Malabar House — an intimate, unhotelly and seductive place to stay. The three suites sing with Anglo-Indian good taste: coloured silk cushions on raised double beds, a unique collection of contemporary Indian art, luxurious linen, controlled blinds, outside bathrooms with sunken showers encircled by pebbles. Two suites have an extra bed on the mezzanine, the smallest has an outdoor deck, and the air conditioning is peaceful. For views, seek out the balcony that overlooks the parade ground — mellow-yellow in the early evening light. Breakfast when you please, on fresh breads and pastries, fruit and eggs and banana and coconut pancakes, smilingly served. For Indian designer clothing, there's an on-site boutique. For dinner — and massage — there's Malabar House. For sport — bikes and a tiny pool. Then retire to the dining/sitting room, chic and inviting with deep orange chairs, books, DVDs, internet and large, lush bowls of fruit.

Price	€150–€220. Family suites €200–€460. Plus 15% tax. Peak season October-April.
Rooms	3: 1 suite, 2 family suites.
Meals	Lunch & dinner €15 at Malabar House, 200m.
Closed	Rarely.
Directions	In Fort Kochi, 200m across Parade Ground from its sister hotel, Malabar House. Airport: Kochi (1 hour).

Price band: D

Mr Isaac Mervin
Trinity at Fort Cochin, Parade Road,
Fort Kochi, Kochi, Ernakulam, 682001

Tel	+91 (0)4842 216 666
Email	reservations@malabarhouse.com
Web	www.malabarhouse.com

Malabar House

Joerg Drechsel, an ethnographic exhibition creator of taste and style, has created a slice of heaven. Old temple carvings cast shadows across lively walls in ochre, turquoise and white, and every piece of furniture has been perfectly chosen. The central courtyard is as Eden might have known it; Joerg built the hotel around a vast vine- and frangipani-clad rain tree. Creeping green vanilla climbs up whitewashed walls, and the lovely, petal-sprinkled plunge pool sits beneath a hanging roof. Tables from the veranda'd restaurant spill out under the trees, bamboo overhangs the open-sided courtyard brushed by sea breezes. Joerg's Spanish wife Txuku concocts the food, a delicate, delectable harmony of east and west. Colonial four-poster teak beds stand opposite vast Keralan masks, subtly-lit works of contemporary art mix with ancient ones. The roof garden suites are the largest, lightest and the most private. Most of the building is new, yet every inch reflects Joerg's commitment to the Keralan vernacular. Old and new seamlessly combine and the luxury is perfectly simple. A calm oasis in this historic harbour city.

Price	€150–€220. Suites €200–€460. Plus 15% tax. Peak season: October–April.
Rooms	17: 11 doubles, 6 suites.
Meals	Lunch & dinner from €15.
Closed	Never.
Directions	Signed from seaside Kochi. Do not get taken to Taj Malabar! Airport: Kochi (1 hour).

Mr Joerg Drechsel
Malabar House, 1/268 & 1/269 Parade
Rd, Fort Kochi, Kochi, Ernakulam,
682001

Tel	+91 (0)4842 216 666
Email	reservations@malabarhouse.com
Web	www.malabarhouse.com

Price band: D

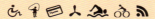

Entry 139   Map 8

Chittoor Palace

Live as a maharaja in your private riverside residence. Built 300 years ago for the Maharaja of Kochi (previously Cochin) when he visited the next-door temple, Chittoor Palace is still owned by his family. Although renovated, little has changed. A golden-pillared portico leads into zen-like gardens surrounded by classically proportioned white buildings with low-slung red roofs, carved balconies and elegant columns. Rooms are stately – teak pillars, polished wood and intricately tiled floors, rosewood four-poster beds, throne-like chairs – and vast. (Bathrooms are less grand, but who cares!) The suite has two balconies (one perfect for sunsets); the downstairs double opens onto the garden, tranquil with mango, teak and tamarind trees, fluttering with birds and dipping to the river. Owner Suresh, a charming and well-to-do accountant, may join you for dinner – vegetarian, classically Keralan – and talk history and traditions. Visit Fort Kochi or Chittoor Temple, or relax in the garden's spring-fed pool. A boat trip from your private jetty is essential. With only two rooms, chances are you'll have the place to yourself.

Price	Full-board Rs10,400. Suite Rs14,700.
Rooms	2: 1 double, 1 suite.
Meals	Full-board only.
Closed	Never.
Directions	Airport: Kochi (29km). Train: Ernakulam (6km).

Price band: C

Suresh Namboothiri
Chittoor Palace, South Chittoor,
Kochi, Ernakulam, 682027

Tel	+91 (0)4842 431 380
Email	thampuran@chittoorpalace.com
Web	www.chittoorpalace.com

Entry 140   Map 8

Old Harbour Hotel

Laze by the pool, sip cocktails under the mango tree: an unusual setting for central Fort Kochi. This 300-year-old colonial building started life as the office of an English tea brokers and manifests a serene fusion of Dutch and Portuguese styles. Now it has been blessed with a sympathetic revival. Interiors are studded with bold local paintings, entertaining artefacts and simple antiques: the effect is both sophisticated and stunning. High-ceilinged bedrooms have deep comfortable beds and big windows for cool breezes. Cushions and curtains are of fine Indian cotton. Chic bathrooms reveal fluffy bathrobes, slippers and towels, and the cottages have open-to-the-sky showers. Windows overlook the ingenious Chinese fishing nets (ancient but still in use: a tourist attraction) or the courtyard garden with its urns full of flowers, pond full of lilies and fountain. Dinners of caught-that-day fish are a pleasure to come home to but it is the staff that are the biggest delight, taking their cue from the owner. A destination for travellers to Fort Kochi in search of contemporary charm and simple good taste.

Price	Rs7,500-Rs10,600. Suites Rs14,600.
Rooms	13: 10 doubles, 3 cottage suites.
Meals	Lunch & dinner from Rs500.
Closed	Never.
Directions	In Fort Kochi, opposite the Chinese fishing nets.

Edgar Pinto
Old Harbour Hotel, 1/328 Tower Road,
Fort Kochi, Kochi, Ernakulam, 682001

Tel	+91 (0)4842 218 006
Email	edgarpinto@yahoo.com
Web	www.oldharbourhotel.com

Price band: D

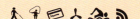

The Brunton Boatyard

The hotel is at once big, grand and simple – like a plantation owner's house. A further appeal lies in its handsome dominance of the waterfront and its position near the Chinese fishing nets. Permission to build in this preservation area is tightly controlled – but not denied to the Casino Group who own this hotel. History has been sympathetically recreated and the large serene spaces resemble a museum of Dutch colonial living – but are far more comfortable. The vaulted lobby walls depict a gallery of the notable worthies of Kochi and the ceiling is overhung with huge fans of Indo-Portuguese origin. Open walkways encircle the central courtyard with its big banyan tree; behind, each room's balcony faces the shipping channel, where tankers cross wakes with ferries and fishing canoes plying their way to the islands beyond: a scene you'll not tire of watching. The pool area is inviting and the restaurants are somewhat soulless, though the food is seriously good. Beautiful bedrooms – splash out on a bigger one – have huge antique bedsteads. Bathrooms are truly sensual. *Free sunset cruises.*

Price	Rs7,590. Suites Rs10,925. Plus 15% tax. Peak season: February; 21 December-10 January.
Rooms	22: 12 doubles, 6 twins, 4 suites.
Meals	Breakfast Rs750. Lunch & dinner from Rs900.
Closed	Rarely.
Directions	At the mouth of the harbour next to Fort Kochi bus station.

Shilendran Mohan
The Brunton Boatyard, 1/498 Fort
Kochi, Kochi, Ernakulam, 682001

Tel	+91 (0)4843 011 562
Email	burtonboatyard@cghearth.com
Web	www.cghearth.com

Price band: C

Entry 142   Map 8

Gramam Homestay

From a bamboo swing, experience the gentle pace of backwaters life on this small island; hard to believe this is only 10km from Fort Kochi. From this sweet and simple homestay wander through the sloping garden, past mango trees and coconut palms, down to the water's edge. Jos, his wife, and two sons live here – all are friendly and welcoming. Light-filled bedrooms have comfy wooden beds and shutters, patterned wall hangings, crisp sheets, fans and mosquito nets. Old mango pots used for salting and storing fruit have been artfully turned into lamp bases, and luggage racks have been created from bamboo. The bedroom at the back of the main house is more private, with its lovely terrace and antique snoozing chairs. Fresh bathrooms are small with hot showers. The family take their environmental responsibilities seriously, support the local community and the new eco cottage under the palms at the edge of the backwaters is a simple delight. Watch the toddy-makers at work, go fishing with the locals, spin off on a bike. The fresh fish, prawn and crab curries are delicious. *Cookery courses.*

Price	Rs4,000. Cottage Rs6,000. Extra bed Rs700. Peak season: September–March.
Rooms	1 + 1: 1 twin. Cottage for 2–4.
Meals	Lunch & dinner Rs300.
Closed	Rarely.
Directions	On North Kumbalangi Island, 10km south of Kochi.

Mr Jos & Lyma Byju
Gramam Homestay, Neduveli House,
North Kumbalangi Island, Kochi,
Ernakulam, 682007

Tel	+91 (0)4842 240 278
Email	keralagramam@vsnl.net
Web	www.keralagramam.com

Price band: C

Philipkutty's Farm

Come to be marooned, in comfort, on an island. Each of these waterfront cottages is solidly built along old architectural lines using tiled overhanging roofs and shuttered windows. One has an open-plan layout with a veranda running around it, others have separate bedroom and sitting area and 'sit outs' in front of the water. The coconut and spice plantation is criss-crossed by hundreds of water channels – enchanting – and all is simplicity and serenity inside: dark wooden ceilings, white walls, some antique furniture. Bedrooms are small but delightful, their heavy wooden doors opening out to water; showers are westernised and luxurious; tiled living areas are open to catch the breeze. The 750-acre island of Puthenkayal was created from land reclaimed by this Syrian Christian family in the 1950s. Gentle Anu and her mother run cookery courses and create exquisite and plentiful Keralan food; meals are communal occasions under the outdoor pavilion. You can be alone or involved, take out punts or just lie back and read. Special indeed. *Cookery courses & farm visits.*

Price	Full-board Rs7,000–Rs9,900. Peak season: October–May.
Rooms	6 cottages for 2.
Meals	Full-board only.
Closed	Rarely.
Directions	From Ambika Market, Church Road for 1km. Boat collects from jetty. 1 hour from Kochi. Airport: Kochi (75km). Train: Kottayam (25km).

Price band: C

Anu Mathew
Philipkutty's Farm, Pallivathukal,
Ambika Market PO, Vechoor,
Kottayam, 686144

Tel	+91 (0)4829 276 529
Email	mail@philipkuttysfarm.com
Web	www.philipkuttysfarm.com

Entry 144   Map 8

Vanilla County

A purple jacaranda tree swathes the front garden in colour and the rich scent of vanilla hangs in the breeze. This is an intimate homestay, where gentle Rani and Baby welcome you like friends and involve you in family and plantation life. A thousand acres of this land were given to your host's grandfather by the local maharaja; the house was built 60 years ago. The new generation are running this vanilla, coffee and rubber plantation organically and delight in showing guests how it all works. Spotless bedrooms are simple not stylish, with concrete floors, patterned Indian bed sheets on wooden beds, and lampshades and coat stands crafted from polished coffee roots. One family room connects via a large private balcony; the rest share verandas. Rani is an excellent cook so you'll enjoy an exquisite chicken biryani with other guests round the large teak dining table. Paintings adorn the walls and there's a small Christian family shrine. This is a wonderful, warm family home so bring the children, cool off in the natural pools and make the most of living on a remote, lush plantation. Magic!

Price	Full-board Rs7,000. Singles 5,750. All local activities included. Peak season: October–March.
Rooms	4: 2 doubles, 2 family rooms.
Meals	Full-board only.
Closed	Rarely.
Directions	Airport: Kochi (100km, 2.5 hours). Train: Kottayam (56km, 1.5 hours).

Baby Mathew & Rani Baby Vallikappen
Vanilla County, Vagamon Road, Mavady Estate, Teekoy, Kottayam, 686580

Tel	+91 (0)4822 281 225
Email	vanillacounty@gmail.com
Web	www.vanillacounty.in

Price band: C

Privacy at Sanctuary Bay

Huge sliding screens give onto the veranda with its bamboo blinds and views across the shimmering lake. This must be one of the most heavenly spots in all Kerala. With its dining room, living room, two bathrooms and air-conditioned suite, this thatched waterfront bungalow is a super-cool retreat. The heritage bungalow, a recently relocated wooden cottage, has two bedrooms, each with an outdoor shower, and separated by a hall. The lovely pool is shared. Both bungalows have private sit-outs and verandas — bucolic spots from which to enjoy a candlelit evening meal, close enough to the lake to be able to dip one's toes in the water. Interiors are colourfully minimalist, typical of the Malabar House ethos to renovate old Keralan buildings with sympathy and simplicity; harmony and symmetry underpin the placing of the few choice ethno-graphic objets. Your chef is present but never overbearing and the food is delicious — delicate curries and fresh juices served as and when you want. You'll see no-one bar the odd passing fisherman, and be disturbed by little other than the wildlife.

Price	€250–€360. Cottage €150–€220 for 2. Peak season: October–April.
Rooms	3: 1 suite for 2. Cottage: 2 doubles.
Meals	Lunch & dinner €30.
Closed	Rarely.
Directions	15-min drive from Cherthala.

Price band: F

Mr Joerg Drechsel
Privacy at Sanctuary Bay, TP111/185
Kannamkara PO, Muhamma,
Thaneermukkom, Alappuzha

Tel	+91 (0)4842 216 666
Email	reservations@malabarhouse.com
Web	www.malabarhouse.com

Discovery

Discovery is a rice boat turned chic houseboat, non-polluting and almost noiselessly powered. It is small, intimate and delightful, ideal for honeymooners or friends. There's a decked sun terrace for lounging, a sitting room with a sofa (that converts into beds), and a super-sleek white-walled suite. (The four staff sleep in separate quarters.) Luxuries include a polished teak floor for a queen-size bed, hot showers and Khadi toiletries, striped sunloungers bedecked with cushions, and gorgeous Keralan-Mediterranean cuisine. Owned by Malabar House, this stylish little boat – 75-foot from top to toe – is moored at Privacy at Sanctuary Bay, on the idyllic shores of Lake Vembanad, nudging the backwaters of Alleppy. On arrival you are ushered into Privacy's private gardens with shimmering pool: yours to share until it's time to board. Then it's off at a stately six knots to explore some of Kerala's loveliest watery corners – alive with egrets, darters, herons, teal, waterfowl, cuckoo, wild duck and Siberian stork. If you bring the children choose December to March: dry, not too hot, sheer bliss.

Price	Full-board €350-€450. Peak season October-April.
Rooms	Cruiser for 2-4 (1 double, 1 sofabed).
Meals	Full-board only. Chef provided.
Closed	Rarely.
Directions	Departure & arrival from sister property Privacy at Sanctuary Bay.

Mr Joerg Drechsel
Discovery, TP111/185 Kannamkara PO,
Muhamma, Thaneermukkom, Alappuzha

Tel	+91 (0)4842 216 666
Fax	+91 (0)4842 217 777
Email	reservations@malabarhouse.com
Web	www.malabarhouse.com

Price band: E

Pamba Heritage Villa

You are greeted at the private jetty, ushered into a verdant garden fringed with palms (try the coconut toddy…) and across to reception on the veranda and a courteous offering of lime water; this is a classic Keralan homestay. Built in 1915 by the owner's landowner grandfather, the mansion's comfy sitting room is shared with family, staff and a 30" TV. Outside is the place to be, in the lush and lovely garden where scenes of Nedumudi village life unfold across the limpid river and hammocks nestle between the big boughs of the breadfruit tree; at sunset this is magical. Big old-fashioned bedrooms in the former rice barn – just one with air con – have fluorescent lights and a teak-wood sobriety; pebble-floor showers with lashings of water are refreshingly open to the sky. Expect to sleep soundly and to be woken by the 6am bustle of the ferries and the happy sounds of Christian worship. Hovering staff serve tasty Keralan dinners; breakfasts are enjoyed on the wraparound veranda. No bells and whistles here but an undeniable sense of old school India charm – especially in the setting.

Price	Full-board Rs3,200-Rs4,000.
Rooms	3 twins.
Meals	Full-board only.
Closed	Rarely.
Directions	Airport: Kochi (85km), Thiruvananthapuram (150km). Train: Alappuzha (10km), Changanassery (18km). Owner can arrange pick-up from these locations.

Price band: B

Rajiv Thomas Kanjooparambil
Pamba Heritage Villa, Kanjooparambil-Umbukadu, Ponga PO, Nedumudi,
Alappuzha, 688512

Tel	+91 (0)4772 762 109
Email	rajiv@pambaheritage.com
Web	www.pambaheritage.com

Emerald Isle

A dug-out canoe ferries you across the Pamba river to the historic wooden bungalow that hides on a little island in the backwaters; all is birdsong and bountiful nature. A sprawling veranda dotted with wicker chairs hugs the contours of this idyllic heritage home, so settle in with a book and cup of sweet milky *chai*: this is a place to just 'be'. Furniture is dark and heavy and much of it original, even the hinges of the carved doors are teak. Vinod's great-grandfather renovated the place years ago and property deeds etched into 250-year-old palm leaves hang in the cool dark living room. Shower rooms are open to the sky and the food is truly delicious. Vinod is gentle and friendly, keen to share the history of this dreamy place. He can organise cookery classes, ayurvedic massage, an overnight trip on the backwaters (on his cousin's boat) or suggest ambles through a maze of canals to the paddy and coconut fields of the estate. Hammocks have been strategically placed en route... a delightfully soporific way to spend your time in India. *House boats available for rent at any time.*

Price	Full-board Rs5,000–Rs5,800. Peak season: August–April.
Rooms	5 doubles.
Meals	Full-board only.
Closed	Rarely.
Directions	Directions on booking. Collection by boat from 'Chathurthiakary Kadav'. Airport: Kochi (95km, 2 hours). Train: Alappuzha (12km, 25 mins).

Mr Vinod Job
Emerald Isle, Kanjooparambil-
Manimalathara, Chathurthiakary PO,
Alappuzha, 688511

Tel	+91 (0)4772 703 899
Email	info@emeraldislekerala.com
Web	www.emeraldislekerala.com

Price band: B

Raheem Residency

All is gentle and serene. Facing the ocean on a quiet Keralan beach, this oasis in Alleppey softens the spirit. The elegant colonial house was built in 1868 and became the home of the Raheems – Muslim/Gujarati traders with links to Gandhi. Today generous Irish ex-journalist Bibi and her Indian business partner Flemin have transformed it into a relaxing, spoiling retreat. Inside are big cool high-ceilinged rooms, pretty antique beds with lush linen, opulent sofas with burnt orange cushions and inlaid coloured glass, and bathrooms that open to the stars. Pad across tiled floors to the courtyard pool after a divine ayurvedic massage; select a book from the library. Guests' privacy is respected and you ring the bell for attention. The restaurant is open to non-hotel guests; from large wicker chairs dine on tasty fresh fish, chicken and vegetarian dishes with western leanings. From here, gaze at the waves rolling, the sun setting – or the cricket. Experience real Indian life – Bibi knows the best places to shop for silk, spices, cotton and gold. Understated luxury and good taste prevail.

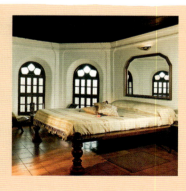

Price	€90-€190. Suite €160-€250. Plus 15% tax. Peak season: October-March.
Rooms	10: 6 doubles, 3 twins, 1 family suite.
Meals	Breakfast €6. Lunch €7. Dinner €12.
Closed	Rarely.
Directions	Airport: Kochi (88km, 1.5 hours). Train: Alappuzha (6km, 10 mins).

Price band: D

Mr Flemin Welben
Raheem Residency, Beach Road,
Alappuzha, 688012

Tel	+91 (0)4772 239 767
Fax	+91 (0)4772 230 767
Email	contact@raheemresidency.com
Web	www.raheemresidency.com

Entry 152   Map 8

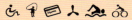

A Beach Symphony

A few years ago Christel and Jan swapped their busy hotel in Spa, Belgium for this cluster of cottages on a palm-fringed beach in Kerala. Every detail has been carefully thought through; elegant Christel has a sharp eye for design and has created a beautiful place to be. The bedrooms are large and lovely, airy and light; walls are washed in ochre, silk bedcovers are piled high with cushions in rich reds and oranges. Expect locally made furniture, teak chairs, low coffee tables with elephants marching around the edges, showers that open to the sky; one cottage has a private plunge pool. Tall vases full of exotic leaves and flowers flash more exuberant colour around. The chef will whip up tasty local dishes for you morning, noon and night – you're looked after beautifully. Cross the sandy garden, duck under the thatched porch and then you're on the beach which belongs to you and the fishermen alone. It's almost a relief to discover when you arrive that there's not a lot to do – giving the excuse you were after to do absolutely nothing. *Cookery courses available.*

Price	Rs7,500–Rs12,500. Peak season: November–April.
Rooms	4 cottages for 2. Child bed available.
Meals	Breakfast Rs250. Lunch & dinner Rs350–Rs750.
Closed	June to mid-August.
Directions	Kochi-Alappuzha highway; turn west at Marari junction. 15km from Alappuzha.

Jan & Christel Arryn
A Beach Symphony, Marari Beach,
Mararikulam, Alappuzha

Tel	+91 (0)9744 297 123
Email	info@abeachsymphony.com
Web	www.abeachsymphony.com

Price band: D

Entry 153   Map 8

Tharavad Heritage Resort

A great setting on the banks of a canal, a 20-minute walk from the sands. More homestay than resort, this is wonderful value. Madhu shares the house with his brother and mother and a stroll around the calm, cool interiors feels like a tour of a lived-in museum: exceptional heirlooms and paintings throughout and everything beautifully polished: an antique rosewood gramophone, a brass and wooden *para* for measuring rice, and a vast rotund brass pot used for mixing oils on a gleaming veranda (Grandfather was an ayurvedic doctor). Each of the bedrooms has its own vintage objet – a big metal safe in one, ornate trinket boxes in another. Showers have gallons of hot water. The warm happy harmony of the house is reflected in your hosts' smiles, and sometimes they join guests for dinner. Local dishes are served in the dining room or outside; the garden is serenely lovely with orchids, tamarinds and huge mango. The fishing town of Alappuzha isn't far – let Madhu help organise boating from there – but far enough away to feel free of urban hum. *More bedrooms & swimming pool planned.*

Price	Rs1,000–Rs2,000. Single Rs800. Apartment: Rs2,000–Rs2,500. Peak season: October–January.
Rooms	7: 4 doubles, 1 single. Apartment: 2 doubles.
Meals	Breakfast Rs125. Lunch & dinner Rs4,000.
Closed	Rarely.
Directions	1km from Alappuzha station near North Police Station Road. Pick-up can be arranged from Kochi or Thiruvananthapuram airports.

Biju & Madhu Mohan
Tharavad Heritage Resort, West of
North Police Station, Sea View Ward,
Alappuzha, 688012

Tel	+91 (0)4772 244 599
Email	info@tharavadheritageresort.com
Web	www.tharavadheritageresort.com

Price band: A

Keraleeyam Ayurvedic Resort

The owner group, SD Pharmacy, has years of experience in ayurvedic health – one excellent reason to include this small resort. Keraleeyam isn't just clinging to the coat tails of the Keralan cash cow, it offers the real thing, and Mr Ramesh comes from a long line of physicians. The 'heritage' cottages – those with air con are a bit boxy in feel – have dark ornate wooden doors, but the best are those constructed entirely of coconut thatching (the locals re-thatch every month) and are great fun, the views from their top-storey verandas reaching over the tranquil backwaters. Tradition meets modernity in their (somewhat jaded) open-air shower rooms; bathe under the stars. The double rooms in the house are small but good: fresh simple furnishings, a gentle bias towards ayurveda and not an ounce of clutter. In the cool dark dining room you may indulge in the great Indian tradition of 'tea and snacks' – and retreat from the heat. Simple western and Chinese food is served too. An idyllic backwater setting, hammocks to dream in, ayurveda to trust in… and excellent value.

Price	Rs1,425. Singles Rs1,140. Cottages Rs1,710–Rs2,280.
Rooms	14: 5 doubles, 9 cottages (for 4, 6 or 8).
Meals	Breakfast Rs171. Lunch & dinner Rs285.
Closed	Never.
Directions	On the backwaters, 3km from Alappuzha station. Airport: Kochi (85km, 1.5 hours).

Mr K Ramesh
Keraleeyam Ayurvedic Resort,
Thathampally PO, Alappuzha, 688006

Tel	+91 (0)4772 231 468
Fax	+91 (0)4772 251 068
Email	mail@keraleeyam.com
Web	www.keraleeyam.com

Price band: A

Motty's Homestay

The first thing you'll notice is Motty's deep infectious chuckle; the second, his eye for beautiful things. Motty and Lali's boutique homestay is crammed with objets d'art from India and beyond, yet his interior designer instinct has made the most of the space – nothing looks busy. With luscious plant-strewn verandas at both front and back you have as much communal space outside as in. Smooth teak pillars hold the front veranda while the one at the back is arched and has a carved jackwood trestle table. The bedrooms, each with its own entrance, are big and private; one has a splendid four-poster and an intriguing collection of walking sticks that splay out at the foot of the bed. Lali's cooking is Keralan and extremely good; communal meals are a highlight and Lali is delighted to share her recipes. Motty can organise rice-barge cruises on the Keralan backwaters (book in advance during the peak season) and, being an impeccable host, ensures everyone has a great time. Charming Alappuzha, or Alleppey, is a five-minute rickshaw away; you'd never know it. *Cookery courses.*

Price	Rs5,000. Half-board Rs6,000. Singles 20% discount. Peak season: November–March.
Rooms	3: 1 double. New annexe: 1 double, 1 twin/double.
Meals	Lunch Rs300. Dinner Rs500.
Closed	Never.
Directions	5 mins from central Alappuzha. Airport: Kochi (90km, 2 hours). Train: Alappuzha (4km, 10 mins).

Price band: C

Motty & Lali Mathew
Motty's Homestay, Murickanadiyil,
Kidangamparambu Rd, Thathampally,
Alappuzha, 688013

Tel	+91 (0)4772 263 535
Email	motty@alleppeybeach.com
Web	www.alleppeybeach.com

Kanjirapally Estate

An atypical farmhouse, a special homestay. Built on a cardamom and coffee plantation bordering the Periyar Tiger Reserve, this angular, 30-year-old building is cool and colourful with bright terrazzo floors, Rajasthani wall hangings and deeply tempting sofas. It's well-kept and well-hung, with a curatorial eye and a fabulous artistic touch: sheer delight. Gita and Mathew, young, sophisticated, interested and involved, champion Slow Food, the slow life and the cultural exchange that their guests bring. Both are passionate conservationists and nature lovers – dog-lovers too – and can take you for bird-spotting walks around the plantation that spreads its forested tentacles across kilometres of steep hillside. (It also plays occasional host to wandering bison from the reserve.) The gardens shine, from the scarlet poinsettia and the riotous cacti in every shape and colour to the three-tiered vegetable garden, a model of sustainability; thought has gone into perfecting each corner. And they can cook up a storm in the kitchen! Guests return. *Guided trekking, rafting, plantation walks & cardamon auctions.*

Price	Half-board Rs7,500. Singles Rs6,000. Peak season: October-February.
Rooms	2 doubles.
Meals	Lunch Rs750.
Closed	Rarely.
Directions	The estate borders the Periyar Tiger Reserve. Directions on booking. Airport: Kochi (128km, 4 hours). Train: Kottayam (65km, 2 hours).

Gita & Mathew Eapen
Kanjirapally Estate, KK Road,
Vandiperiyar PO, Vandiperiyar,
Idukki, 685533

Tel   +91 (0)4869 252 278
Email kanjirapallyestate@hotmail.com

Price band: C

Entry 157   Map 8

Windermere Estate

Cool relief from the heat and stickiness of the coast, here in Munnar. Sprays of bougainvillea and morning glory cover the garden walls of this stunning spot, perched above miles of steep-sided tea estates and wooded slopes. It is green beyond imagination and as colourful as a Devonshire spring garden. The stable-like buildings are not particularly well soundproofed but perfectly comfortable, the cheaper rooms are being done up and the new planters' villas are generous with their space. Splash out on a room with a dreamy view. There is a long shaded terrace with wicker chairs and bicycles to borrow. You might find an embroidered alpine milkmaid watching you from the dining room wall, but the setting is stunning, the tranquillity total and the early morning or evening guided walk through the plantation takes you into a world of birdsong and arboreal paradise; return to tea and cakes. The trees are vast buttressed giants that play host to hundreds of species of birds and wild bee colonies, beneath which sprout the jungle-like plants. Breakfasts are good but evening meals are aimed at mild European palates.

Price	Rs6,850–Rs8,850. Cottages Rs7,650–Rs10,250. Villas Rs10,250–Rs14,250. Plus 15% tax. 25% discount June–August. Peak season: October–March.
Rooms	18: 10 doubles, 6 cottages, 2 villas.
Meals	Packed lunch Rs300. Lunch Rs400. Dinner Rs600.
Closed	Rarely.
Directions	From Kochi, cross Headwork's Bridge; right 2km before Munnar, pass Pothamedu viewpoint; 500m, entry thro' tea garden. Airport: Kochi (160km, 3 hrs).

Price band: D

Dr Simon John
Windermere Estate, Pothamedu, Munnar, Idukki, 685612

Tel	+91 (0)4865 230 512
Fax	+91 (0)4865 230 978
Email	info@windermeremunnar.com
Web	www.windermeremunnar.com

Entry 158   Map 8

Paradisa Plantation Retreat

Cicadas and calling birds, peace and tranquility in the Periyar Wildlife Sanctuary – and at this remote village guest house on the point of a tree-rich valley. Your attentive host, Simon, took on this challenging project in 1994; now the 26-acre site has its own access road. Set around are several private cottages, with panelled walls and ceilings in rich red and brown teak; Chettinad-style antique pillars add grandeur to the entrances and the smell of sweet honeysuckle infuses the air. With low-level lighting and lots of dark wood the rooms feel a touch sombre, but private verandas have comfortable recliners and the mood is relaxed and friendly. Home-cooked food in the open-sided, view-filled thatched restaurant is sometimes accompanied by classical costumed performers. Treks in search of wild elephants can be arranged, there's 7am yoga by the pool (lovely small classes) and ayurvedic massages at a nearby therapy centre. Or clamber to the top of the hill and watch the eagles soar off towards the sea. Crafted out of salvaged relics and with exquisite views, Paradisa has an unmistakable charm.

Price	Rs10,500–Rs12,600. Cottage Rs20,000–Rs24,000 for 4. Singles Rs9,450–Rs11,340. Plus 15% tax. Peak season: 20 December–10 January.
Rooms	10: 8 doubles. Cottage: 2 doubles.
Meals	Lunch & dinner Rs950. Plus 12.5% tax.
Closed	Mid-May to mid-July.
Directions	On the Kottayam/Kumilly road at Murinjapuzha; signed. Airport: Kochi (140km, 3.5 hours). Train: Kottayam (80km, 2 hours).

Mr Simon Paulose
Paradisa Plantation Retreat,
Murinjapuzha PO, Murinjapuzha, Idukki,
685532

Tel	+91 (0)4692 701 311
Email	paradisa@rediffmail.com
Web	www.paradisaretreat.com

Price band: E

Entry 159   Map 8

Amritara - Shalimar Spice Garden

A spectacular drive to get here, a garlanded welcome on arrival and kind helpful staff to take you to the thatched teak-clad huts (some detached) dotted among the trees. The setting is beautiful and secluded, the resort merging with the spice gardens that encompass it. All the cottages are different; there are coloured glass windows, patterned hangings, white walls, fresh flowers, comfy beds and beautiful bathrooms filled with potions. There is a touch of zen about the place: beams of sunlight illuminate the old spice tree in the lobby that lies across a wooden bridge; Ganesh the elephant god wears a garland of flowers. Wander through the ornamental spice gardens, take a book to the peaceful treehouse. You breakfast on mango, grape or pineapple juice and scrambled eggs at rough granite-topped tables outside, or, if you prefer, on your bedroom veranda. Dine at tables for two, order snacks by the pretty pool, enjoy an ayurveda massage by the open fire. All this and the Periyar Tiger Reserve 5km away – you may not see a tiger but wild elephants are common. Tranquil and mountain-cool.

Price	Rs6,000–Rs17,500. Plus 15% tax. Peak season: October-March; 20 December-10 January.
Rooms	20: 10 doubles, 10 cottages for 2.
Meals	Lunch & dinner from Rs750. Restaurants 5km.
Closed	Rarely.
Directions	Bus: Kumily (5km). Airports: Kochi/Thiruvananthapuram (4–5 hours).

Mr Abdul Gafoor
Amritara - Shalimar Spice Garden,
Murikkady PO, Kumily, Idukki, 685535

Tel	+91 (0)8041 306 352
Fax	+91 (0)8041 306 357
Email	reservations@anantara.in
Web	www.amritara.co.in

Price band: E

Entry 160   Map 8

Villa Jacaranda

The breakfast cloths are hand-embroidered, exquisite garlands of jasmine scent the bedrooms and frangipani flowers float in giant copper vessels: of such detail dreams are made at the serene Villa Jacaranda. This purpose-built guest house opened its stylish but sensuous doors in 2002 and has been charming guests ever since. There are sun-washed bedrooms, rattan-sprinkled verandas, delicious shower rooms and a tranquil garden with not a leaf out of place. North Beach is a 12-minute walk from here, in this wonderfully laid-back, hippy-chic corner of Kerala where tempting wares line the cliff top, and seashell-rich South Beach is even closer; the walks are spectacular. Return to a deckchair on your private terrace with a rattan blind to protect you from the sun; the top terrace (Room 4) glimpses the sea. Inside, white walls merge with pastel borders, floor tiles are inset with marble, and beautiful Aboriginal and Indian art hints at exotic travels. A perfect place to write, read or dream, with the added joy of fresh breakfasts made to order and ayurvedic massages to replenish the soul. The owner speaks excellent English.

Price	Rs3,300–Rs5,000. Plus 15% tax. Peak season: November–February.
Rooms	4 doubles.
Meals	Restaurant opposite.
Closed	End April to end July.
Directions	Situated on south cliff, near main temple. Airport: Thiruvananthapuram (80 mins). Train: Varkala (10 mins).

Mr Ajay Ojha
Villa Jacaranda, Temple Road West,
South Cliff, Varkala,
Thiruvananthapuram, 695141

Tel	+91 (0)4702 610 296
Email	villajacaranda@yahoo.co.in
Web	www.villa-jacaranda.biz

Price band: C

Varikatt Heritage

Minutes from the busy streets of Thiruvananthapuram, step through the door and back in time to the British Raj. Sundowners on the veranda, hunting trophies on the wall, whirring ceiling fans overhead. You half-expect a young Victorian, Miss Blanket, to appear (she fell in love with a tea-planter and followed her heart to find him, building this bungalow in the 1850s). Ever since they left, the house has remained with the same Indian family – and the sense of history remains. Antique rosewood furniture and family pieces sit beneath wood panelled ceilings, and big bedrooms have a genteel air, like the guest rooms in a favourite uncle's house. Rugs are scattered on tiled floors, cabinets gleam with china. It's very much 'look and touch' and Colonel Kuncheria (retired, Ghurkha Rifles) will delight in telling you their stories. Explore the city, then return to a walled garden strutted by hens, fragrant with nutmeg and sage, cinnamon and mango, and dozens of orchids lovingly tended. Cooking is the Colonel's pride and joy and he and his wife will join you for dinner – and may leave you with a riddle to ponder. What a treat.

Price	Rs3,500-RsRs5,500. Peak season: November-February.
Rooms	4: 2 doubles, 2 suites.
Meals	Lunch & dinner from Rs300.
Closed	Never.
Directions	50m from Cantonment Police Station, nearr the Secretariat; with big brown gates. Airport: Thiruvananthapuram (6km, 15-20 mins). Train: Thiruvananthapuram (3km, 10 mins).

Colonel Roy Kuncheria
Varikatt Heritage, Punnen Road,
Thiruvananthapuram, 695039

Tel	+91 (0)4712 336 057
Email	sales@varikattheritage.com
Web	www.varikattheritage.com

Price band: C

Entry 162   Map 8

Graceful Homestay

Helped by her brother Giles and his wife Elsy, Sylvia is high energy and smiley, a self-confessed workaholic. Through her work with the humanitarian organisation CARE she has travelled widely, gathering tales along the way. At the end of a suburban street, a whitewashed mass of arches and verandas give her modern house a colonial air, and Sylvia's collection of handicrafts – from Tanzanian wood carvings to metal work from Kosovo – cover the walls. Artefacts from Tajikistan are a recent addition. Meals are wonderfully relaxed affairs on the big balcony, but when Sylvia is off on her travels, Giles and Elsy, who live in the original family home on the other side of the lush garden, take over. Accept an invitation to eat at their place – Elsy is a wonderful cook of Keralan cuisine. Things are truly relaxed here, the family are always on hand, and the best thing is, you can be as independent as you like. The bustling centre of Thiruvananthapuram may be minutes away, but gazing out across a carpet of palms to the thin blue line of the Arabian Sea, you'd never know it. Great value.

Price	Rs1,500-Rs2,500.
Rooms	4 doubles.
Meals	Lunch & dinner Rs250.
Closed	Rarely.
Directions	From Thiruvananthapuram, taxi to Kumarapuram, or pick-up. Then Pothujanam road; 400m to Philip's Hill. House within compound. Airport/train: Thiruvananthapuram.

Ms Sylvia Francis
Graceful Homestay, PHRA 20-21, Philip's
Hill, Pothujanam Road, Kumarapuram,
Thiruvananthapuram, 695011

Tel	+91 (0)4712 444 358
Email	southernsafaris@yahoo.co.in
Web	www.gracefulhomestay.com

Price band: B

Gayatry (Traditional Cottages)

His wife and his neighbours thought he'd gone crazy, but Mr Ramesh longed to bring back something from his birthplace in Kottayam. And if that something was a traditional Nera house (dismantled, transported for hundreds of miles and rebuilt on top of his own home) then so be it. It worked. In fact, it worked so well that this veterans' tennis champion (he gives lessons) is now in the process of building another, this time in the garden, a little smaller, but with marvellous views of residential gardens and the cool mountains in the distance. You soon forget that you are perched atop the Rameshes' house: among the engulfing teak and foliage, this could be a treehouse, all warm with the woodiness of mango and jackfruit trees. Beneath the rafters, patter in bare feet around a spacious bedroom; and while the kitchen and bathroom may not be fancy, they make each house a great base for couples on longer stays. Breakfast or reading on your terrace are fine things, but best is spending time with Mr Ramesh and his delightful wife Rani, who loves people and all things Thiruvananthapuram. Special. *10-minute taxi to town.*

Price	Rs1,500.
Rooms	2 houses for 2.
Meals	Breakfast included. Restaurants 4km.
Closed	Rarely.
Directions	Airport: Thiruvananthapuram (13km). Train: Pangode Military (6km).

Price band: A

Mr and Mrs Ramesh
Gayatry (Traditional Cottages), T.C.
8/1828 Gayatry, Parakovial, Thirumala,
Thiruvananthapuram, 695006

Tel	+91 (0)4712 358 935
Email	ramesh_gayatri@yahoo.co.in

Friday's Place

Play safe and stay in the Tsunami House — it's hydrodynamically designed! Like a sophisticated treehouse it's Mark's "honeymoon house" with a bed suspended from the rafters and breathtaking treetop views. Your eco retreat in the backwaters of Kerala is Mark's dream; kingfishers swoop, parakeets nestle and there are plenty of beasties. A ferry arrival is the start of this Robinson Crusoe adventure; garlands and melon juice welcome you, Mark entertains you and his 'Man Friday', Jose, attends to your every need. The two spacious treehouse cottages raised on steddle stones are reached via thrillingly steep open stairs; the smaller two cottages have charming little verandas. Inside are generous beds with sturdy rubber mattresses, colourful mosquito nets, washbasins and solar fans. Lather yourself with ayurvedic soaps in the beautiful, communal, rainwater shower, then dine on fresh fish and river crabs in a space that doubles up for yoga; or retreat to your terrace. Water flows, birds trill, there's river swimming for the brave and a disco for dancers — way down the canal. A tranquil, tropical and exotic retreat. *Minimum stay three nights.*

Price	Full-board £105–£150. Singles £60. Peak season: October-March.
Rooms	5: 1 treehouse. 2 treehouses, 2 cottage suites, sharing shower.
Meals	Full-board only.
Closed	Rarely.
Directions	Boat transfer at Poovar Island Resort Welcome Area near Poovar Excise check post. Airport: Thiruvananthapuram (30km).

Mark Reynolds
Friday's Place, Poovar Island, Attupuram, Uchekkada, Thiruvananthapuram, 699506

Tel	+91 (0)4712 133 292
Fax	+44 (0)1428 741510
Email	amphibious_robinson_crusoe@hotmail.com
Web	www.fridaysplace.biz

Ethical Collection: Environment; Community. See page 264.

Price band: C

Wild Palms on Sea

An intimate guest house on a beautiful fishermen's beach — watch your supper being caught. It's run by gracious, humorous Justin and Hilda. White sands, swaying palms, a curvaceous pool, a profusion of flowers… gardening is Hilda's passion. Her other is masterminding a delightful staff at this, the family's second venture into the hospitality world. Built on the site of Justin's old family home, the main part of the hotel is new, and blends well into the landscape. The sitting room has a cosy family feel, the dining room overlooks the sea and a wide circular staircase meanders up to light, airy, traditional bedrooms with terraces: just what you need in the Keralan heat. Bed linen is snowy, mattresses are firm, water is solar-heated, bathrooms are unswish and sparklingly clean. Start the day with a scrumptious fruit smoothie, end it with an ayurvedic massage and a wholesome Keralan dinner washed down with a beer (there's fish and chips, too). Just 16km from the airport, a remarkably peaceful place from which to discover small villages — and miles and miles of undiscovered beaches.

Price	Rs1,795–Rs2,195.
Rooms	17 doubles & suites. Extra beds.
Meals	Lunch from Rs80. Dinner from Rs125.
Closed	Rarely.
Directions	Directions on booking.

Price band: B

Hilda & Justin Pereira
Wild Palms on Sea, Beach Road,
St Xavier's College PO, Puthenthope,
Thiruvananthapuram, 695586

Tel	+91 (0)4712 756 781
Email	wildpalms@vsnl.net
Web	www.wildpalmsonsea.com

Entry 166   Map 8

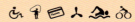

Karikkathi Beach House

Foreign diplomats come here for a break from the social whirl. Mr Sajjad's Beach House (now become two) is an unusual concept in the Indian travel scene. Both houses sit on a stunning part of terraced shoreline overlooking the ocean, the small shared beach shaded by swaying palms. Both houses have two double bedrooms and a cosy sitting room in between (you may book just one room or the house). The project was fuelled by Sajjad's despair at the burgeoning desecration of Kerala's coastal beauty so his houses, Swiss architect-designed, employ local materials and natural colours. The roof is palm thatch on lashed wooden poles, the floors are red tiles and the shuttered windows open to the horizon. The beds are comfortable, with crisp white sheets, mozzie nets and cotton throws; the shower rooms are spacious; the sea breezes are cool. There's a 'boy' on call and a chef comes to cook when and what you want — perhaps generous portions of fresh fish laced with local herbs and spices, lovingly served and accompanied by waves crashing on the shore. Pure escapism. *Wooden canoe & snorkel hire next door.*

Price	Rs7,920–Rs10,560 for 2. Peak season: November–April.
Rooms	2 houses for 2-4 (each with 2 doubles).
Meals	Full-board extra Rs990 p.p.
Closed	June.
Directions	Just before Surya Samudra Beach Garden, on main road 6km south of Kovalam. 5-min walk among palm groves from temple at Mulloor.

Mr Shaina Sajjad
Karikkathi Beach House, Mulloor
Thottam, Pulinkudi, Thiruvananthapuram

Tel	+91 (0)4712 400 956
Email	karikkathi@yahoo.co.in
Web	www.karikkathibeachhouse.com

Price band: D

Bangaram Island

As you sweep over this archipelago of reef-protected islands you'll catch your breath at the view. The whole experience is a taste of heaven, from the coconut drink served on arrival to the trip to the outer reefs (and diving) that follows early-morning yoga. This island is restricted to 100 residents so you get to know your fellow guests well: Italians and Brits, mostly. Staff are friendly too, serving delicious salads and fish curries with big smiles, lighting mozzie coils enthusiastically and keeping rooms spotless; volleyball games between staff and guests are an engaging extra. As for the shared houses, don't expect hot water or air con but ceiling fans and sea breezes, firm mattresses and open-air showers; for privacy we recommend the individual cottages aimed at families. Let the birds wake you and the waves lull you to sleep – no bed is further than 75 metres from the sea. Breakfast is 'full English', lunch is Indian, cocktails are international, dinner is served under the stars. There's a beach shack bar, badminton on the sands and an ayurvedic centre with blissful treatments and… hot showers!

Price	Full-board Rs8,500-Rs12,750.
Rooms	26: 23 twins/doubles in 5 thatched houses; 3 family cottages for 4.
Meals	Full-board only.
Closed	Rarely.
Directions	Fly from Kochi to Agatti Island, then boat to Bangaram Island (or helicopter during monsoon, mid-May to mid-September).

Price band: D

Shilendran Mohan
Bangaram Island, Lakshadweep
Tel   +91 (0)4843 011 562
Email   shilendran@cghearth.com
Web   www.cghearth.com

Karnataka

SwaSwara

Undulating hills give way, the jungle recedes to blue corduroy and Gokarna keeps its promise. Spread exclusively over 30 acres of lush paddy fields, coconut groves and tropical kitchen gardens, with 'Om' beach and its hippies the other side of the fence, SwaSwara prizes environment, solitude and the self. The Konkani stone cottages are simple but spacious and unusual too, each with a small garden, open-air sitting room and a rooftop meditation hideout to salute and farewell the sun. Your own slumber, behind drawn muslin, challenges notions of space in probably the largest beds in India. Feed the body first with baked pastries or dosas for breakfast, a prescribed ayurvedic thali for lunch, and finally with a magical four-course seafood dinner on the beach (no meat, and wine the only type of alcohol). The chefs offer private cookery lessons, while delightful manager Anjali will help walk off excess. For it is soul food that really matters here, with classes every day in hatha yoga, chanting and laughing, led by the swami inside the centrepiece blue meditation dome. Pampering has never been so pure. *Minimum stay five nights.*

Price	Full-board €900 per person per week. Plus 12% tax. Includes transfers & activities.
Rooms	27 cottage suites.
Meals	Full-board only.
Closed	Never.
Directions	Airport: Dabolim (3.5 hours).

Shilendran Mohan
SwaSwara, Om Beach, Gokarna,
Udupi District

Tel	+91 (0)4843 011 562
Email	swaswara@cghearth.com
Web	www.swaswara.com

Price band: D

Entry 169   Map 8

Terrace Gardens Guesthouse

Bangalore's (or Bengaluru's) first ever B&B has all the benefits of being bang in the middle of India's most cosmopolitan city, yet provides refuge from the bedlam. Set in a genteel tree-lined suburb, it is a breath of fresh air after the congestion and chaos a mere block away. With numerous terraces and a working garden centre brimful of carefully collected plant species, it delivers on the promise of the name. While the kitsch garden 'adornments' might make a garden gnome collector reel, the rooftop space, low night lighting and al fresco eating areas are a luxury in this choc-a-block metropolis. Rooms are varied and eclectic. Expect, in one block, clean-cut contemporary in red leatherette sofas, smoked glass showers, steel fridges and snappy uplighting, and 70s retro in another (chintzy curtains, floral paintings). All shine. Staff are wonderfully calm and helpful, breakfasts on the rooftop are tasty and your host, the effusive Kausalya, is a real 'people person'. Guests love the *me casa tu casa* feel of India's only 'gnomestay' – right in the heart of town.

Price	Rs1,800–Rs3,000. Singles Rs1,600–Rs1,850. Suites Rs3,300–Rs3,800. Plus 12% tax.
Rooms	21: 15 doubles, 3 singles, 3 suites.
Meals	Restaurants close by.
Closed	Never.
Directions	Off MG Road. Directions on booking.

Mrs Shankar
Terrace Gardens Guesthouse, 15 Brunton
Rd Cross, Bangalore 560025

Tel	+91 (0)8025 584 797
Fax	+91 (0)8025 591 047
Email	terracegardens@vsnl.net
Web	www.terracegardensguesthouse.com

Price band: B

Villa Pottipati

A 'home from home', as the staff call it proudly, minutes from the centre of Silicon City. This wonderfully restored heritage property that dates from 1873 flourishes an impressive entrance porch, elegant verandas and a tranquil country-house feel. Nor is there a shortage of modern enticements; you get laundry service, air conditioning and broadband in every room. Lunch is traditional Indian, served under the giant shivalinga tree; dinner is French, prepared by a chef from Puducherry and the food is delicious. Each serenely elegant room – the lightest are upstairs – feels like the master bedroom of a private house yet each is unique: a sitting area here, a mezzanine there, a private veranda; warm brown tones, local cottons, irresistibly deep baths (in most) and dark polished colonial pieces; some open to the cool outdoor pool. There's a wonderful courtyard with umbrellas and old mango trees for shade, and small parterres of crotons and seasonal flowers; these tree'd gardens help keep city bedlam at bay. Comfortable, beautiful and welcoming, Villa Pottipati is a joy.

Price	Rs3,500–Rs6,000. Plus 12% tax.
Rooms	8: 4 twins, 1 single, 3 triples.
Meals	Breakfast Rs200. Lunch & dinner Rs400. Plus 4% tax.
Closed	Rarely.
Directions	Airport: Bangalore (35km). Train: Bangalore (4km, 15 mins). Hotel is in Malleswaram district.

Price band: C

Mr Kannan P
Villa Pottipati, 142, 8th Cross,
4th Main Road, Malleswaram,
Bangalore, 560003

Tel   +91 (0)8023 360 777
Email   villapottipati@yahoo.com
Web   www.neemranahotels.com

Soukya Holistic Health Centre

The smiles are life-affirming, the health care is rejuvenating and the ayurvedic herbs are grown on site. In India's 'silicon valley', an hour's drive from Bangalore (now Bengaluru), is one of the best holistic centres in Asia. It is also the fulfilment of Dr Issac Mathai's dream, whose vision is to provide healthcare to all people (he runs a free clinic in town) and to heal using natural resources; the team here offer yoga, hydrotherapy, massage, nutrition and compassion. Not for the faint-hearted – no alcohol, smoking or meat – but cosseting and pampering by a dedicated staff and feasting on the freshest foods ever: dosas and idlis, pomegranate, pineapple and papaya, soups, salads and dhal of the day. Lovely spacious bedrooms in Keralan-style buildings have been individually decorated by wife Suja, with kingsize beds, desks, armchairs and, in some, outdoor showers. Floor-to-ceiling windows lead to private gardens vibrant with palms, ponds, birds and butterflies. There's an open-air dining hall, a thatched *shala* for yoga and a swimming pool – if your ayurvedic programme allows. Special.

Price	Full-board Rs9,900–Rs14,900. Singles Rs7,900–Rs12,900. Suites Rs24,700.
Rooms	25: 21 doubles, 4 suites.
Meals	Full-board only.
Closed	Never.
Directions	Airport: Bangalore (50 mins). Airport pick-ups arranged.

Dr Issac Mathai
Soukya Holistic Health Centre, Soukya
Rd, Samethanahalli, Whitefield,
Bangalore, 560067
Tel   +91 (0)8028 017 000
Email   info@soukya.com
Web   www.soukya.com

Price band: D

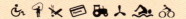

Shreyas Yoga Retreat

Pull through gates, enter landscaped grounds, be welcomed with a marigold garland and a cocktail by serene, white-robed staff. As you fill in a questionnaire about your mental and physical health, realisation dawns that this is no regular luxury hotel! Neither fawning nor pretentious, it is, simply, impeccable. Your stay is meticulously planned in terms of diet and treatments... be soothed by ayurvedic massage and exquisite food, guided meditation and a rejuvenating spa, contemplative spots scattered around the grounds, pukka astanga and hatha yoga twice a day and, if you choose, afternoons spent in the organic vegetable garden getting your hands dirty (and buffing your karma squeaky clean). Of course you can come just to soak up the atmosphere, stroll through the coconut groves, navel-gaze by the lotus-scudded ponds, snooze on the veranda (of your flawless tent or cottage), sunbathe on the white-cotton-swathed sunbeds by the pool or browse the exceptionally well-stocked library. Birds sing, frangipani wafts on the breeze. Welcome to heaven!

Price	Full-board £250-£285. Singles £190-£250. Yoga & sound meditation classes included.
Rooms	12: 3 cottage suites, 8 tents, 1 cottage for 5.
Meals	Full-board only.
Closed	Never.
Directions	Airport: Bangalore (50km, 1 hour). Transfers available on request.

Price band: E

Pawan Malik
Shreyas Yoga Retreat, Santoshima Farm, Gollahalli Gate, Nelamangala, Bangalore, 562123

Tel	+91 (0)8027 737 102
Email	reservations@shreyasretreat.com
Web	www.shreyasretreat.com

prs calm

Converted by the Premchand family as one of their own holiday retreats, "prs calm" is a slick, well thought out modernist secret on the outskirts of Mysore. With views of Lalitha Mahal Palace and the Chamundi hills beyond, there's a boutiquey vibe going on: a clean use of space, light from the atrium lobby, and carefully chosen objets d'art sharing walls with exquisite paintings by contemporary Indian artists. The rooms are perfectly designed, simple yet balanced, with all the necessities, from WiFi to writing bureaus. Service is excellent, meals are exceptional, fresh and innovative, and the chef is proud enough to invite you to watch him at work – a rare phenomenon. Your hospitable host, P K Suraj, is a modest mine of information and there's loads to do in and around town; the walk up the 1,000 steps to the Chamundeswari Temple for sunset is fabulous. There's an open flower-dense garden to lounge about in, with bowers and shady seating, and a beautiful glass-walled hall that's used for cultural evenings, conferences and conventions. Not a destination in itself but a hospitable and quietly special put-up.

Price	Rs5,000. Singles Rs3,800.
Rooms	5: 3 doubles, 2 twins.
Meals	Lunch & dinner from Rs550.
Closed	Rarely.
Directions	From Mysore Sports Club towards 'Sangoli Rayanna Circle' ('Chamundi Hills Circle'). Take Lalitha Mahal Palace road. prs calm on right after 0.30km.

Mr P K Suraj
prs calm, 25/65 Lalitha Mahal Palace Road, Nazarbad, Mysore District, 570011

Tel	+91 (0)8212 475 900
Fax	+91 (0)8212 475 933
Email	suraj@prs-group.com
Web	www.prscalm.com

Price band: C

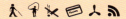

Entry 174   Map 8

The Green Hotel

Once used as a film set, this palace on the outskirts of Mysore was built around 1910 by the Maharaja for his unmarried sisters. Very nice it is too – not too big, with space and character, a taxi ride out of town, although noisy: the hotel is close to a busy junction. Rooms in the main house are easily the best – from the small Writer's Room to the large Maharani suite with four-poster and antiques, rooms are full of interest; the ground-floor 'Bollywood' rooms display framed panels of Indian film stars. Rooms in the garden annexe are plainly but pleasantly furnished and overlook the lawns. The garden is most fragrant and lovely at breakfast time and after dark (but mind the monkeys don't get your bananas!). In the shaded restaurant area, candlelit at night, the delicious food is Indian, Chinese or continental. Relax on the veranda or pick a window seat; there are books and games to dip into. There's also a travel desk manned by delightful staff. The hotel aims to be a model of sustainable tourism – hence the name – and all profits go to Indian charities and environmental projects.

Price	Rs2,950–Rs6,250. Garden annexe: Rs2,250–Rs3,750. Plus 10% tax. Peak season: October–March.
Rooms	31: 6 doubles, 1 suite. Garden annexe: 19 doubles, 5 suites.
Meals	Lunch & dinner Rs250–Rs500.
Closed	Rarely.
Directions	Leaving Mysore on the Madikeri road, hotel signed on right, 75m after Basappa Memorial Hospital. Your landmark is the old Premier Film Studios.

J Hilel Manohar
The Green Hotel, Chittaranjan Palace,
2270 Vinoba Road, Jayalakshmipuram,
Mysore, 570012

Tel	+91 (0)8214 255 000
Email	thegreenhotel@airtelmail.in
Web	www.greenhotelindia.com

Price band: C

Entry 175   Map 8

Rainforest Retreat

Rustic wild perfection in 20 acres of bird-bright rainforest. Orchids dangle from trees, pineapples abound, there's bamboo, hibiscus, ferns, silver oak – and when it rains it pours. Sujata, botanist, and Anurag, molecular biologist, are passionate about their eco retreat and fascinating to talk to. Sujata, or a trained guide, takes guests on free guided walks around the three-valley organic spice plantation (cardamom, coffee, pepper, vanilla, medicinal plants), explaining the benefits of bio-diversity and the methods employed to preserve it. The project was initiated with a grant from the NGS in 1997 and the proceeds of the guest house go towards an NGO; they also teach local farmers about organic farming. Three cottages hold two bedrooms each, not luxurious but lovely, with ladders to little galleries, wall hangings and open fires; tents under thatched covers have double cane beds. There are photo-voltaic panels for electricity, wood-burners for morning bucket showers and a brilliantly simple system that channels methane from cow to kitchen. Star-lit dinners, home-grown, are served around the camp fire. *Trekking.*

Price	Full-board Rs3,000-Rs4,000. Tents Rs2,000. Peak season: October-January; April-May.
Rooms	8: 6 doubles in 3 cottages, 2 tents.
Meals	Full-board only. Madikeri 20-min drive.
Closed	July/August.
Directions	Airport: Mangalore (150km, 4 hours). Train: Mysore (135km, 3 hours).

Drs Anurag & Sujata Goel
Rainforest Retreat, Kaloor Road,
Galkibeedu Village, Madikeri,
Kodagu, 571201

Tel	+91 (0)8272 201 428
Email	rainforestours@gmail.com
Web	www.rainforestours.com

Ethical Collection: Environment;
Community; Food.
See page 264.

Price band: B

Four Winds

The Colonel's enthusiasm for India and Kodagu (or Coorg – the 'Scotland of India') is infectious. Pradeep, as he likes to be called, is a remarkable man and easy company – the main reason for including his house in this book. It's a small modern bungalow with just two bedrooms (one is yours), an office and a dining and sitting room. It's simple and cosy, with pleasant views to the hills and few rules. The bed is comfy, you have a window onto a verdant garden, jolly curtains, good lighting, a basic bathroom, plenty of books. Outside is a small sit-out in the shade of a mango tree; the sitting room, shared with your host, is tiny, traditional, with wooden sofas and check covers, dark red floor and rug. If you choose to dine out the Colonel will take you into town. From arranging tours of the coffee estates to trekking, birdwatching, fishing and golf, Pradeep can organise it all; he'll even ferry you around if you are lucky. (He also collects guests who arrive by bus.) This is no obvious tourist destination, just a human encounter with the best of modern India. And good value.

Price	Rs3,000. Peak season: November–May.
Rooms	1 double.
Meals	Lunch & dinner Rs300.
Closed	Rarely.
Directions	2km from Madikeri centre on road to Mysore. The Colonel will pick you up, or direct you in more detail.

Lt Col K G Uthaya
Four Winds, Mysore Road, Madikeri,
Kodagu, 571201

Tel	+91 (0)8272 225 720
Email	speedy8@rediffmail.com

Price band: B

Serenity Homestay

Leave the town, the roads and your troubles behind for this 1920s villa and four acres of garden filled with orchids, honeysuckle and powder-puff roses – a haven of clean living and contemplation. Three dalmatians greet you and smiling, funny, passionate Monique settles you in. Come to paint, walk, read, retreat, splash in the swimming hole or join in yoga and meditation. Monique and her helpers provide salads and Indian and continental dishes as and when you want them – and rustle up romantic picnics with champagne. There are four distinct areas here: the villa, the cottage (with kitchenette), the family bungalow at the back (with a fun feel and a private garden), and a tented camp some distance away. Expect terracotta floors, low beds, open fires (it gets cold at night); the best rooms have colourful paintings and a Mediterranean feel. All is simple and homely, with something to suit everyone. This homestay is run as a charitable retreat with a hippie vibe, and the coffee's good too: Serenity is on an organic coffee estate and the views down the valley are exquisite.

Price	Rs1,500-Rs3,000. Singles Rs800. Peak season: October-May.
Rooms	Villa: 2 doubles. Bungalow: 3 doubles; 1 double sharing bath. Cottage for 4-7. Tents available.
Meals	Lunch & dinner Rs200-Rs500. BYO alcohol.
Closed	Rarely.
Directions	Directions on booking. Airport: Mangalore (140km, 3 hours). Bangalore (260km, 7 hours). Train: Mysore (128km, 3 hours).

Monique Somaya
Serenity Homestay, Krishnaraj Villa, Post Box 76, Madikeri, Kodagu, 571201

Tel	+91 (0)8272 224 976
Email	monique@bsnl.in
Web	www.serenityhomestay.com

Ethical Collection: Environment; Food. See page 264.

Price band: B

Entry 178   Map 8

The School Estate

Secret bowers and immaculate lawns, honeysuckle, rosewood, white cedar and wild fig: the gardens are luxuriant and the coffee bushes decorate 200 acres. The estate's comforts are decidedly luxurious and Rani's bright welcome a blessing after the drive to get here. This big attractive house, built by a German missionary, has huge old-fashioned carpeted bedrooms and a wonderful feel. There are antique rosewood beds with embroidered bedspreads, themed colours, pretty antiques, garden flowers and horticultural pictures. Large bathrooms are a little antiquated but perfectly fine, and two garden rooms share a covered veranda with a sofa – let the birds serenade you. There are many deliciously shady nooks outside, and the whole garden for the children to play in. Rani wears the traditional pinned sari and can recount many a Coorg yarn; Mr Aiyapa may whisk you off on plantation strolls, or to the elephant camp nearby; for quiet English moments there's a century-old pool table. Meals are exquisite, with dangerously good puddings; dine beneath the gaze of the ancestors or in the garden by candlelight… you'll be smitten.

Price	Full-board Rs12,000. Peak season: September–June.
Rooms	4: 3 doubles, 1 family room.
Meals	Full-board only.
Closed	Rarely.
Directions	From Mysore to Periyapatna. After Periyapatna cross., left to Sidapur. Right at Engilkere; tarmac road to bungalow. Airport: Bangalore (228km, 5 hours). Train: Mysore (90km, 2 hours).

Mrs Rani Aiyapa
The School Estate, Siddapur, Kodagu
Tel   +91 (0)8274 258 358
Email   school1@sancharnet.in

Price band: C

Tamil Nadu, Puducherry & Andaman Islands

Mayuram Eco Lodge

Paddy fields dotted with palms meet the Western Ghats – this is a beautiful place. Rajesh is a bubbling source of ideas on rainwater harvesting and other environmental issues and is re-establishing an indigenous forest on his estate. Close at hand are walks in wooded hills and among lakes – and the joy of swimming in mountain streams. Come when the rains have cooled the plains. The wide variety of habitat makes this a superb place for birdwatchers. US-educated Rajesh used his skills as an architect to design his guest house around a court with an ornamental pool, in keeping with the vernacular, and has the bedrooms opening onto a generous balcony that overlooks the estate. The farm is some distance from a main road so you do need to be certain you know where you are going. If Rajesh is not there himself he passes special pre-requests on to the servants; they may not speak much English but there is the most wonderful cook who cannot do enough to help you. Excellent Indian food is served in the small library. Serenely simple: a gem.

Price	Full-board Rs4,000. Peak season: October–March.
Rooms	4 doubles.
Meals	Full-board only.
Closed	Rarely.
Directions	135km from Thiruvananthapuram; 235km from Kochi. Directions on booking.

Mr Rajesh George
Mayuram Eco Lodge, Kallarackal Farm,
Govindaperri Village, Kadayam, Tirunelveli

Tel	+91 (0)4842 335 673
Fax	+91 (0)4842 343 474
Email	info@thegreenappleexperience.com
Web	www.mayuramlodge.com

Price band: B

Pallam Palace

From the winding road clinging to the Western Ghats, lime-green vistas full to bursting unfurl below. A tiny road wiggles through a village, then the track wends ever upwards, through a working coffee and pepper estate to end before an avenue of stately trees and an 18th-century palace built on holistic Vaastu principles. The building exudes a blissful quietude. Rooms, courtyards and verandas are multiple and wonderful in shape and style, lattice screens deflect torrential rains and encourage breezes, and minimalist design is enlivened by splashes of rich colour from paintings, linens and sweet vases of flowers. Soft-spoken Francis Fry is the man behind all this elegant beauty, and his passionate and unobtrusively compassionate approach touches staff, animals and all who stay; the place shines with bonhomie. Food from the gardens is mouthwateringly delicious, bedrooms are languorous and mattresses divine. Extravagant wildlife includes giant squirrels and barking deer, a cacophony of treetop birdlife soothes the soul and a swim under the tiered waterfall will stay in the memory for ever. *Opening September 2010.*

Price	Full-board Rs9,000. Singles Rs5,500. All activities included.
Rooms	6: 5 doubles, 1 single.
Meals	Full-board only.
Closed	Rarely.
Directions	From Dindigul, 3km before Vathalangunda, right onto W. Ghat Road. Thro' Pulavelli, left at Manjel Parappu, into village, left up cobbled road. Taxi essential.

Francis Fry
Pallam Palace, Rajakad Estate,
Manjel Parappu, Dindigul, 624212
Tel   +91 (0)4542 224 324
Email   robeshpg@gmail.com

Price band: C

Entry 181   Map 8

Lakeside

Discover the beautiful realities of rural southern India. English-born Peter and Dorinda Balchin, whose modest bungalow is tucked into colourful gardens overlooking Kamaraj Lake, greet guests as friends. This is warm-hearted homestay living, with the focus on the surroundings and local life, not deluxe extras. Choose a main house room or a cottage – 1980s-styling, built of local stone – with bedrooms a charming mismatch of furniture, a touch outdated, clean and colourful with tiled floors, high ceilings and authentic avocado bathrooms. Eat simply but well (Indian or continental) in luscious surroundings: the lake-view veranda for breakfast, the roof terrace for dinner. Indeed, with abundant gardens – a swirl of bougainvillea, alamandas, mango and papaya trees – and exotic bird and butterfly life on tap, you might stay here all day. But the Balchins, and the previous owner, a pioneer of the region's educational and environmental projects, have unrivalled local knowledge and will arrange guided nature walks and village visits. An unhurried Indian experience that sings its eco credentials beautifully.

Price	Rs2,200. Singles Rs1,500. Half-board Rs3,050 for 2; full-board Rs3,850.
Rooms	11: 5 twins/doubles, 6 cottage suites.
Meals	Breakfast Rs150. Lunch Rs250. Dinner Rs400.
Closed	April/May.
Directions	Dindigul towards Kodaikanal to Sembatti village, then Palani; 1st left towards Athoor. Ask for 'Boys Town', then towards Wild Rock. Arrange to be met in Athoor, or Dindigul.

Price band: B

Dorinda Balchin
Lakeside, Athoor, Dindigul, 624701
Tel   +91 (0)9894 563 935
Email lakeside@aol.in
Web   www.lakeside.co.in

Cardamom House

A retired British doctor, a traveller and a talker with comedic flair, Chris has poured energy into creating his utopia; his staff wear the broadest smiles and the whole place sweeps you into a warm embrace. The house stands at the foot of a steep hill, huddled in a horseshoe of scrub hills with views from the pretty garden across the lake to the Western Ghats. Divided between three buildings, bedrooms are a picture of taste and restraint – tiled floors, white linen, solar-powered showers, fresh flowers on bedspreads. Covered verandas crouch beneath bougainvillea cascading in every colour, creating hidden spots in which to escape into a book; the rooftop terrace sits beneath a nocturnal frenzy of stars. Ultimately, the feeling is of conviviality, of sharing the treat of discovering a moment of true happiness in the remote heart of rural India. Chris is passionate about the environment and social responsibility, guided trips to the village support the local community, and staff are in charge of the developing organic vegetable garden – the food is multicultural and exceptional. *Minimum stay two nights.*

Price	Rs3,300–4,100. Suite Rs4,000–5,000. Extra bed Rs1,500. Peak season: December–March.
Rooms	7: 6 doubles, 1 suite.
Meals	Breakfast Rs300. Lunch Rs450. Dinner Rs500.
Closed	April to mid June.
Directions	2km after Sembatti x-roads, on Madurai-Coimbatore road, left for Athoor, signs for house. Airport: Madurai (70km, 2 hrs). Train: Dindigul (27km, 45 mins).

Dr Christopher Lucas
Cardamom House, Athoor,
Dindigul, 624701

Tel	+91 (0)4512 556 765
Email	chrislucas@cardamomhouse.com
Web	www.cardamomhouse.com

Ethical Collection: Environment;
Community.
See page 264.

Price band: B

Cinnabar

Come to be cosseted – warm, positive, engaging Bala and Vasu love looking after guests and sharing their home. He is an organic fruit and vegetable farmer – their farmland garden is enchanting – and makes superb gourmet cheese (an Indian rarity). They designed and built their home themselves, and have added on two comfortable bedrooms behind the main house. Plump duvets conquer cold, blackwood floors are insulated with coconut coir and much of the water is rain-harvested. There are pine ceilings, appliqué bedcovers in beige and white, Vasu's watercolours and sweet touches: homemade chocolates, fresh flowers, a booklet about the fruit trees in the garden. You share the family sitting room and may meet daughter Vidya and three-legged Hero (the dog). A log fire smoulders in the evenings and Vasu cooks superb contemporary cuisine with a European slant. As-delicious breakfasts will set you up for the day and include their own bread, coffee, honey and milk. Bala can take you on walks, arrange golf and tennis, drop in on the local quiltmaker, show you another side to this busy hill station. A perfect homestay.

Price	Half-board Rs5,000. Peak season: May.
Rooms	2 doubles.
Meals	Half-board only.
Closed	Rarely.
Directions	From Kodaikanal Lake, right at telephone exchange, left into Chettiar Road, 300m on right. Airport: Madurai (129km, 3 hours). Train: Kodai Road (80km, 2 hours).

Ethical Collection: Food.
See page 264.

Price band: C

Bala Krishnan
Cinnabar, Chettiar Rd, Kodaikanal,
Dindigul, 624101
Tel   +91 (0)4542 240 220
Email cinnabarfarm@yahoo.com
Web   www.cinnabar.in

Entry 186   Map 8

The Bangala

After a bumpy drive to get here, bliss to step out of the car and into the arms of this heritage hotel. The town of Karaikudi is the centre of the Chettiars, a small coterie of families who wielded immense influence under the Raj, and their 'palaces' are thick on the ground in a scattering of dusty villages – imagine turning the corner to be met by an avenue of faded villas, mansions and mini-palaces from every era. The sparkling Bangala, more villa than hotel, is one of these, just a 15-minute walk from town, and run with kindness, charm and discretion. The atmosphere is fabulous old world with a strong Art Deco bias; imagine charming old family photographs and beautiful wooden doors with massive old keys. The Bangala is one of the few places that serves genuine Chettinad food (as is the custom, on banana leaves); so good is the food that many come for the Chettinad lunch alone. Evening meals are served in a beautiful dining room on old English china. All feels elegant, stylish and comfortable, like a country house whose owner, even when absent, is there in spirit. *Pool planned for 2010.*

Price	Rs4,000–Rs7,100.
Rooms	25: 12 doubles.
	New wing: 13 twins/doubles.
Meals	Breakfast Rs300. Lunch & dinner Rs500.
Closed	Rarely.
Directions	At the beginning of Devakottai Road, in the Senjai area.
	Airport/train: Trichy & Madurai (90km).
	Train: Chennai (428km).

Mrs Meenaksh Meyyappan
The Bangala, Devakottai Road, Senjai,
Karaikudi, Sivaganga, 630001

Tel	+91 (0)4565 220 221
Fax	+91 (0)4424 934 543
Email	thebangala@gmail.com
Web	www.thebangala.com

Price band: C

Entry 187   Map 9

Visalam

Extraordinary houses, extraordinary stories. Chettinad – land of the palatial houses – was chosen by the Chettiars (traders fleeing the weather of coastal south India) to showcase their wealth. Unusually, Visalam was built for a woman (daughters usually moved into husbands' houses) and has a feminine grace in its Art Deco curves. A sprawl of vast bays, stepped gables and classical pillars, the 1930s mansion's interiors are cool and serene: teak ceilings, tiled floors, shuttered windows and Art Deco furniture. The house is leased from the original owner's great-granddaughter and care has been lavished on its restoration – traditional egg plaster walls, handmade tiles; new slips seamlessly into old. Bathrooms are deluxe. Stately bedrooms with high raftered ceilings, white walls and teak furnishings have an uncluttered calm. Wake to breakfast by the pool or under the bougainvillea; take dinner on the veranda… Chettinad is known for its cuisine. Knowledgeable staff will show you the region including its skilled craft workers. Five-star comfort in a flawless restoration. *Cookery & craft courses.*

Price	Rs5,625.
Rooms	15: 9 doubles, 6 twins.
Meals	Lunch Rs650–Rs750.
	Dinner Rs800–Rs900.
Closed	Rarely.
Directions	Directions on booking.

Price band: C

Shilendran Mohan
Visalam, Local Fund Road,
Kanadukathan, Karaikudi, Sivaganga

Tel	+91 (0)4565 273 301
Fax	+91 (0)4565 273 111
Email	visalam@cghearth.com
Web	www.cghearth.com

Chettinadu Mansion

Slip through the gated entrance, under the white portico and into another world. This amazing, and gracious, 126-room mansion – in a village of 26 palatial Chettiar mansions – took ten years to complete at the beginning of the last century. In Russian-doll fashion, double doors open to reveal yet another marbled hall, yet another courtyard. Size is everything; the Marriage Hall, with its Italianate floor and inky granite pillars, is 70-feet long. You could spend half a day marvelling at ornamental ceilings, graceful archways, teak furnishings and decorative tiled floors. Bedrooms overlook the central courtyard on one side, with a street-side balcony on the other – a delightful spot for watching village life before retreating to the grandeur of a teak-carved bed. Ceilings disappear heavenwards, walls are painted and tiled in jewel-bright colours. White sheets, glass-topped tables and traditional clocks complete the elegant picture. Dip into the pool, work out in the gym, dine on wonderful Chettinad food before enjoying the sunset from the roof terrace. Mr Chandramouli is a true gentleman.

Price	Rs5,800. Singles Rs4,400.
Rooms	11 doubles.
Meals	Breakfast Rs300. Lunch & dinner Rs600.
Closed	Rarely.
Directions	Airport: Trichy (80km, 2 hours). Train: Chettinadu (3km, 5 mins).

Mr Chandramouli
Chettinadu Mansion, SARM House
(Behind Raja's Palace), TKR Street,
Kanadukathan, Sivaganga

Tel	+91 (0)4565 273 080
Email	info@deshadan.com
Web	www.chettinadumansion.com

Price band: C

Entry 189   Map 9

Bungalow on the Beach

Breathe in the sea air from your balcony, watch the fishermen in their boats, and the sunsets – heaven. Tranquebar (Tharangambadi) is a historic curiosity, the only Danish outpost in the Indian sub-continent. This small but elegant heritage hotel, opposite the Danish fort, next to a Hindu temple overhanging the sea, fuses the Tamil vernacular with Danish colonial architecture; its grand proportions and serene air will charm you. The 16th-century building is surrounded by well-tended lawns and frangipani, with a pool and a modest restaurant at the back; the service is willing if slightly unpolished but there are no other choices nearby. The entrance hall is cavernous and a new teak staircase leads to a blue and white panelled drawing room; the vast bedrooms are named after Danish ships that stopped here. Pretty patterned bedcovers set the theme, while pastel pinks and turquoises enliven white walls, dark-wood four-posters and stripped floors; all has been beautifully restored. Upstairs rooms have wide views from their balconies, and privacy. Continental breakfast can be served on the terrace.

Price band: C

Price	Rs3,500–Rs5,000. Gate House Rs3,000. Nayak House Rs1,000–Rs2,000. Plus 12.5% tax.
Rooms	17: Main House: 7 doubles, 1 twin; Gate House: 4 doubles, 1 twin, 1 triple; Nayak House: 2 doubles, 1 twin.
Meals	Breakfast Rs150. Lunch & dinner Rs350. Plus 8% tax.
Closed	Rarely.
Directions	Head inside the Danish Fort; hotel next to fort by the sea. Airport: Chennai (300km, 6 hrs). Train: Nagapattinam (24km, 45 mins).

Mr Devan
Bungalow on the Beach, 24 King St, Tharangambadi, Nagapattinam, 609313

Tel	+91 (0)4364 288 065
Email	sales@neemranahotels.com
Web	www.neemranahotels.com

Entry 190 Map 9

Kurumba Village Resort

An entrance between 'the fourth and fifth hairpin bends' gives a clue as to the spectacular setting. Surrounded by rainforests, sitting amongst gardens and spice trees, these views, scents and sounds will have you reeling. Watch the clouds swirl around the treetops from your dining table; wake to birdsong; send monkeys flying as you explore the maze of paths (often steep). You have a ringside view of the forest from your floor-to-ceiling windows; cool, white and spacious with tiled floors, bamboo furnishings and splashes of orange and lemon, suites have a contemporary chic, while pyramidal roofs and tribal ornaments add local colour. The simple elegance ensures nothing detracts from the kaleidoscopic world of nature that (almost) invades your room. Even bathrooms – crisp, modern, part open to the skies – have jaw-dropping windows. While away your time with binoculars on your veranda or floating in the infinity pool but don't miss the guided treks and tea estate tours. Food is delicious and abundant (Indian and continental). Gentle staff, sensational setting.

Price	Full-board Rs6,500. Double-storey suites Rs7,500.
Rooms	19: 17 cottage suites, 2 double-storey suites.
Meals	Full-board only.
Closed	Rarely.
Directions	Airport: Coimbatore (60km, 1.5 hours). Train: Mettupalayam (18km)

Sanjay Awatramani
Kurumba Village Resort, Ooty-
Mettupalayam Road, Hillgrove Post,
Kurumbadi, The Nilgiris, 643102

Tel	+91 (0)9323 421 823
Email	nilgiris@kurumbavillageresort.com
Web	www.kurumbavillageresort.com

Price band: C

Entry 191   Map 8

Footprint Bed & Breakfast

In a genteel street in south Chennai, near the boutiques, spas and global cuisines of Chamiers Road, is a modern set of apartments, a sanctuary B&B. Meet Rucha and Ashish, as keen to reveal to you the delights of Chennai as they are to welcome you here. In the two communal sitting and dining areas are sofas to sink into and an airy mix of contemporary western and South Asian styles. There are papers, magazines and travel books to entertain you, framed handmade prints to delight you, free WiFi to inform you and, in each minimalist bedroom, satellite TV. All has been thoughtfully considered; you get a choice of air con (remote controlled) or easy-to-open mosquito-netted windows; there's even a balcony for smokers. Bed linen is unusually crisp, rooms are city-peaceful, showers are hot and guests get a choice of pillows. To set you up for a trip to the city's museums and temples or a day's shopping (seek out saris and beautiful handblock cotton prints), the caretaker produces breakfast, delicious full-western or Indian, and served, should you like that, in your room. *Linked with Barefoot, Andaman Islands.*

Price	Rs3,000. Plus 10.3% tax. Long-stay prices on request.
Rooms	9 twins/doubles. One extra mattress per room.
Meals	Restaurants 5-minute walk.
Closed	Never.
Directions	South Chennai, near ITC Park Sheraton Hotel.

Price band: B

Rucha and Ashish Gupta
Footprint Bed & Breakfast, 2B Gayatri Apartments, 16 South Street, Sriram Nagar, Alwarpet, Chennai

Tel	+91 (0)9840 037 483
Email	rucha@footprint.in
Web	www.footprint.in

Hotel de L'Orient

In the pastel charm that is colonial Puducherry you could forget this is India. The hotel, formerly the French Department of Education, is a beautiful 18th-century mansion whose restoration has won a UNESCO award. Bedrooms are decorated with antiques, statuettes, rhinestone-studded oleographs and Savonnerie-style dhurries from the looms of Jaipur. From the vast and superior Chandernagore Suite to the crow's nest of Gingy (reached via a steep, ladder-like stair), each room is rich in individual character (and life's dull essentials are secreted away in dowry chests and teak cupboards). For a private terrace with pillared recess and terracotta floor, choose the Karikal Suite. Ground-floor rooms do get some noise (restaurant music, breakfast clatter) so go for a loftier, window-shuttered room with a balcony. These overlook the white sun-dappled courtyard where Creole food – a blend of French and Tamil – is elegantly served, as well as French breakfasts of tropical juices and jams. It's a romantic place, just two streets away from a sunset stroll along the promenade.

Price	Rs3,000–Rs6,500.
	Peak season: September–March.
Rooms	16: 4 doubles, 10 twins, 2 suites.
Meals	Lunch Rs350–Rs450.
	Dinner Rs350–Rs450.
Closed	Rarely.
Directions	In central Puducherry.
	Airport: Chennai (160km).
	Train: Puducherry (2km).

VJ Daniel
Hotel de L'Orient, 17 Rue Romain
Rolland, Puducherry, 605001

Tel	+91 (0)4132 343 067
Fax	+91 (0)4132 227 829
Email	sales@neemranahotels.com
Web	www.neemranahotels.com

Price band: C

The Dune Eco Beach Hotel

Scattered over a 30-acre swathe of Tamil Nadu coastline (interspersed with an organic farm, an ayurvedic spa, a tennis court, a jogging track, lush gardens, amazing pool and 47 dwellings of every description, each unique), this is one of the most creative, quirky and eco-groovy holiday villages in India. Built from reclaimed colonial houses, Chettinad palaces and planters' mansions, dwellings range from stylish, minimalist, air-conditioned villas to artists' houses with playful interiors to breezy thatched shacks near the beach. Bathrooms have open showers and aromatic oils, there are compost loos (good green fun!), private outdoor spaces and free bikes for all (you need them). Post-tsunami, trees, flowers and shrubs are being tirelessly replanted, organic fruit and vegetables joyfully grown, hens and cows nurtured; the seven-acre farm is brilliant for kids. Breakfasts are feasts of dosas, vadas, pancakes, patisserie and platters of fresh fruit; laid-back dinners are delectable. No loungers or life guards on the beach but the ocean frontage is fabulous, the buzz is irresistible and the staff are a delight.

Price	Rs5,500. Cottages Rs7,950. Houses Rs11,950. Villas Rs18,250.
Rooms	47: 17 doubles, 15 cottages for 2, 4 houses for 2, 11 villas for 2.
Meals	Lunch & dinner Rs500–Rs900.
Closed	Never.
Directions	East Coast Road (ECR) from Chennai. At Pondicherry ECR toll gate signs for The Dune. Airport: Chennai (2.5 hours). Train: Villupuram (1 hour).

Price band: C

Mr Sunil Varghese
The Dune Eco Beach Hotel,
Pudhukuppam, Keelputhupet,
Puducherry, 605014

Tel	+91 (0)4132 655 751
Email	booking@epok-group.com
Web	www.thedunehotel.com

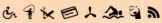

Barefoot at Havelock

The best places are the hardest to reach and this is one remote retreat. Forget clichéd coconuts and palms, listen instead to forest birds in acres of hanging orchids and tall mahua trees, a two-minute stroll from the most perfect white beach. No TVs, no phones, just stunning star-studded skies and sunsets over the Andaman Sea. The rough thatched eco cottages are made from bamboo, wood and palm leaves, and draw their water from the camp's own spring. The hardwood villas have floor-to-ceiling windows on three sides, shady verandas and opaque jungle-shower roofs that pull light in from the forest canopy; seven fan-cooled suites are on their way. Dine by candlelight on floor cushions at low tables accompanied by jazz and the sound of the ocean; the food is local fusion, organic, delicious and if, perchance, you tire of it they open a second restaurant soon. There's heaps to do: yoga or massage, kayaking around uninhabited islands, snorkelling or diving (book early), scootering here and there, bathing in the lagoon, swimming with elephants in the sea. And the breakfast parathas are delicious.

Price	Rs5,000–Rs12,000.
	Singles Rs4,500–Rs11,500.
	Suites Rs10,800–Rs13,800.
Rooms	19 cottages & villas for 2-4.
Meals	Lunch & dinner from $12.
Closed	Rarely.
Directions	Fly to Port Blair Airport. Ask for details of boat transfers when booking.

Samit Sawhny
Barefoot at Havelock, Beach No 7,
Radhanagar Village, Havelock Island,
Andaman Islands

Tel	+91 (0)4424 341 001
Email	reservations@barefootindia.com
Web	www.barefoot-andaman.com

Price band: D

Entry 195   Map 9

Sri Lanka

The Mud House

Under a hat of palm thatch sits a mosquito-swathed bed, a lantern to peer by and a branch for your clothes. Nearby is a western sink and loo, a dining hut just for you, and a shower and hammocks in open grounds: a cluster of eco huts is allotted to each couple, far enough apart to ensure privacy. Earthman Kumar (the manager) is blissed out by this place and delighted to show you why; nothing is too much trouble. He'll lead you to giant crocodiles and purple herons, white-throated kingfishers and bright butterflies, take you swimming in local rivers, bike or tuk-tuk you to historic temples, and invite you to pick the produce. Delectable labour-intensive Sri Lankan curries made by a local family are cooked and served with oodles of love. Staying here is like diving into nature: wake to a riot of peacocks, monkeys and frogs, join the water buffalo for a lily-strewn bathe, fall asleep to swishing trees under a canvas of stars. In the words of one guest: "It's romantic without trying to be"… just avoid harvest times when a neighbour's tractor works through the night. For families and nature lovers it's paradise.

Price	Full-board $180. Singles $110. Most guided excursions included.
Rooms	10 huts.
Meals	Full-board only. Full-board for your driver included.
Closed	Rarely.
Directions	Arrange to be met in Anamaduwa.

Tom Armstrong
The Mud House, Pahaladuwelweva,
Anamaduwa, Anuradhapura

Price band: C

Tel	+94 (0)7730 161 91
Email	info@themudhouse.lk
Web	www.themudhouse.lk

Alankuda Beach

Leave the perfunctory little towns behind and wash up at a golden sand peninsula and a turquoise sea: Alankuda's setting is supreme. It's a funky set-up created in 2006, a cool compound of sun-bleached wattle, daub and thatch cabanas off a corridor of coconut matting. It's more glamorous than luxurious and shabby-chic in style. You get a gorgeous chill-out dining area with sensational views of sparkling infinity pool and glittering sea, a beach shack with hammocks, an ocean swing, twig-woven screens, vibrant cushions everywhere. The door-less cabanas are open to the elements and the sound of the sea, and their bamboo-spout showers (refreshingly cold!) are a pad away in each private garden; mattresses for kids lie under a mosquito canopy. The villas are grander in dimension and much more substantial. Come November to April before the seas get choppy and the winds rise; come above all to gawp at whales and pods of dophins – thrilling! Marine activities are organised daily, an all-inclusive treat. The food is terrific too, served buffet style in terracotta urns, fresh from the sea.

Price	Full-board $120-$300 for 2. Villa $240-$600 for 4. Extra bed $40. Plus 12% tax. Expeditions included.
Rooms	6: 4 cabanas for 2-4, 2 villas for 4–10.
Meals	Full-board only.
Closed	Rarely.
Directions	Directions on booking.

Viren Perera & Giles Scott
Alankuda Beach,
Alankuda, Kalpitiya, Puttalam
Tel   +94 (0)7735 070 88
Email   info@alankuda.com
Web   www.alankuda.com

Price band: D

Entry 197   Map 10

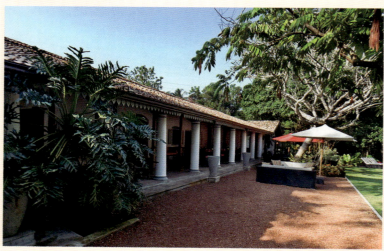

The Wallawwa

Ten minutes from the airport: tall jackfruit and mango trees, coffee bushes and strelitzia frame a gracious croquet lawn and a secluded pool. 'Wallawwa' is Sinhalese for the primary home of an aristocratic family and this generously proportioned manor house has real pedigree. Built 200-plus years ago for the head chieftain of Galle, it was later occupied by the RAF, then bought by a Kandyan lawyer with a passion for gardening and books (his gardens and library remain); now it's a super-luxe post- or pre-plane sanctuary with ten cool suites peppered around a central courtyard. Entrepreneurial Brit with an eco-heart Mike Davies has combined his loves of cutting edge design, quirky style and deep comfort with his well-trodden travel know-how. An international menu that would be at home in the hippest eateries of Sydney or New York is served under the lengthening shadows of the veranda, and your tropical-styled room (the spacious garden suites with thick stripy outdoor sofas) will provide you with the comfiest bed in the land – providing the coolly tranquil spa hasn't floored you first.

Price	From $140. Suites from $180.
Rooms	14: 4 twins, 10 suites.
Meals	Lunch from $7. Dinner from $15.
Closed	Rarely.
Directions	Directions on booking.
	45–min drive from Colombo.

Ethical Collection: Food.
See page 264.

Price band: D

Henry Fitch
The Wallawwa, Minuwangoda Road,
Near Negombo, Kotugoda, Colombo

Tel   +94 (0)1122 810 50
Email   enquiries@thewallawwa.com
Web   www.thewallawwa.com

Max Wadiya

Behind high white walls on the road to Galle, a gracious lawn links two colonial-style villas and sweeps to the beach. The ocean's roar becomes your companion: beyond the garden gate lie miles of light golden sands and safe swimming. Beautiful coastline greets you from sea-view verandas in the luxury suites and upstairs rooms; the room downstairs opens to the gorgeous gardens. Here are dining gazebos, hammocks and coconut palms – relax with a juice from the bar. All is unpretentious, light, clean and wonderfully homely; the suites in the newer villa are vast, with kitchenettes and sofas. Terracotta tiles team with cream walls, teak and jackfruit wood, four-poster mosquito-netted beds and bright jewel colours – but note, you sleep close to the main road and the rumbling railway. Smiling, kind and super-calm, manager Rangan oversees delectable Sri Lankan and fusion dishes, with local fish and meat, papayas and bananas from the grounds. A lovely launch pad for southern Asia's largest buddha, and World Heritage Galle. But it's the ocean that is the biggest pull.
Ayurvedic massage, yoga & cookery classes.

Price	Full-board $210–$300.
Rooms	5 suites in 2 villas.
Meals	Half-board available on request.
Closed	Mid-May to mid-July.
Directions	2km south of Ambalangoda. 85km south of Colombo on Galle Road, 25km before Galle.

Ruth Max
Max Wadiya, Galle Road (Parrot Junction), Madampe, Galle

Tel	+94 (0)9122 579 26
Fax	+94 (0)9122 575 10
Email	max.wadiya@gmail.com
Web	www.maxwadiya.com/home.html

Ethical Collection: Environment; Community.
See page 264.

Price band: D

The Sun House

This is a place that encourages drifting – from elegant sitting room to breezy bedroom, from cool pavilion to tropical garden. Gleaming white, wrapped around by verandas and privacy, yet a short stroll from Galle, this former merchant's house has a stylish colonial charm and a joyfully eclectic touch. It was the first boutique hotel in Sri Lanka. Sofas are huge, artwork is bright, and books, objets and glorious flowers beautify shelves and tables. Bedrooms are chic airy spaces of vibrant colour and gorgeous attention to detail: pretty baskets, antique towel rails, white mosquito drapes. Some have balconies or verandas, all have stunning views, and the Cinnamon Suite, up sisal-covered stairs, is open-plan and spectacular, with 360 degree views over Galle and a bathtub on the balcony: gaze at the stars or watch the wildlife. After a day at the Fort or on the beach, slip into the sparkling pool, enjoy up-country tea or house cocktails, then dine by candlelight on some of the island's finest cuisine. Manager Henri is fabulously flamboyant, service is friendly, perfect. A blissfully romantic getaway.

Price	$175–$260.
Rooms	7: 4 doubles, 1 twin, 2 suites.
Meals	Breakfast SLRs1,200. Lunch SLRs1,500. Dinner SLRs2,950.
Closed	Rarely.
Directions	Directions on booking. 3-hour drive from Colombo.

Price band: D

Geoffrey Dobbs
The Sun House,
18 Upper Dickson Road, Galle

Tel   +94 (0)9143 802 75
Fax   +94 (0)9122 226 24
Email info@thesunhouse.com
Web   www.thesunhouse.com

Entry 202   Map 10

The Dutch House

High above the hustle of Galle — yet only minutes away — is this sanctuary of understated style. Cool but not edgy, luxurious but not showy, it exudes space, calm and undeniably good taste. The one-storey house, built in 1712, classically proportioned, elegantly colonnaded and surrounded by manicured gardens, is so airy and peaceful you feel utterly private, even when the house is full. Light-filled rooms are a sophisticated marriage of antique and modern: writing desks and contemporary art, polished floors and soft sofas. Suites have an easy-going grandeur with four-poster beds, silk taffeta curtains, fine Dutch antiques and huge doors opening to luscious grounds. Bathrooms, with claw foot baths and wooden washstands, add a delicious colonial touch. Breakfasts are indulgent, served anytime, anywhere. Explore rainforests, tea plantations and beaches — if you can pull yourself away from the perfect croquet lawn and the infinity pool below, resplendent with greenery and views to the Indian Ocean. Drift next door to sister hotel The Sun House for an exquisite candlelit dinner. Stately, spacious, calming.

Price	$320.
Rooms	4 suites.
Meals	Lunch SLRs1,500. Dinner SLRs2,950.
Closed	Rarely.
Directions	Directions on booking.
	3-hour drive from Colombo.

Geoffrey Dobbs
The Dutch House,
23 Upper Dickson Road, Galle

Tel	+94 (0)9143 802 75
Fax	+94 (0)9122 226 24
Email	info@thesunhouse.com
Web	www.thedutchhouse.com

Price band: E

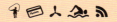

Entry 203   Map 10

Kahanda Kanda

High on a hill, overlooking a tea plantation, is Kahanda Kanda – KK, as it is known by its engagingly charismatic staff. If KK were a movie it would be *Casablanca*: classic, classy and utterly memorable. Designer-owner George bought the 12-acre plot in 1999, a fitting backdrop to his tropically sumptuous talent. The open-air *umbalama* is one gorgeous hangout – for lounging and gazing on the luscious coco-palm canopy – while the dining area exudes a minimalist chic; intimate dining tables can also be set up at small stunning spots on request. You might breakfast by the black and turquoise infinity pool (on fresh fruits and delectable hot pancakes), then indulge in a little massage or yoga, take a tuk tuk to Galle Fort (the World Heritage Site is 20 minutes away) or spin off to the beach. In the huge, open-plan, light-filled suites, windows are lined with wooden louvres, polished concrete floors gleam in double-showered wet rooms half open to the sky, and hand-loom throws in mulberry and ochre dot white mosquito-netted four-posters and Barcelona chairs. Heaven in Sri Lanka.

Price	$235–$350.
Rooms	5: 3 villa suites, 2 suites.
Meals	Lunch $22. Dinner $30.
Closed	Rarely.
Directions	140km from Colombo.

George Cooper
Kahanda Kanda, Angulugaha, Galle
Tel   +94 (0)9122 867 17
Email manager@kahandakanda.com
Web   www.kahandakanda.com

Price band: E

Saffrons Beach Villa

Be the queen of the beachside scene. It's a first for this coast, this world-class villa, glass framed and ocean-fronting. With its dramatic cutaway walls and ceilings, streamlined Danish furniture and colour-contrast throws, giant carp pond and, on a coco-palmed lawn, towering light installation, it was intended as an über-glam holiday spot for a successful Aussie media couple. But the budget went OTT, resulting in its conversion from divine villa to divine hotel. No sign of sour grapes: Ian and Bryan gladly show you, cocktail in hand, around the two lofty storeys, happy to share their palatial pad and the talents of their world-cuisine chef. They are also serious greenies, having installed a humidity harnessing system for the drinking water, contributed equipment to local schools, and distributing their coconut harvest to villagers. Gaze beachside from the breakfast pavilion (the occasional hum of the local train in the distance) as you contemplate the day ahead: yoga on the lawn, a siesta in the hammock, a quick ocean dip. Or a bath in the majestic egg-shaped beach-view tub upstairs. *Minimum stay three nights.*

Price	Low season from $299 per suite; high season $775–$990 for whole villa.
Rooms	Villa for 6 (3 suites).
Meals	Lunch $16. Dinner $22.
Closed	Rarely.
Directions	Directions on booking.

Bryan Smith
Saffrons Beach Villa, Habaraduwa, Galle

Tel	+94 (0)9122 827 77
Fax	+94 (0)9122 826 76
Email	bryan@smithemail.com
Web	www.saffronsbeachvilla.com

Price band: E

Taprobane Island

Wade through rolling surf – or atop an elephant! – to this tear-shaped islet jutting out from the emerald waters of Sri Lanka's south coast. Stone stairs bring you to a neo-Palladian mansion, a jewel in the ocean, built in 1927 by a bohemian count. Eight verandas encircle a salon spilling over to rambling gardens, dining tables are placed for once-in-a-lifetime views, attentive staff and talented chef are to hand... there are day beds, banquettes, outdoor sofas, an infinity pool over the ocean and massages on request. Just add lapping tides and moonlight for the ultimate in indulgence. Comfort blends with a delightful aesthetic in the salon, with its high vaulted ceilings and cushiony sofas in a palette of cream and white. Five spacious bedrooms are similarly gorgeous: bright silk on four-poster beds and lamps highlighting vivid hangings on pristine white walls, antique wooden chairs, scatter cushions. You can see the flower-speckled coast opposite but the island is exclusively yours and there's nothing between you and the South Pole. Absolute privacy, total peace and as romantic as luxury can get.

Price	$1,000-$2,200.
Rooms	Villa for 10 (4 doubles, 1 twin).
Meals	Full-board extra $40 p.p. (optional).
Closed	Rarely.
Directions	200 yards off the coast of Weligama Bay; 30 mins south of Galle; 3.5 hours south of Colombo.

Geoffrey Dobbs
Taprobane Island, Weligama, Galle

Tel	+94 (0)9143 802 75
Fax	+94 (0)9122 226 24
Email	info@thesunhouse.com
Web	www.taprobaneisland.com

Price band: F

Entry 206   Map 10

India is vast: there are so many contrasts and such diversity. With a billion people it can seem noisy and chaotic – and yet an immense serenity and peace can be found. Seventeen major regional languages, hundreds of dialects, a sophisticated civilisation that goes back 5,000 years and the place where four major religions – Hinduism, Jainism, Sikkism and Buddhism – were founded. Then there are the historical and colonial influences, the many cuisines, and the rich variety of landscape, vegetation and wildlife. You can visit stunning coastline, tree-rich hills, vast plains, deserts, and snowcapped peaks.

Some states are so large that one section is dramatically different from another. We tell you a little about the regions below; a good travel guide will tell you far more.

You may notice that large swathes of the country do not include any of our Special Places, particularly the central and northern regions. The reasons vary: a lack of good accommodation; undeveloped tourism; extreme living conditions; a sparse terrain; political instability.

Assam, Sikkim & West Bengal

The Brahmaputra River feeds Assam's lush valleys and more than half of India's tea is grown here. In the stunning grasslands of the World Heritage Kaziranga National Park you may be lucky enough to see one-horned rhinos, Hoolock gibbons and elephants.

Peaceful Sikkim is dominated by the snow-capped peaks of India's highest mountain, Kanchenjunga (8,586m); in this tiny and beautiful state are richly decorated Buddhist monasteries, lime-green rice paddies, orange groves, mountain lakes and smiling, gentle people. You need a permit to visit Sikkim.

In West Bengal lie the Raj-era hill stations of Darjeeling and Kalimpong and the wildlife-rich Sunderbans. The state capital Kolkata (formerly Calcutta) is the intellectual heartbeat of the nation.

Best time to visit: Assam November-April. Sikkim mid-October to mid-December; March to late May. West

Photo: The Brunton Boatyard, entry 142

Bengal October-March (lower plains); October-December & March-May (hills).

Himachal Pradesh, Ladakh & Punjab

The 'Abode of Snow', Himachal Pradesh borders Ladakh, the Punjab and Tibet. Its mountain landscape is thick with oak, deodar and pine at lower altitudes, alpine meadows higher up. The Kangra Valley is filled with apple orchards and is the seat of the Tibetan government-in-exile in Dharamsala. 'Queen of Hills' Shimla (Simla) was declared the summer capital of the British Raj in India.

Ladakh, to the north, is a high-altitude desert and its capital, Leh, was once the central trading point between the Punjab and central Asia, Kashmir and Tibet.

The vast, dry plains of the Punjab were transformed by the 'Green Revolution' of the 1960s and this area now produces much of India's wheat, rice and dairy products. Punjabi culture has its own language, religion, cuisine and music. Revel in the beauty of the awesome Golden Temple – the very heart of Sikh religion – at Amritsar.

Best time to visit: Himachal Pradesh mid-May to mid-October; late December-March. Ladakh May-October. Punjab October-March.

Uttar Pradesh & Uttarakhand

Uttar Pradesh is not only the cultural heartland of Islam, famous for the soul-stirring Taj Mahal and other great Islamic monuments, but also the spiritual heartland of Hinduism – the holy and vibrant city of Varanasi lies on the sacred Ganges River.

In Uttarakhand watch the flickering candles float down the Ganges at Haridwar and be mesmerised by the chanting at sunset; spot tigers in the Corbett National Park, go river-rafting in Rishikesh or on superb treks in the Kumaon mountains; or visit the popular hill stations of Mussoorie and Nainital. Best time to visit: October-March.

Delhi & Haryana

India's crazy capital, Delhi, is the transport hub of northern India and home to 16 million people; it's a fascinating and challenging place that teems with paradoxes. Modern cars and

Photo: Kalmatia Sangam Himalaya Resort, entry 35

buses, cycle rickshaws and the odd elephant pack out the roads; shopping malls rub shoulders with souk-like bazaars; smart neighbourhoods sit alongside desperate slums.

Haryana surrounds Delhi on three sides, and the flat and fertile river plains mean a lush green landscape.

Best time to visit: October-March.

Rajasthan

The largest state in India, glorious Rajasthan is also one of its most popular tourist destinations. Incredible images abound: men in red, yellow and orange turbans with coiffed moustaches, women in dazzling mirrored saris, children with bells on their ankles, ambling camels, beggars, vibrant colours. In the 'Golden City', the desert fortress town of Jaisalmer, are incredible carved balconies, mirror mosaics, elephantine entrance gates, latticed screened havelis. From a rooftop in the 'Pink City', Jaipur, gorge on Indian sweets and watch the fireworks during the Diwali festival. In the 'Blue City', Jodhpur, square houses are painted blue – visit the coloured-glass fort. Pushkar is a pilgrimage site with 400 temples and a holy lake, and its camel fair in November is one of the most colourful spectacles on earth. Find tigers, leopards and sloth bears in Ranthambhore National Park.

Best time to visit: mid-October to mid-March.

Gujarat

Gujarat is immensely friendly, off the tourist trail, and claims a third of India's coastline; its culture has been influenced by the Dutch, Portuguese, British, Mughals, Arabs and Parsis. The capital Ahmedabad has been a major centre for India's textile trade since the 15th century – visit the fabulous Calico Museum. Or learn about the hand-made embroidery in Kutch from elaborately dressed villagers in mirrorwork dresses and heavy silver bracelets. Officially Gujarat is one of India's 'dry' states, though you can buy beer and wine in most hotels.

Best time to visit: October-March.

Madhya Pradesh & Maharastra

Tourists tend to overlook this state even though it has some of the best heritage sites in India and is friendly and relatively hassle-free. Madhya Pradesh (MP) also has the highest percentage of forest in India and over 20% of the world's endangered tigers; you can see them in three of the national parks (Kanha, Pench and Bandhavgarh).

India's second most populous state, Maharastra, contains the glitzy state capital of Mumbai (Bombay) with its vast slums and skyscrapers, western luxuries and Bollywood films. Or head up to one of the hill stations where Mumbai-ites go to cool down.

Best time to visit: Madyha Pradesh

September-February.
Maharastra October-March (coast); September to mid-June (hills).

Goa

The smallest yet one of the richest states in India, laid-back Goa's culture stems from its Portuguese colonial past. There are whitewashed churches, crumbling forts and yellow, ochre, green or indigo houses with white trims. The Goans are extremely friendly and make tourists very welcome. The state capital Panaji (Panjim) is in the northern part and attracts many of India's Catholic pilgrims. The market town of Mapusa and the vibrant flea market at Anjuna are also highlights. North of Mandrem you will find the Goa of your dreams: a scattering of coco-huts, and fishermen's boats pulled up on the sands. In the south, Palolim beach is renowned for its beauty. Head inland and explore Goa's wildlife sanctuaries and the splendid Dudhsagar Falls.

Best time to visit: October-March.

Kerala & Lakshadweep

A narrow strip of land between the Arabian Sea and the Western Ghats, Kerala is a mosaic of inland waterways and lakes smothered in lilac water hyacinths, swaying palm trees by lime-green paddies, heady spice plantations and fascinating rituals. An idyllic way to travel from Alappuzha (Alleppey) is by rice barge. In Kochi (Cochin) you can forage in the antique shops for a glimpse of Jewish, Keralan, Portuguese and British culture or watch fishermen demonstrate their ingenious Chinese fishing nets. Head for the hills and the spice plantations and see how tea, coffee, vanilla, cloves, cardamom, rubber and pepper grow. In villages further north you may see the Theyyam, an all-night holy dance where the performers experience a trance-like state. Here, visit thriving Calicut, the remote northern beaches and the tourist-quiet Wayanad Wildlife Sanctuary. Chill out on the palm-fringed beaches at Varkala and Kovalam and book in for some ayurvedic massage to rub away any remaining tension. Dive off unspoilt Bangaram Island, whose coral atolls are home to hundreds of varieties of dazzling reef fish.

Best time to visit: October-March.

Karnataka

Karnataka stretches from the white-sand beaches of the Arabian Sea to the tree-covered steeps of the Western Ghats where coffee, spices and fruit flourish – and also the dusty plains of the Deccan Plateau. Bustling Bengaluru (Bangalore) is the IT and call-centre capital of India. In the Kodagu (Coorg) area you will meet the friendly people from this distinct ethnic group; they delight in sharing their unique culture, and their delicious tangy pork-rich cuisine. In Mysore buy silks and sandalwood or visit the traditional Amba Vilas Palace.

Best time to visit: September-February.

Tamil Nadu, Pucucherry & Andaman Islands

Tamil Nadu is culturally and physically beautiful, extremely friendly and relatively unspoilt. Cool off in the hill-stations of Ooty and Kodaikanal on the way to busier Kerala and have fun in Chennai (Madras) the 'Detroit of South Asia'. Hike in the Nilgiri Hills, and visit the fascinating Chettinad region with its 18th-century mansions.

Puducherry (Pondicherry), established as capital of all the French territories in India in 1674, has tree-lined boulevards, Catholic churches, colonial mansions and chic cafes. Stroll along the 3km seafront, the St Tropez of southern India, and visit the Gandhi statue and the famous Sri Aurobindo Ashram.

Snorkel through the mangroves on that still relatively untouched paradise, Havelock Island – or swim with elephants in the crystal-clear sea.

Best time to visit: Tamil Nadu and Puducherry December-February. Andaman Islands December-April.

Sri Lanka

Style meets substance on this pretty little gem. Sri Lanka ('Venerable Island') lies 31km off the southern shores of India, but, with its Buddhist heart, its uniquely intricate cuisine and its history as a trading port flanked by West Asia and the Far East, it is no mere drop in the ocean. The capital Colombo sees itself as a new international hub, burgeoning with chic eateries and boutiques. From there it's an inland trip through jungly trails to the emerald heights of Kandy – the country's 'Vatican' and seat of the ancient Sinhala kings – before passing on to world heritage sites with millennia-old Buddhist relics, testament to the country's spiritual core. Meander through the vertiginous heights of traditional tea country in Nuwara Eliyah, where high teas are taken by cosy fires in colonial plantation homesteads as the mists gather over the horizon. Or snake down the pristine west coast, with its azure seas and blond sands. Bear witness to European history in Galle, a 16th-century colonial fort, or catch gnarly surf breaks in sheltered coves, where, as the sun sets, you can buy supper straight from the wide-smiled fishermen on the beach. Up and down the coast, ayurveda, yoga and meditation retreats, elephant and tiger safaris and whale-watching adventures will keep you coming back for more.

Best time to visit: October–April.

Photo: The Dutch House, entry 203

Getting around

India has one of the biggest rail networks in the world, and probably the busiest in terms of passenger numbers, so train journeys are a great way to see the country and meet people. An excellent beginner's guide to train travel in India can be found at www.seat61.com/India.htm. The Indian Railways website gives train times and fares, although it can be confusing to use (www.indianrail.gov.in). Many routes get fully-booked, especially at weekends, so do book in advance if possible. One of the easiest ways to do this is to organise an 'Indrail' pass – this allows you to pre-book some or all of your travel via the UK's IndRail agency (SD Enterprises, www.indiarail.co.uk). You can also book train tickets online using the government-sponsored service at www.irctc.co.in, although there is a limit to the number of journeys you can book each month (currently ten).

In Sri Lanka too, trains are a cheap, safe and enjoyable way to get around. The official Sri Lanka Railways website is www.railway.gov.lk.

You can also organise a car and a driver, or a taxi, and you can make use of the vast network of internal flights. The owners in this guide are a great resource when booking a car and driver; they often know the best local companies (with excellent and knowledgeable drivers) and get good prices. Note that many hotels do not have drivers' facilities so the car may have to double up as the driver's bedroom. Taxis are a cheaper option for shorter journeys, and don't forget the trusty rickshaw – ideal for whizzing round cities.

Place names

Many towns in India have changed their names in recent years, for example Alleppey (now Alappuzha), Cochin (Kochi), and Pondicherry (Puducherry). We have generally used the new names, but both names are often still in common (and official) usage. Transcription from a different alphabet can also lead to variations in spelling, so do check carefully.

Visas and health

You need a visa to enter India; applications are handled by the India Visa Application Centre (http://in.vfsglobal.co.uk). The easiest way to apply for a visa is by post; allow at least two weeks for its return. Visitors to Sri Lanka do not need visas. You will also need immunisation – and possibly anti-malarial medication – before you go; contact your local doctor for advice.

Culture clashes

The beaches in India and Sri Lanka are undeniably beautiful but for fishing communities they are both workplace and home. Scantily clad tourists can cause offence, and topless sunbathing is intolerable. Local women seldom bare their skin and would certainly be grateful if you followed their example –

particularly around religious sites. Communities visited by tourists sometimes complain that their children are abandoning school to hound tourists for money. So, although it may go against your instincts, please do not give money, sweets or trinkets to school children. Leave donations with established charities instead.

Water scarcity & responsible tourism

India is suffering. Rainfall is declining, monsoons are failing, water tables are falling and crops and livestock are suffering. It is a problem exacerbated by deforestation, by extravagant use of water and poor conservation practices. Although Indian communities have coped with poor rains and semi-arid climates for generations, the Indian population growns apace and the introduction of western technologies and tastes has stretched resources to breaking point. The growth of tourism in India is also playing its part. Hotels in the desert of Rajasthan, embellished with water gardens and infinity pools, are drilling ever further into the ground to slake their thirst, while nearby villages find their communal taps running dry and their animals dying. It is a savage irony. India's tourism brings in the foreign exchange needed to fuel its growth, yet many of her people are suffering as a result. A more considered approach to tourism is required. Be sensitive to your surroundings – and do not run baths in the desert!

Getting involved

There are hundreds of charitable organisations needing help. We are keen to endorse the work done by SCAD (Social Change and Development) which dedicates itself to helping the poor, neglected, marginalized and under-privileged, eg. the landless agricultural workers, saltpan workers, gypsies, lepers, the physically disabled and rural women and children. In the UK, SCAD is supported by Salt of the Earth (www.salt-of-the-earth.org.uk).

Tigers

It is a sad fact that the wildlife population in India is rapidly decreasing, particularly the majestic tiger, now mainly found in Madhya Pradesh, Assam, Rajasthan and Uttarakhand. The prolific growth of India's tiger tourism industry is also threatening the parks' very resources and the survival of the tiger. We only recommend lodges in the wildlife parks that are members of TOFT (Travel Operators for Tigers, www.toftigers.org), an organisation set up to create responsible tourism practices in wilderness areas.

Photo: Misha Ostromecki, www.mishaphoto.co.uk

Many of you may want to stay in environmentally friendly places. You may be passionate about local, organic or home-grown food. Or perhaps you want to know that the place you are staying in contributes to the community? To help you we have launched our Ethical Collection, so you can find the right place to stay and also discover how each owner is addressing these issues.

The Collection is made up of places going the extra mile, and taking the steps that most people have not yet taken, in one or more of the following areas:

• **Environment** Those making great efforts to reduce the environmental impact of their Special Place. We expect more than energy-saving light bulbs and recycling – in this part of the Collection you will find owners who make their own natural cleaning products, properties with solar hot water and biomass boilers, the odd green roof and a good measure of green elbow grease.

• **Community** Given to owners who use their property to play a positive role in their local and wider community. For example, by making a contribution from every guest's bill to a local fund, or running pond-dipping courses for local school children on their farm.

• **Food** Awarded to owners who make a real effort to source local or organic food, or to grow their own. We look for those who have gone out of their way to strike up relationships with local producers or to seek out organic suppliers. It is easier for an owner on a farm to produce their own eggs than for someone in the middle of a city, so we take this into account.

How it works
To become part of our Ethical Collection owners choose whether to apply in one, two or all three categories, and fill in a detailed questionnaire asking demanding questions about their activities in the chosen areas. You can download a full list of the questions at www.sawdays.co.uk/about_us/ethical_collection/faq/

We then review each questionnaire carefully before deciding whether or not to give the award(s). The final decision is subjective; it is based not only on whether an owner ticks 'yes' to a question but also on the detailed explanation that accompanies each 'yes' or 'no' answer. For example, an owner who has tried as hard as possible to install solar water-heating panels, but has failed because of strict conservation planning laws, will be given some credit for their effort (as long as they are doing other things in this area).

We have tried to be as rigorous as possible and have made sure the questions are demanding. We have not checked out the claims of owners before making our decisions, but we do trust them to be honest. We are only human, as are they, so please let us know if you think we have made any mistakes.

The Ethical Collection is still a new initiative for us, and we'd love to know what you think about it — email us at ethicalcollection@sawdays.co.uk or write to us. And remember that because this is a new scheme some owners have not yet completed their questionnaires — we're sure other places in the guide are working just as hard in these areas, but we don't yet know the full details.

Ethical Collection online

There is stacks more information on our website, www.sawdays.co.uk. You can read the answers each owner has given to our Ethical Collection questionnaire and get a more detailed idea of what they are doing in each area.

You can also search for properties that have awards.

Ethical Collection in this book

On the entry page of all places in the Collection we show which awards have been given.

A list of places in our Ethical Collection is shown below, by entry number.

Environment

7 • 21 • 35 • 51 • 63 • 66 • 80 • 136 • 165 • 176 • 178 • 183 • 201

Community

7 • 21 • 35 • 51 • 63 • 66 • 80 • 165 • 176 • 183 • 201

Food

6 • 21 • 51 • 66 • 136 • 176 • 178 • 186 • 200

Photo: Kalmatia Sangam Himalaya Resort, entry 35

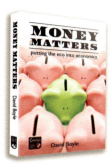

Money Matters
Putting the eco into economics
David Boyle
£6.99

This well-timed book will make you look at everything from your bank statements to the coins in your pocket in a whole new way. It holds the potential to change your life. In a world where the richest man is able to amass a fortune of over $50 billion, but over half the population of the planet live on less than $2 a day, this book discloses alternative and fairer ways. In his pithy and well argued style, author David Boyle sheds new light on our money system and exposes the inequality, greed and instability of the economies that dominate the world's wealth.

Money Matters is an easy-to-understand guide that demystifies the economic system that has us all caught in its tentacles, from hedge funds to hyperinflation, credit cards to the credit crunch.

Do Humans Dream of Electric Cars?
Your journey to sustainable travel
£4.99

It is estimated that there are over 600 million motor vehicles being driven on the streets of the earth. This figure is expected to double in the next 30 years. But oil is running out and bio-fuels are no longer seen as a viable alternative to fossil fuels.

This guide provides a no-nonsense approach to sustainable travel and outlines the simple steps needed to achieve a low carbon future. It highlights innovative and imaginative schemes that are already working, such as car clubs and bike sharing and is published to coincide with Sustrans's Change Your World Campaign 2009.

Sustrans is the UK's leading sustainable tranport charity. Their vision is a world in which people choose to travel in ways that benefit their health and the environment.

The Big Earth Book £12.99
Updated paperback edition

This book explores environmental, economic and social ideas to save our planet. It helps us understand what is happening to the planet today, exposes the actions of corporations and the lack of action of governments, weighs up new technologies, and champions innovative and viable solutions.

What About China? £6.99
Answers to this and other awkward questions about climate change

A panel of experts gives clear, entertaining and informative answers arguing that the excuses we give to avoid reducing our carbon footprint and our personal impact on the earth are exactly that, excuses.

The Book of Rubbish Ideas   £6.99

Every householder should have a copy of this guide to reducing household waste and stopping wasteful behaviour. Containing step-by-step projects, the book takes a top-down guided tour through the average family home.

Ban the Bag £4.99
In May 2007 Modbury in Devon became Britain's first plastic bag-free town. This book tells their story and highlights the struggles.

One Planet Living £4.99
Based on 10 guiding principles, which address key human needs, this little book suggests easy, ingenious and affordable ways in which we can lessen our impact on the planet and other people.

Little Food Book £6.99
Original, stimulating mini essays about what is wrong with our food today, and about one of the greatest challenges of the new century: how to produce enough food without further damaging our health and our environment.

To order any of the books in the Fragile Earth series call +44 (0)1275 395431 or visit www.fragile-earth.com

If you have any comments on entries in this guide, please tell us. If you have a favourite place or a new discovery, please let us know about it. You can return this form or visit www.sawdays.co.uk.

Existing entry

Property name: _____

Entry number: _____   Date of visit: _____

New recommendation

Property name: _____

Address: _____

_____

Tel/Email/Web: _____

Your comments

What did you like (or dislike) about this place? Were the people friendly? What was the location like? What sort of food did they serve?

_____

_____

_____

_____

Your details

Name: _____

Address: _____

_____

                                Postcode: _____

Tel: _____   Email: _____

Please send completed form to:

IND, Sawday's, The Old Farmyard, Yanley Lane, Long Ashton, Bristol BS41 9LR, UK

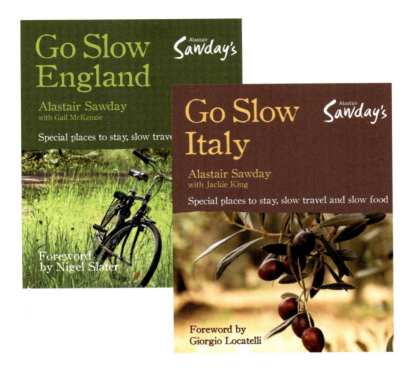

Special places to stay, slow travel and slow food

The Slow Food revolution is upon us and these guides celebrate the Slow philosophy of life with a terrific selection of the places, recipes and people who take their time to enjoy life at its most enriching. In these beautiful books that go beyond the mere 'glossy', you will discover an unusual emphasis on the people who live in Special Slow Places and what they do. You will meet farmers, literary people, wine-makers and craftsmen – all with rich stories to tell. *Go Slow England* and our new title *Go Slow Italy* celebrate fascinating people, fine architecture, history, landscape and real food.

RRP £19.99. To order either of these titles at the Reader's Discount price of £13.00 (plus p&p) call +44(0)1275 395431 and quote 'Reader Discount IND'.

"*Go Slow England* is a magnificent guidebook" *BBC Good Food Magazine*

1 Other place   Rajasthan **2**

3 ### Apani Dhani Eco-Lodge

4 Here your conscience and your corpus can be at peace. The principles are 'eco' and 'low impact', rooted in Ramesh's deep concern for the disappearing local heritage and the damaging effects that tourism can have. Ramesh lives here with his extended family, the sounds and smells of their lives providing a gentle backdrop to this beautiful and tranquil setting. The rooms are a cluster of traditional huts with mud-rubbed walls, thatched roofs and earthy colours. Wooden furniture and intriguing *objets* in russet-toned alcoves create an understated feel; bathrooms have gleaming white tiles and polished chrome. Everything you need is here though luxuries are few, and alcohol plays no part. Fabulous vegetarian food (seasonal, and from the organic garden) is served on leaf plates under a bougainvillea-clad pagoda in the circular courtyard that's the hub of the place. Visitors delight in Ramesh, a pleasant, well-travelled man of principle, who believes in the importance of harmonious living. Cookery classes, artisan workshops and guided treks, too. *5% room rate to community projects.*

5	Price	Rs850–Rs1,095.
6	Rooms	8: 3 doubles, 5 twins.
7	Meals	Breakfast Rs150. Lunch Rs225. Dinner Rs275.
8	Closed	Never.
9	Directions	Near Kisan Chatrawas off Nawalgarh bypass, on road from Sikar to Jhunjhunu. Train & bus: Delhi & Jaipur. Bus: Bikaner & Jodhpur.

Mr Ramesh C Jangid
Apani Dhani Eco-Lodge, Old Jhunjhunu
Road, Nawalgarh, Sikar, 333042
Tel   +91 (0)1594 222 239
Email   enquiries@apanidhani.com
Web   www.apanidhani.com

Ethical Collection: Environment; Community; Food. See page 264.   **10**

Price band: A **11**

12   Entry 51   Map 1 **13**